ECONOMIC CHALLENGES FACING MIDDLE EASTERN AND NORTH AFRICAN COUNTRIES

Also by Nemat Shafik

PROSPECTS FOR MIDDLE EASTERN AND NORTH AFRICAN
ECONOMIES: From Boom to Bust and Back?

REVIVING PRIVATE INVESTMENT IN DEVELOPING
COUNTRIES: Empirical Studies and Policy Lessons (*editor with*
A. Chhibber and M. Dailami)

Economic Challenges Facing Middle Eastern and North African Countries

Alternative Futures

Edited by

Nemat Shafik

Foreword by Heba Handoussa

in association with
ECONOMIC RESEARCH FORUM FOR THE
ARAB COUNTRIES, IRAN AND TURKEY

First published in Great Britain 1998 by
MACMILLAN PRESS LTD
Houndmills, Basingstoke, Hampshire RG21 6XS and London
Companies and representatives throughout the world

A catalogue record for this book is available from the British Library.

ISBN 0–333–71398–2 hardcover
ISBN 0–333–71399–0 paperback

First published in the United States of America 1998 by
ST. MARTIN'S PRESS, INC.,
Scholarly and Reference Division,
175 Fifth Avenue, New York, N.Y. 10010

ISBN 0–312–17632–5

Library of Congress Cataloging-in-Publication Data
Economic challenges facing Middle Eastern and North African countries
: alternative futures / edited by Nemat Shafik.
p.   cm.
Includes bibliographical references and index.
ISBN 0–312–17632–5 (cloth)
1. Middle East—Economic policy.   2. Africa, North—Economic
policy.   3. Economic forecasting—Middle East.   4. Economic
forecasting—Africa, North.   5. Middle East—Economic
conditions—1979–   6. Africa, North—Economic conditions.
I. Shafik, Nemat.
HC415.15.E27 1997
338.956—DC21   97–13673
                                                              CIP

© Economic Research Forum 1998

This book is printed on paper suitable for recycling and made from fully managed and sustained forest sources.

10   9   8   7   6   5   4   3   2   1
07   06   05   04   03   02   01   00   99   98

Printed and bound in Great Britain by Antony Rowe Ltd, Chippenham, Wiltshire

To Talaat Shafik

Contents

List of Figures and Tables   ix

Foreword by Heba Handoussa   xi

Notes on the Contributors   xii

1   Economic Challenges Facing Middle Eastern and
     North African Countries: An Overview
     Nemat Shafik   1

PART I   PERSPECTIVES FROM THE MAGHREB

2   Adjustment, Strategic Planning, and the Moroccan
     Economy
     Bachir Hamdouch   13

3   Competition Policies and Deregulation in Tunisia
     Mohamed Hedi Lahouel   25

PART II   PERSPECTIVES FROM THE MASHREQ

4   A Vision for Egypt in 2012
     Heba Handoussa and Hanaa Kheir-El-Din   53

5   The State and the Private Sector in Jordan
     Taher H. Kanaan   78

6   The Palestinian Economy: Alternative Futures
     George T. Abed   101

7   Reconstructing Lebanon's Economy
     Georges Corm   116

8   Syria: Strategic Economic Issues
     Nabil Sukkar   136

PART III PERSPECTIVES FROM TURKEY, SUDAN, IRAN, AND THE GULF

9 Determinants of Economic Growth in Turkey
   Sübidey Togan   159

10 Sudan: Toward a Strategic Vision for Peace and
   Development
   Ibrahim A. Elbadawi   178

11 Structural Adjustment and the Iranian Economy
   Massoud Karshenas   202

12 Policies and Economic Potential in the Countries of
   the Gulf Cooperation Council
   Hossein Askari, Maha Bazzari, and William Tyler   225

Index   257

List of Figures and Tables

Figures

9.1 GDP growth, Turkey, 1950–94   160
11.1 Per capita income, Iran and various regions, 1955–92   203
11.2 Per capita income, Iran, Republic of Korea, and Turkey,
      1955–92   204
11.3 Manufacturing output, employment, and productivity,
      Iran, 1963–90   208
11.4 Real wages and the cost and price structure in
      manufacturing, Iran, 1963–90   210

Tables

2.1 Macroeconomic indicators, Morocco, various years   15
3.1 Restricted and liberalized imports, Tunisia, 1983–94   27
3.2 Unrestricted imports, Tunisia, 1987–93   28
3.3 Domestic production protected by quantitative
     restrictions, Tunisia, 1987–93   29
3.4 Nominal domestic protection by sector, Tunisia, 1983–90   31
3.5 Effective domestic protection by sector, Tunisia, 1980–90   32
5.1 Gross domestic product in the public and private
     sectors by economic activity, Jordan, 1990–92   80
5.2 Value as added in the public and private sectors, Jordan,
     1985–90   81
5.3 Public financing, various countries, 1991   82
A5.1 Performance of public shareholding companies listed
      in the Amman Financial Market, 1981–90   98
A5.2 Public entities and employment   99
7.1 Inflation rates and exchange rates, Lebanon, 1989–94   124
8.1 Destination of Syrian exports, 1991–93   144
8.2 Access to health services, safe water, and sanitation,
     Syria, 1988–93   147
8.3 External financing, Syria, 1977–89   150
8.4 External debt ratios, Syria, 1989–93   151
10.1 Economic indicators and gross domestic product, Sudan,
      fiscal 1971–91   179
10.2 Macroeconomic indicators, Sudan, 1971–94   181

10.3   Costs of civil war in Sudan   185
10.4   Four stages of agricultural transformation   192
11.1   Structure and growth of the manufacturing sector in
        Iran, Turkey, and Republic of Korea   209
11.2   Macroeconomic indicators, Iran, 1988–93   214
12.1   Economic indicators, Gulf Cooperation Council, 1970–93 226
12.2   Required savings rates with different life of oil reserves,
        size of nonoil economy, and rates of real return   231
12.3   Actual life of oil reserves, size of nonoil economy, and
        national and required savings rates, GCC   231
12.4   Trade and current account balances, GCC, 1980 and
        1992   234
12.5   Revenues, expenditures, and budget balances, GCC,
        1970–92   237
12.6   Fuel, electricity, and water subsidies, GCC, 1980–92   239
12.7   Expatriate labor as a share of total labor force, GCC,
        1975–90   245
12.8   Population structures, GCC, 1960–90   248
12.9   Actual and projected growth rates for water
        consumption, GCC, 1980–2000   251
12.10   Projected consumption of desalinated water, GCC,
        1995–2015   253

Foreword

The Economic Research Forum for the Arab Countries, Iran and Turkey (ERF) is an independent, nonprofit networking institution based in Cairo that promotes and funds policy-oriented research. The ERF develops and coordinates research activities for a core constituency of research fellows primarily from the region but also operating out of institutions elsewhere in the world. An important part of the ERF's mandate is to contribute to capacity building in economic research and to the policy debate in the Middle East and North Africa.

This volume of country studies on key issues facing economies in the region is the third to be published by the ERF as part of its efforts to disseminate the findings of ongoing research on the Arab countries, Iran, and Turkey. This book is complemented by a companion volume of thematic studies by international scholars titled *Prospects for Middle Eastern and North African Economies: From Boom to Bust and Back?*. The papers here provide an important local perspective on the broader themes outlined in the companion volume. The implications of changes in the world economy, in the role of the private sector, and in the need for human resource development are analyzed at the country level by leading development thinkers in the region. Nowhere else will readers find such a combination of contemporary empirical work and policy insights on such a large number of economies in the Middle East and North Africa. We hope that both books will contribute to the debate in the region about its economic future and inform policy decisions in these countries in the coming years.

This book and its companion volume could not have been produced without the efforts of a number of people. Gillian Potter, the publications director of the ERF, helped identify publication outlets for the books. Nemat Shafik helped plan the workshop in Tunisia and commissioned many of the papers. Paul Holtz, of American Writing Corporation, edited the manuscript. Azeb Yideru kept track of numerous authors around the world with great efficiency. Without the efforts of these people, this important book and its companion volume would not have seen the light of day.

HEBA HANDOUSSA
Managing Director
Economic Research Forum
for the Arab Countries, Iran and Turkey

Notes on the Contributors

George T. Abed is Senior Advisor in the Fiscal Affairs Department at in the International Monetary Fund.

Hossein Askari is chair of the Department of International Business, School of Business and Public Management, at the George Washington University.

Maha Bazzari was a summer intern at the World Bank when this volume was written.

Georges Corm is an independent economic and financial consultant based in Paris and Beirut.

Ibrahim A. Elbadawi is Research Coordinator of the African Economic Research Consortium in Nairobi.

Bachir Hamdouch is Professor of Economics at the National Institute of Statistics and Applied Economics in Morocco.

Heba Handoussa is Managing Director of the Economic Research Forum for the Arab Countries, Iran and Turkey.

Taher H. Kanaan is Vice President of Computer and Communication Systems in Amman.

Massoud Karshenas is Reader in Economics in the School of Oriented and African Studies at the University of London.

Hanaa Kheir-El-Din is Chair of the Economics Department at Cairo University.

Mohamed Hedi Lahouel is Professor of Economics at Faculté de Sciences Economiques in Tunis.

Nemat Shafik is Research Fellow at the Economic Research Forum for the Arab Countries, Iran and Turkey and manager of the Private Sector Team in the Middle East and North Africa Region at the

World Bank. While editing this book she was a visiting associate professor at the Wharton School of the University of Pennsylvania.

Nabil Sukkar is Managing Director of the Syrian Consulting Bureau for Development and Investment in Damascus.

Sübidey Togan is Dean of the Faculty of Economics, Administrative, and Social Sciences at Bilkent University.

William Tyler is lead economist in Middle East and North Africa Country Department II at the World Bank.

1 Economic Challenges Facing Middle Eastern and North African Countries: An Overview

Nemat Shafik

Middle Eastern and North African countries face enormous economic challenges as the twenty-first century approaches. Stagnant real wages, deteriorating competitiveness, and rapidly growing populations and labor forces have left most countries in the region unable to deliver higher living standards to much of society. Yet the opportunities facing the region have never been greater – world trade is growing rapidly, capital flows to developing countries have never been higher, and regional integration options are many as a result of the evolving peace process and the European Union's proposal for a free trade area in the Mediterranean. Why, after nearly a decade of negative per capita income growth, has the region been unable to muster sufficient reform momentum to sustain economic progress? Do important differences across countries hold lessons for the future? What are the social consequences of economic stagnation, and how might future adjustment costs be managed to protect the poor? How have individual countries in the region defined the challenges ahead? And what issues must be addressed to realize a more prosperous future?

This volume presents the results of work sponsored by the Economic Research Forum for the Arab Countries, Iran, and Turkey (ERF) and by the World Bank to help answer these critical questions. Most of the papers in this volume were presented at a workshop held in Tunis in June 1995 that brought together economists, human resource specialists, and environmentalists from almost every country in the region to discuss the major long-term issues facing the Middle East and North Africa. Thematic papers on the changing international context, human resource development, the role of the private sector, and the environment appear in a companion volume called *Prospects for Middle Eastern and North African Economies: From Boom to Bust and Back?* (Shafik, 1997). This volume presents country

1

studies by scholars in the region that analyze the implications of international developments at the local level, the key policy challenges facing governments, and the political and institutional obstacles to reform. The country studies that appear in this volume fall into three broad groupings – the Maghreb (Morocco and Tunisia), the Mashreq (Egypt, Jordan, Palestine, Lebanon, and Syria), and Turkey, Sudan, Iran, and the Gulf.

THE MAGHREB

Morocco and Tunisia face two key issues: their emerging integration with Europe and their need to move from adjustment to sustainable and shared growth. Both countries have negotiated free trade agreements with the European Union under its Mediterranean policy. The basic objective of this policy is to incorporate the Mediterranean countries into the European economic area with the ultimate goal of creating a free trade zone in the region by 2010 (see Diwan, Yang, and Wang, 1997; Hoekman, 1997). Achieving this goal will require that partner countries lower trade barriers and substantially increase the competitiveness of local firms and the productivity of labor. The European Union will help pay for a portion of these adjustment costs through assistance to the private sector in its partner countries, financing infrastructure and supporting poverty alleviation, rural development, and environmental protection.

Morocco and Tunisia are among the most advanced reformers in the Middle East and North Africa. As a result both countries have higher levels of per capita income growth than other countries in the region, which has helped create jobs and reduce poverty (World Bank, 1995). Unlike many other countries in the region, Morocco and Tunisia maintain low capital-labor ratios because labor markets give investors incentives to create jobs. Moreover, the low-wage jobs created in export-oriented industries have helped reduce poverty by nearly half (van Eeghen, 1997). Still, social tensions linger because real wages have not risen substantially, public services have been curtailed, and social inequities persist (particularly in Morocco).

Integration with Europe will require further structural reforms in competition and labor market policies. In Chapter 3 Mohamed Hedi Lahouel shows that even Tunisia's relatively liberal policies stymie the competitiveness of firms through import licensing, tariff protection, investment restrictions, and price controls in certain sectors. Bachir

Hamdouch's analysis of Morocco (Chapter 2) emphasizes that integration with Europe must occur as the same time as integration with the world economy to maximize the benefits to the Moroccan economy. For both countries, managing the adjustment costs and social dislocations that greater competition and integration will bring (especially in manufacturing) will be a key policy issue, particularly given the ongoing civil strife in neighboring Algeria.

THE MASHREQ

The external environment for countries in the Mashreq is determined by developments in the world economy as well as by economic relations with Europe and the ongoing peace process (Riordan and others, 1997). For the "front line" states the peace process is a constant source of economic uncertainty whose resolution is essential to a more prosperous future. Regional peace would improve investment performance, allow economies of scale to be exploited, and create new economic opportunities. But the path to peace will be fraught with pitfalls that have major economic consequences.

These issues are most apparent in Chapter 6 by George Abed. Abed describes two possible scenarios for Palestine's economic future – an incremental and a fundamental approach. Incrementalism in the peace process, he argues, will have adverse economic effects in the form of low growth, persistent unemployment, and continued dependence on foreign aid. By contrast, a more rapid, fundamental approach to the political negotiations combined with well-designed economic reform could set the stage for increased foreign investment, rapid growth, a sharp drop in unemployment, and a sustainable budget deficit.

Jordan's prospects are also closely tied to the resolution of regional conflicts and to its ability to use its free trade agreement with Europe to attract investment and create competitive firms. In Chapter 9 Taher H. Kanaan assesses Jordan's progress in rethinking the role of the public sector in the economy and in encouraging greater private investment. He argues that privatization makes sense where markets are competitive; commercialization of state-owned enterprises is preferable where markets are imperfect. Moreover, transactions costs must be lowered if private sector performance in Jordan is to improve – including legislative reforms that govern company establishment, investment incentives, stock exchange operations, and taxation and trade procedures (Anderson and Martinez, 1997).

Lebanon has achieved macroeconomic stability, but the situation is fragile because of the enormous investment requirements of the government's ambitious reconstruction program. In Chapter 7 Georges Corm describes the challenge of reconstruction in Lebanon given the growing inequality of incomes and the weakness of the state. He argues that the massive reconstruction program will be jeopardized by two key factors: the risk of fiscal and monetary imbalances and the unmet social needs of the poor. Raising tax revenues must be an important element of any future strategy to ensure that Lebanon's tradition of laissez-faire policies and entrepreneurialism is complemented by a social safety net and the creation of opportunities for all groups in society.

Syria has grown relatively rapidly in recent years as a result of oil discoveries that have supplanted past aid flows from the Gulf countries and the former Soviet Union. In Chapter 8 Nabil Sukkar points out that the Syrian economy's prospects depend crucially on slowing rapid population growth, reducing high levels of military spending, accelerating economic reform, and improving the quality of human resources. Sukkar argues that Syria has numerous integration options – Lebanon, Iraq, the Euro-Mediterranean partnership – that could lay the ground for greater links with the world economy. But any reform and integration strategy will also have to resolve Syria's sizable arrears to the former Soviet Union, the World Bank, and Western European export guarantee agencies.

For a large country like Egypt, domestic policies will be the main determinant of how the economy copes with an increasingly competitive world economy and greater integration with Europe. Egypt's recent achievements in macroeconomic stabilization are laudable, but some of the more politically difficult reforms (like privatization of some sectors, labor market reform, and competition policy) are still pending. The consequence has been lackluster growth, insufficient to absorb the growing number of new entrants into the workforce and inadequate to reduce current levels of poverty.

In Chapter 4 Heba Handoussa and Hanaa Kheir-El-Din take a long-term perspective by envisioning what the Egyptian economy could achieve by 2012, and then work back from those targets to needed investment and policy reforms. They emphasize the need to shift the focus toward microeconomic and social sector reforms that will increase productivity and reduce poverty. They also identify a series of measures needed to improve the performance of Egyptian exporters by promoting a shift toward higher value-added products and more diversified markets. These measures will be essential if Egypt is to achieve the growth rates and social objectives outlined in the chapter.

TURKEY, SUDAN, IRAN, AND THE GULF

Turkey is an interesting case because, relative to most Middle Eastern and North African countries, it has had considerable success in exporting manufactures and is quite advanced in its integration with Europe, having agreed on a customs union rather than only a free trade agreement. In Chapter 9 Sübidey Togan examines the sources of growth in Turkey, emphasizing the importance of productivity gains in explaining the country's export success and growth performance. Turkey's export promotion policy relied on several instruments – a competitive exchange rate, preferential access to credit for exporters, fiscal incentives, and reduced protection. Togan estimates that the productivity gains resulting from exposure to greater competition, investment, and innovation explained 42 percent of Turkey's growth during 1978–92. But although Turkey has been able to create an outward-oriented export sector, it has not been able to improve the operations of poorly performing public enterprises, whose losses are putting enormous pressure on the government deficit and threatening macroeconomic stability. This will be a key issue for Turkey's economic future.

Sudan is one of the tragedies of the Middle East and North Africa – a poor country with great potential that, because of political strife, has grown poorer over time. In Chapter 10 Ibrahim A. Elbadawi assesses the costs of the ongoing conflict in Sudan, including lost oil revenues, agricultural devastation, large military outlays, and destruction of physical, human, and social capital, particularly in the South. Elbadawi also considers Sudan's long-term prospects once the civil war is resolved. He outlines a development vision that relies on policies to promote growth, measures to achieve agricultural transformation and economic diversification, initiatives to foster regional cooperation, and government efforts to reduce poverty and income inequality.

Postrevolutionary Iran has experienced a sharp drop in per capita incomes as a result of severe external shocks – the protracted war with Iraq, the freezing of Iranian assets, economic isolation, and the drop in oil prices after 1986. In Chapter 11 Massoud Karshenas describes the government's response to these shocks, in the form of extensive interventions in markets for foreign exchange, credit, and goods. The reform program launched under the first Five-Year Plan (1989–93) dismantled many of these controls but was ultimately unsuccessful because inflationary pressures arose and a large gap between the official and parallel market exchange rate emerged. Karshenas argues that successful future reform in Iran will require strengthening institutions (such as state firms and charitable foundations that have commercial roles), imposing hard budget constraints on public enterprises, and preventing the overexpansion of credit.

Economic performance in the Gulf countries is determined by events in oil markets; development in these economies is essentially a by-product of how oil resources are managed. With long-term projections of petroleum prices remaining flat, oil economies will have to do more with less if living standards are to be maintained as populations continue to grow rapidly (see Riordan and others, 1997). In Chapter 12 Hossein Askari, Maha Bazzari, and William Tyler outline the key policy tradeoffs facing the six economies of the Gulf Cooperation Council. Given the nature of resource extraction, the need for greater savings to generate future income streams is central, particularly in countries – such as Bahrain, Oman, and Qatar – with low levels of oil reserves. Kuwait and the United Arab Emirates have maintained adequate levels of savings to sustain living standards once oil reserves are depleted, while Oman and Saudi Arabia have had savings rates that were adequate in some years, inadequate in others.

Oil, mineral, and natural gas industries in the Gulf Cooperation Council countries are still enclaves, with few links to the rest of the economy. Such isolation is problematic. Askari, Bazzari, and Tyler emphasize the need to reconfigure the role of the state in these economies away from distributing oil revenues to citizens and toward relying on infrastructure and incentives to promote the private sector. Subsidies must be cut, laws must be clearly written, goods and factor markets must be liberalized, and clear economic policies must be implemented to create a healthy business environment. These efforts must be complemented by measures that increase the flexibility of labor markets, slow population growth, and make more rational use of the Gulf Cooperation Council's limited water resources.

YESTERDAY'S ACHIEVEMENTS, TODAY'S PREDICAMENT

The country studies in this volume paint a fairly bleak picture of economic performance over the past decade in the Middle East and

North Africa. Still, some important exceptions provide hope for the future. Economic policies in much of the region looked similar to those in other developing countries during the 1960s and 1970s, but in many countries the availability of rents postponed the structural reforms that Asian and Latin American countries undertook during the 1980s. The availability of oil enabled countries to pursue inward-oriented strategies, protecting the industrial sector and subsidizing energy at the expense of efficency and the environment (Mohtadi, 1997). The most extreme example comes from the Gulf, where extensive subsidies and transfers have created vested interests that even now are resisting reform. Perhaps the only exception is Lebanon, with its laissez-faire tradition and weak state, but even there the civil war created a peculiar type of protection that must be dismantled. Most countries in the Maghreb and the Mashreq face considerable vested interests in the statist policies of the past.

The achievements of the era of statism, from the 1960s to the mid-1980s, should not be understated. Growth rates in the region were among the highest for countries at their level of per capita income (Page, 1997). Income inequality was low for countries growing so rapidly, and poverty levels are still well below those in East Asia and Latin America (van Eeghen, 1997). Social indicators have also improved dramatically. A Middle Eastern child born in 1990 could expect to live thirteen years longer than his or her parents. Infant mortality more than halved over twenty-five years – from 151 deaths per 1,000 live births in 1965 to 61 per 1,000 in 1991. Primary enrollment improved markedly, from 61 percent in 1965 to 98 percent in 1991. And adult literacy went from 34 percent in 1970 to 53 percent in 1990, with particular progress in the oil-exporting countries.

But many of these past successes were the outcome of easier times, not statist policies. During 1960–85 oil prices were high, the world economy was buoyant, and competition was less fierce. The high rates of investment that were possible during the oil boom are no longer sustainable, and without higher domestic savings and massive improvements in productivity, living standards will not improve. The current system provides few incentives for households to save and for firms and workers to be productive. Gross savings rates in Middle Eastern and North African countries are about 10 percentage points of GDP lower than in countries like Indonesia, Malaysia, and Thailand – and in many countries adjustments for natural resource extraction result in negative net savings rates (Larsen, 1997). In many countries firms are protected from international competition: average

collected tariffs in the region (with the exception of the Gulf Cooperation Council countries, which are quite open) are higher than in most
countries in East Asia and Latin America. In Algeria, Egypt, Jordan,
and Syria educated workers account for 60–80 percent of the unemployed and have skills and expectations that are out of sync with the
labor market (Golladay, Berryman, Avins, and Wolff, 1997). In the
Gulf public sector employment has often become the means for transferring oil wealth to citizens, undermining the incentives for nationals
to take productive jobs in the private sector.

Still, there are causes for optimism. There is some evidence of
economic recovery, with higher oil prices and many countries reaping
the gains from earlier reforms. The diversity of economic strategies in
the region is probably greater today than at any time in recent history.
Some of the most advanced reformers – Jordan, Morocco, Tunisia,
Turkey – have reaped considerable rewards, with more jobs, less
poverty, booming exports, strong growth performance, and increased
foreign investment. Although these results were achieved with some
adjustment costs (such as unemployment), these costs were offset in
the long run by greater job creation in the rest of the economy. It is no
accident that these were the first four countries in the region to sign
association agreements with the European Union and that they are
the best prepared to compete at an international level.

The prospects for the rest of the region depend critically on whether
these early reformers serve as examples to their neighbors or whether
adverse external circumstances and domestic political constraints
result in continued stagnation. The implications for the region and
for the rest of the world are enormous. Continued stagnation will fuel
further political discontent and extremist voices that will destabilize
the region. But the road to prosperity is also possible – with economic
reform expanding opportunities and raising living standards – albeit
with some political obstacles along the way (see Waterbury, 1997).
The papers in the volume suggest possible future paths for the countries in the region. Hopefully, the perspectives of these distinguished
scholars will contribute to the debate about the economic future that
will have to occur among the region's citizens as they enter the twenty-
first century.

References

Anderson, Robert E., and Albert Martinez, 1997. "Supporting Private Sector
    Development in the Middle East and North Africa," in Nemat Shafik

(ed.), *Prospects for Middle Eastern and North African Economies*, London: Macmillan.

Diwan, Ishac, Chang-Po Yang, and Zhi Wang, 1997. "The Arab Economy, the Uruguay Round Predicament, and the European Union Wildcard," in Nemat Shafik (ed.), *Prospects for Middle Eastern and North African Economies*, London: Macmillan.

Golladay, Frederick L., Sue E. Berryman, Jon Avins, and Laurence Wolff, 1997. "A Human Capital Strategy for Competing in World Markets," in Nemat Shafik (ed.), *Prospects for Middle Eastern and North African Economies*, London: Macmillan.

Hoekman, Bernard, 1997. "The World Trade Organization, the European Union, and the Arab World: Trade Policy Priorities and Pitfalls," in Nemat Shafik (ed.), *Prospects for Middle Eastern and North African Economies*, London: Macmillan.

Larsen, Bjorn, 1997. "Environment and Natural Resource Management in the Middle East and North Africa Region," in Nemat Shafik (ed.), *Prospects for Middle Eastern and North African Economies*, London: Macmillan.

Mohtadi, Hamid, 1997. "Environmentally Sustainable Development in the Middle East and North Africa," in Nemat Shafik (ed.), *Prospects for Middle Eastern and North African Economies*, London: Macmillan.

Page, John, 1997. "From Boom to Bust – and Back? The Crisis of Growth in the Middle East and North Africa," in Nemat Shafik (ed.), *Prospects for Middle Eastern and North African Economies*, London: Macmillan.

Riordan, E. Mick, Uri Dadush, Jalal Jalali, Shane Streifel, Milan Brahmbhatt, and Kazue Takagaki, 1997. "The World Economy and Its Implications for the Middle East and North Africa, 1995–2010," in Nemat Shafik (ed.), *Prospects for Middle Eastern and North African Economies*, London: Macmillan.

Shafik, Nemat (ed.), 1997. *Prospects for Middle Eastern and North African Economies*, London: Macmillan.

van Eeghen, Willem, 1997. "Poverty in the Middle East and North Africa," in Nemat Shafik (ed.), *Prospects for Middle Eastern and North African Economies*, London: Macmillan.

Waterbury, John, 1997. "The State and Economic Transition in the Middle East and North Africa," in Nemat Shafik (ed.), *Prospects for Middle Eastern and North African Economies*, London: Macmillan.

World Bank, 1995. *Claiming the Future: Choosing Prosperity in the Middle East and North Africa*, Washington, D.C. : World Bank.

Part I

Perspectives from the Maghreb

2 Adjustment, Strategic Planning, and the Morocco Economy

Bachir Hamdouch

Morocco has been struggling with economic policy since 1993, when a decade of structural adjustment efforts came to an end. Although adjustment was beneficial in terms of macroeconomic balance and structural reform, it had adverse consequences for infrastructure development and the social sector. Such struggles are nothing new. They are, in fact, ever-present dilemmas for policymakers who, after having transformed an economy, must determine whether to continue with adjustment or to accelerate growth, in order to ease adjustment's impact. This chapter assesses the strategic dimensions of this conflict within the Moroccan framework. Two key issues are emphasized: prospects for domestic growth and development (in particular, the roles of the state and the private sector) and external issues (in particular, the relationship with the European Union).

For ten years (1983–93) Morocco implemented a structural adjustment program with the technical and financial support of the International Monetary Fund and the World Bank (Hamdouch, 1990b; Moroccan Economic Association, 1994). The program was introduced to address the serious macroeconomic imbalances that developed in the Moroccan economy during the late 1970s and early 1980s. These imbalances, which were provoked by external shocks, were magnified by inadequate policy responses. Two earlier stabilization efforts – the 1978–80 Triennial Plan and the 1980–83 Adjustment Program – failed because their indeterminate economic policies wavered between stabilization and growth.

THE ADJUSTMENT POLICY

By mid-1983 Morocco was compelled to adopt a two-pronged structural adjustment program. The first part, a stabilization and medium-term reform program supported by the International Monetary Fund, lasted through 1993. It was intended to address internal and external macroeconomic imbalances and to liberalize the economy. The second part was a series of sector adjustment programs that covered most economic sectors (agriculture, industry, foreign exchange, public enterprises, the financial sector, transportation, energy, water) and some social sectors (education, training, health, housing). Two structural adjustment loans, in 1988–90 and 1992–94, were provided to augment these efforts.

Achievements

The structural adjustment program achieved impressive results in terms of both macroeconomic balance and economic reform. Macroeconomic imbalances were drastically reduced by the end of the first phase of the program (1988). The balance of payments deficit, which had amounted to 12.3 percent of gross domestic product (GDP) in 1982, became a 2.3 percent surplus (Table 2.1). The public deficit fell from 9.7 percent to 4.5 percent of GDP during the same period. The annual inflation rate fell from 10.5 percent to 2.3 percent.

The balance of payments deficit reemerged during the second phase of the adjustment program, although by 1993 it was contained at 2.2 percent of GDP. External reserves amounted to about five months of imports by the end of 1992. The public deficit continued to decline, to about 3 percent of GDP. Inflation shot up, but was still below 6 percent at the end of the program. After having increased during the first phase, external debt stabilized at $21 billion. Finally, during the 1980s real GDP growth was about 3.8 percent a year, and per capita income increased by more than 1 percent a year.

The structural adjustment program introduced five major economic reforms:

- *Economic liberalization.* Most prices of goods and services were freed. Quantitative restrictions on external trade were removed. Customs duties were lowered drastically (the maximum rate went from 400 percent to 35 percent) and consolidated by Morocco's adherence to the General Agreement on Tariffs and Trade (GATT) in 1987. The system of subsidies, which had a negative impact on exports, was reformed.
- *Exchange control liberalization.* The dirham has been convertible since the beginning of 1993 for current operations and for operations involving nonresidents' capital.

Table 2.1 Macroeconomic indicators, Morocco, various years (percent unless otherwise indicated)

Indicator	1982	1984	1986	1988	1990	1991	1992	1993
Balance of payments (share of GDP)	-12.3	-7.8	-1.3	2.3	-0.8	-1.5	-1.5	-2.2
Consolidated government budget deficit (share of GDP)	-9.7	-6.6	-4.8	-4.5	-4.4	-3.1	-2.1	-3.0
Inflation rate	10.5	12.5	8.8	2.3	6.7	8.2	5.7	5.2
External debt (billions of U.S. dollars)	12.4	14.0	18.8	21.1	20.6	21.1	21.3	21.0
External debt/GDP	83.4	118.5	106.0	94.6	77.0	72.0	78.0	77.0
External debt service/exports of goods and services	43.2	33.2[a]	36.4	26.1	21.3	25.9	23.7	30.7
	1971–80	*1981–85*	*1986–90*	*1990*	*1991*	*1992*	*1993*	*1994*[b]
Change in GDP	5.6	3.3	4.3	3.8	5.9	-4.0	-1.1	11.3
Change in per capita income	3.1	0.6	1.6	1.4	3.6	-6.0	-3.0	9.4

a 1985.
b Preliminary data.
Source: Bank Al-Maghrib, various years; World Bank, 1995; Centre Marocain de Conjoncture, 1995.

- *Tax reform.* The tax system was modernized and simplified into three main taxes: a corporation tax, a general income tax, and a value-added tax.
- *Monetary policy liberalization and financial sector reform.*
- *Public enterprise reforms and privatization.*

The last two reforms are under way and have progressed less rapidly than the others.

Constraints

There are three main constraints to structural adjustment: those relating to implementation of the adjustment program, those relating to adjustment itself, and adjustment's economic and social costs.

Implementation

The problems relating to implementation of the structural adjustment program were both technical and sociopolitical. Implementation was not always carried out in a regular and harmonious manner, which led to delays. There was also a lack of coordination, especially during the first phase, between the general adjustment program and the sector adjustment programs, and also among the sector adjustment programs. This lack of coordination led to some incoherence between the policies that were adopted (Hamdouch, 1990b).

The adjustment process

Adjustment itself is also being questioned. To begin with, adjustment was performed by reducing absorption. In fact, the closing of the resources gap (from more than 13 percent of GDP in 1982 to 5 percent in 1992) was achieved by lowering public and private consumption and public investment. Likewise, at the external level three-quarters of the reduction in the resources gap resulted from reduced imports of goods and services.

Furthermore, adjustment of public finances was not intended to raise incomes (30 percent of the balancing effort) as much as it was intended to lower expenditures (70 percent of the balancing effort) — especially investment expenditures (60 percent of the balancing effort). The share of current expenditures in GDP was not lowered substantially, but they were structurally transformed into lower operating costs and consumption subsidies, with much higher interest rates on the public debt. The structure of public deficit funding was changed in favor of internal funding, especially of a nonmonetary kind. This in turn required tapping into private savings and raising interest rates.

Economic and social costs

The economic and social costs of adjustment were felt in three main areas. First, adjustment caused the growth rate to fall – from 5.6 percent during the 1970s to 3.8 percent during the 1980s – because it was based on a reduction of internal demand that the negligible increase in exports was unable to offset (World Bank, 1995). Absorption was also cut by lowering real wages, freezing public employment, reducing public investment, and discouraging private investment (Hamdouch, 1990b; Karshenas, 1994).[1]

Second, the lowering of public investment and operational expenses had a negative impact on the development and operations of both economic infrastructure and social facilities. These setbacks delayed the provision of basic infrastructure (transportation, telecommunications, and so on) and social sector services (education, training, health, housing). Such delays have a considerable impact on the poor segments of society.

Finally, adjustment aggravated unemployment. The unemployment rate in urban areas rose from 11 percent in 1982 to 16 percent in 1992, and reached even higher levels during the interim (Direction de la Statistique, 1992, 1993). The rate is even higher for women (more than 25 percent in 1992) and for fifteen- to twenty-four year olds (more than 30 percent). The rate is even higher for fifteen- to twenty-four year olds who have completed secondary school or more (more than 70 percent in 1993).

CHALLENGES AND STRATEGIC OPTIONS

Morocco has not had a program with the International Monetary Fund since 1993, when the dirham became convertible for current operations (it was already convertible for the capital operations of nonresidents). In addition, the last reschedulings of foreign debt were in 1990 (the London Club) and 1992 (the Paris Club). The country has continued to work with the World Bank, however, within the framework of sector adjustment programs and the second structural adjustment loan (1992–94).

Challenges

Internal

Although, in principle, everything was expected to run smoothly by 1993, the economic situation was – and remains – clouded by social tension. This tension has persisted since the first adjustment attempt in 1978. It can be attributed to the increase in unemployment, the reduction in purchasing power of wage earners, and the downswing of social services. Even economic upturns – like the successful 1994 cereals campaign that led to an exceptional 11.3 percent increase in GDP – do not have the expected economic or psychological impact (Centre Marocain de Conjoncture, 1995). On the other hand, the 1995 drought is considered a national catastrophe and will reduce GDP by some 5 percent. These circumstances reflect the brittleness of the economy, whose level of activity changes from year to year in accordance with climatic conditions. Although agriculture now accounts for just 15–20 percent of GDP, its importance is much greater in human terms: nearly half the population is rural, in addition to the new city dwellers who maintain close ties with rural areas.

Thus the first challenge is to improve the economic and social climate and to sever the link between economic growth and climatic uncertainties. Faster growth could help achieve these goals, but would in turn create two new challenges – that of accelerating growth in an economy geared to moderate growth rates and that of accelerating growth within a stable macroeconomic framework.[2] The experience and benefits gained from ten years of structural adjustment must be preserved.

Strong growth could, however, make it easier to speed the development of economic infrastructure and social services. Morocco's human development indicators are much lower than those of countries with similar per capita incomes (UNDP, 1995).

A second area of concern is environmental deterioration, which is causing precious natural resources (such as water) to fall in short supply while overexploited ones (like the sea) might become totally exhausted. Although the government is becoming more aware of the need for environmental and natural resource protection, the work is only beginning. The energy deficit is already serious and tends to be self-perpetuating: more than 90 percent of consumption is provided by imports (Al-Maghrib Bank, 1993). The only hope for a domestically sustainable fuel source lies in renewable, clean energies (solar, wind, and so on).

External

External challenges arise from the rapidly changing international context. The world economy, driven by globalization and regionalization, is developing into an increasingly deregulated and liberalized framework in which the private sector plays an ever greater role.

Globalization will proceed in one of two ways. If it follows an orderly route – as with the liberalization of trade under GATT – all the expected profits will accrue to the world economy, although these profits will not be evenly distributed (Goldin, Kudsen, and Van des Mehsbrugghe, 1993; IMF, 1994). If it is disorderly, monetary and financial shocks will result from the lack of coordination among the economic policies of the main players, in a financial framework characterized by deregulation and the absence of a real international monetary and financial system.

Regionalization is also gaining momentum. Having started from a horizontal integration of economies at similar levels of development, it is heading for a broader, more vertical approach. Thus the European Union is establishing a Euro-Mediterranean free trade area by integrating the Central and Eastern European countries and by cooperating with the Mediterranean ones. Similarly, two other blocs are emerging: a U.S. bloc centered around the United States (the North American Free Trade Agreement) and an Asian one centered around Japan and China (Association of Southeast Asian Nations).

For Morocco these developments provide both opportunity and hazards. The opportunity is to profit from the dynamic effects of the liberalization of international trade (especially after the adoption of the final act of the Uruguay Round) or regional trade (the Euro-Mediterranean agreement). The hazards are that Morocco might be marginalized in either or both spaces, or that it might suffer the negative effects of international financial disorders (such as the Mexican peso crisis at the beginning of 1995). Seizing the opportunity while avoiding the hazards is the strategic challenge.

Internal strategic options

The approach adopted by Morocco – in tandem with the World Bank – to overcome the deadlock that followed the structural adjustment program was to double the growth rate to 7–8 percent. Slower growth would make it impossible to overcome the lag in social and infrastructure development, to reduce poverty, and, most important, to reduce unemployment – which had the potential to rise from 16 percent in fiscal 1993 to 20–22 percent by 2000 (based on an annual growth rate of 4 percent). A growth rate of 8 percent, on the other hand, would help keep unemployment at 10–12 percent.

What is needed?

Achieving growth of 7–8 percent will require an investment rate of 27–30 percent of GDP by 2000, a 5–8 point increase over current rates. This would widen the gap with the savings rate (17 percent of GDP during 1991–93), which could rise from 5–10 percent of GDP (World Bank, 1995). This gap will be difficult to bridge, but the authorities believe that they can do so by increasing internal (private and public) savings and by attracting foreign capital. Foreign capital, however, represents just 2 percent of GDP (notwithstanding a sizable upswing to $500 million in fiscal 1994). Its rising inflow must be sustained until it reaches $1 billion.

The following measures are being adopted to mobilize the necessary additional savings:

- Stringent budgetary policies.
- Faster economic reforms – especially in the financial sector – and privatization.
- A restructured institutional framework that reforms the working code, the code of trade and companies, and the judicial system, and that unifies the advantages and investment regulations already contained in the common law system that no longer require official approval to go into force.

What is also needed, however, is a model of development that achieves short-term goals while protecting long-term interests – a model of sustainable development.

Achieving sustainable development

The concept of sustainable development is grounded in the fact that accelerated growth is a necessary but insufficient means of addressing economic and social challenges. Unless development is carried out carefully, acceleration of growth can aggravate problems – such as distributional inequality or environmental damage – that will ultimately cause growth to falter.

Growth must therefore be integrated with a broader framework, that of sustainable development. Sustainable development takes into account the physical environment (pollution, nonrenewable resources), the social environment (civil unrest, employment, basic needs, welfare distribution), and the regional and international environment (peace in the Maghreb and cooperation with the Middle East and Europe). Growth that favors sustainable development is macro-economically, sociologically, ecologically, and globally balanced.

At least two conditions are required for Morocco's sustainable development. First, a medium- and long-term framework of information, consultation, programming, and coordination must be established. The objective is to formulate – starting from a consensual vision of development – plans that forecast the necessary reforms, policies, and actions, and to place them within a coherent, comprehensive program.

The second requirement is a transparent definition of the areas requiring action, the rules of the game, and the roles of the public and private sectors. These distinctions should not exclude joint fields of action (such as research and development, training, and infrastructure development) and flexible approaches. The East Asian economies, where the state's hand is visible, active, and efficient, are instructive in this regard. Economic policies and, in particular, industrial policies are closely linked to international competitiveness and economic success (World Bank, 1993).

A tripartite advisory committee comprising representatives of the government, the private sector, and the World Bank was established in 1994 to work toward these goals and to develop action plans to develop Morocco by 2020. Three growth poles have been selected and studied thus far: infrastructure and public services, social sectors, and the competitive sectors of production. Identifying the competitive sectors of production will reveal the links between internal and external strategy options and suggest how the two can be addressed using a global strategy.

External strategic options

The international environment and increasing globalization, regionalization, and liberalization pose hazards to Morocco's development strategy and require that strategic choices be made. Morocco enjoys privileged relations with the European Union, with which it conducts 60 percent of its foreign trade (nearly 80 percent of agricultural exports) and from which it receives 70 percent of foreign investment, 80 percent of tourism revenues, and where more than 90 percent of Moroccan citizens living abroad are settled (BMCE, 1995; European Union, 1995).

Morocco's ties to Europe date to a 1976 cooperation agreement that grants preferential treatment to Moroccan exports. Under the agreement most industrial products are exempted from customs duties and agricultural products are subject to reduced customs tariffs. Preferences have eroded over the years, however, and will gradually disappear in the aftermath of the Uruguay Round. Thus the Round will result in a real loss of income for Morocco, Tunisia, and other countries of the Mediterranean (Fontagn and Péridy, 1995). Given the shift in circumstances, Morocco must decide whether it will remain anchored to Europe or break away, to profit from the potential export opportunities provided by GATT.

So far Morocco has opted to retain ties with Europe, and to defend the privileges its exports have on European markets. However, the prospect of signing a free trade accord with the European Union, within the framework of the accelerated growth strategy, seems to indicate a desire to open up to the international market. In any case global economic changes and the history of Moroccan relations with the European Union do not leave any space for a choice. It cannot be either Europe or the international market; it must be both Europe and the international market.

Morocco must develop its relations with Europe within the framework of a Euro-Mediterranean free trade area in order to avoid marginalization in the world economy. At the same time it must diversify its economic relations by looking at destinations other than the North and Europe. Doing so will require developing a competitive economy at the global level. This will entail tackling the numerous determinants of international competitiveness – development of human and physical capital, strengthening of environmental protection, and so on. Increased competitiveness would help lower the trade deficit, which reached $3 billion a year during 1992–94, and thus to service foreign debt (another $3 billion) without impinging on the viability of the balance of payments (Centre Marocain de Conjoncture, 1995).

CONCLUSION

The next few years are critical ones for Morocco's future. Numerous internal and external challenges require a long-term strategic framework whose objective is speedy but sustainable economic development. The private sector must play a greater role, possibly even replacing the state as the engine of growth. The state must set the stage for and help implement the new model of development. And external relations should both strengthen relations with Europe and open Morocco to the rest of the world. Achieving these objectives will not be easy and will require a sustained, long-term effort in many interrelated areas together with, above all, a revolution in mentality and behavior. Such is the price of success.

Notes

1. Especially during the middle of the period, private sector activity was inhibited by the Treasury's monopoly of money creation and private savings and by positive and exaggerated real interest rates (Hamdouch, 1990a).
2. Morocco's only phase of accelerated growth since independence took place during the 1970s. It led to the first structural adjustment program (Hamdouch, 1990b).

References

Al-Maghrib Bank, various years. *Annual Report*, Rabat.

BMCE (Banque Marocaine du Commerce Extérieur), 1995. *Information Bulletin* 218 (May), Casablanca.

Centre Marocain de Conjoncture, 1995. *Bulletin*, 13 (May).

Direction de la statistique, 1992, 1993 Annuaire Statistique du Maroc, Ministere Charge de la Population, Rabat, Royaume du Maroc.

European Union, 1995. "Letter of Information of the Delegation of the European Commission, in the Kingdom of Morocco," 128, Rabat.

Fontagné, Lionel, and Nicolas Péridy, 1995. "Uruguay Round and PVD, The North African Case," *Revue économique*, 46(3): 703–15.

Goldin, Ian, Odin Knudsen, and Dominique van der Mensbrugghe, 1993. *Trade Liberalisation: Global Economic Implications*, Paris: OECD and World Bank.

Hamdouch, Bachir, 1990a. "Investment Policies in Morocco," in Said El-Naggar (ed.), *Foreign and Intratrade Policies of the Arab Countries*, Washington, D.C.: International Monetary Fund.

————1990b. "Politiques de Développement et d'Ajustement au Maroc, à l'Epreuve de la Crise," Rabat. Société Marocaine de Editeurs Réunis.

IMF (International Monetary Fund), 1994. "International Trade Policies: The Uruguay Round and Beyond," Washington, D.C.

Karshenas, Massoud, 1994. "Structural Adjustment and Employment in the Middle East and North Africa," *Economic Research Forum Working Paper* 9420, Cairo.

Ministry of Population, 1993. *Social Indicators*, Rabat : Statistics Department.

————Various years. *The Active Population*, Rabat.

Moroccan Economic Association, 1994. "Evaluation of a Decade of the
   Structural Adjustment Program," *Moroccan Economic Association Journal*,
   special issue.
UNDP (United Nations Development Programme), 1995. *Human Develop-
   ment Report*, New York: Oxford University Press.
World Bank, 1993. *The East Asian Miracle*, A World Bank Policy Research
   Report, Washington, D.C. : World Bank.
————1995. *Claiming the Future: Choosing Prosperity in the Middle East
   and North Africa*, Middle East and North Africa Region, Washington,
   D.C.: World Bank.

3 Competition Policies and Deregulation in Tunisia[1]

Mohamed Hedi Lahouel

Tunisia's economy was highly regulated from independence in 1956 until 1986, at which point macroeconomic and external payment difficulties, along with the constraints of central control, prompted major policy changes. So far reform has involved the removal of barriers to competition, notably in trade and investment. In addition, most price controls have been removed, many state-owned enterprises have been privatized, and deregulation of banking has advanced considerably. During the period of structural adjustment (1986–94) Tunisia became the first southern Mediterranean country to sign a free trade agreement with the European Union, committing itself to total removal of tariff and non-tariff barriers on all imports (except agricultural products), and it became a full member of GATT (the General Agreement on Tariffs and Trade). Under the Uruguay Round Tunisia committed itself to the progressive removal of quantitative restrictions on imports and of binding on most tariff lines. Despite such progress, reform in many areas has been either inadequate or slow in coming. If Tunisia is to improve its economic performance, the climate of competition must be enhanced through further reform.

The removal of barriers to competition is an essential component of policies aimed at improving economic performance. Until Tunisia instituted its structural adjustment program in 1986, barriers to competition were numerous. Practically all private undertakings were subject to state intervention, including investment programs, imports of goods and services, and pricing. Public enterprises dominated most economic activities and benefited from easy bank credit as well as all kinds of government subsidies. State intervention greatly limited the functioning of markets, leaving little room for competition.

Given the size of the Tunisian economy – the country has a population of less than 9 million people and a per capita income of about $1,700 – efforts to encourage competition have little meaning unless foreign trade is liberalized. Tunisia has made significant progress in this respect, but the protection of domestic firms by tariff as well as nontariff barriers remains relatively high.

To promote competition, investment incentives must be as unbiased as possible; horizontal objectives such as efficiency, the reduction of regional disequilibria, and environmental protection must be guiding principles; and barriers must be removed for both domestic and foreign investors. The Tunisian regulatory system has been significantly reformed in the direction of investment liberalization, but it still has serious restrictions and distortions that, in particular, affect totally exporting offshore firms.

A liberalized economy relies on its pricing system, which is supposed to encourage the efficient allocation of resources. Not only is price regulation incompatible with liberalization, but it often wastes human and nonhuman resources. Since 1986 Tunisia has made major strides toward the lifting of administrative price fixing, but liberalization needs to be taken further.

Competition should also be promoted in services such as transportation, telecommunications, and finance. Some of these services have been virtually monopolized by state-owned enterprises whose heavy losses the treasury and banking sector have had to bear. Despite the policy shift of the last few years, the pace of liberalization in these activities remains slow.

TRADE LIBERALIZATION

Tunisia's import regime is based on licensing, which until recently was very restrictive and still an important policy tool, and on tariff protection, which has been reduced over the past few years but is still relatively high.

Quantitative restrictions and licensing

Until the middle of 1994 imports were regulated by a positive list. The regulatory system consisted of a free regime under which import operations required a certificate, delivered more or less automatically, and a restricted regime that required administrative authorization, a license, or an import card, depending on the import, the size of the applying firm or importer, and its needs. The positive list enumerated the goods free of restriction; all goods not included were submitted to the second regime. In August 1994 a new foreign trade law (Law 94–41) was enacted; it unified authorization procedures and, more important, replaced the positive list with a negative one limited to the goods still under restriction.

The policy of liberalization that took root in the mid- 1980s paved the way for Tunisia to become a full member of GATT in 1990. During the Uruguay Round Tunisia committed itself to the progressive removal of quantitative restrictions and their replacement by import duties and to the binding of tariffs, albeit at relatively high rates, on most tariff lines.

The removal of import licensing has been gradual. In 1986 more than 94 percent of imports (in terms of tariff lines) were licensed. Trade reform started seriously in 1987 when the share of liberalized imports rose to 20 percent in terms of tariff positions (Table 3.1) and to almost 32 percent in terms of import value (Table 3.2). During the first two years of structural adjustment (1987–88) reform focused on the liberalization of imported raw materials and semiprocessed and capital goods. By the end of 1988 almost 40 percent of imports were unrestricted; the share of free imports was much higher for capital goods (about 70 percent) than for other goods, but 54 percent of imported raw materials (excluding energy) and semiprocessed goods were also unrestricted. For consumer goods the share of unrestricted imports reached 41 percent in 1987 (though this figure includes clothing used mainly by offshore textile firms in their exporting activities, which have been exempt from licensing since the beginning of the 1970s).

Table 3.1 Restricted and liberalized imports, Tunisia, 1983–94

Type	1983	1986	1987	1988	1989	1990	1994
Restricted imports							
Number of tariff lines	6598	7966	6781	5963	4747	4045	1646
Share of total number of lines (percent)	78.3	94.2	80.0	69.8	56.7	48.3	27.4
Unrestricted imports							
Number of tariff lines	1827	489	1694	2577	3629	4331	4367
Share of total number of lines (percent)	21.7	5.8	20.0	30.2	43.3	51.7	72.6
Total number of tariff lines	8425	8455	8475	8540	8376	8376	6013

Source: IQE, 1994; GATT, 1994.

Since 1988 licensing has been gradually removed from food products, energy, and consumer goods. For all goods the share of unrestricted imports in terms of tariff lines stood at almost 73 percent as of

Table 3.2 Unrestricted imports, Tunisia, 1987–93
(share of unrestricted imports in the value of total imports)

Import	1987	1988	1989	1990	1991	1992	1993
Food	0.9	0.4	2.5	9.4	19.6	28.9	41.5
Energy	0.0	0.0	15.4	17.5	23.9	94.1	99.7
Raw and semiprocessed materials	37.0	54.2	65.1	82.7	82.9	85.9	86.1
Capital goods	40.5	69.6	77.9	73.5	76.2	94.6	80.3
Consumer goods	41.2	31.7	54.9	66.1	78.9	91.0	70.4
Total	31.8	39.4	53.0	64.0	72.2	84.2	76.8

Source: IQE, 1994.

April 1994 and at more than 76 percent after the publication of the negative import list in August of that same year. In terms of value, liberalized imports reached almost 77 percent of total imports in 1993; energy has been partially liberalized, whereas food imports are still largely regulated by licensing (see Table 3.2). However, in the case of energy public enterprises still hold an import monopoly, which means that the removal of licensing should not be interpreted as a significant measure of liberalization.

It is more useful to assess the extent of liberalization in terms of the share of domestic production not protected by import licensing, since the aim of liberalization is to promote competitiveness by exposing domestic firms to foreign competition and inducing resource reallocation based on comparative advantage. In this light the pace of liberalization was slow at the beginning of structural adjustment, with the share of unlicensed domestic production not exceeding 6 percent and 14 percent of total production, respectively, in 1988 and 1989 (Table 3.3). Food, textiles, and mining remain overly protected by import licensing. The removal of quantitative restrictions accelerated in 1992, with almost half of domestic production facing unrestricted imports. According to World Bank data this share rose to 60 percent in 1993 and 83 percent in 1994. By the end of 1995 liberalization will be extended to other goods representing an additional 8.5 percent of domestic production. Once this projected liberalization is implemented, licensing will be limited to basic subsidized goods and luxury products representing less than 8.5 percent of domestic production.

However, other estimates based on the negative list published in August 1994 show lower rates of liberalization in domestic production. The removal of import licensing has affected only about

Table 3.3 Domestic production protected by quantitative restrictions, Tunisia, 1987–93 (percent)

Sector	1987	1988	1989	1990	1991	1992	1993
Manufacturing	96.6	94.0	85.6	68.4	—	—	—
Food	99.8	99.6	95.6	83.9	—	—	—
Chemicals	94.4	93.7	90.2	50.9	—	—	—
Textiles	98.5	97.8	93.6	90.5	—	—	—
Electrical and machinery	90.3	88.0	61.3	53.8	—	—	—
Agriculture	97.3	98.4	98.3	85.5	—	—	—
Mining	99.3	98.4	98.3	85.5	—	—	—
Total economy	97.0	94.7	87.5	71.9	70.3	52.5	40.0

—Not available.
Source: World Bank data; Central Bank of Tunisia data.

54 percent of domestic production for agriculture and fishing and there are no plans to liberalize the rest. Cereals, most vegetables, and live cattle are still protected by licensing. Less than 53 percent of manufactured goods have been liberalized; within the sector, 61 percent of textiles and leather goods continue to be highly protected. Far more progress has been made in removing import restrictions on mechanical and electrical products; in these areas liberalization has reached almost 82 percent of domestic production. By contrast, 60 percent of domestically processed food products are still protected by heavy licensing. Finally, more than half of chemical products are still required to receive import authorization. Commercial policy also restricts mining and energy products – the degree of liberalization in this area is less than 26 percent in terms of domestic production. Moreover, the sector is dominated by public enterprises with a quasi-import monopoly.

For the whole economy import liberalization stands at about 50 percent of total domestic production, much lower than the 83 percent stated in the 1995 budget. The authorities plan to liberalize garments by the end of 1995, which will almost totally remove import restrictions on textiles, clothing, and leather products. This move will increase the degree of liberalization for manufacturing from the current 53 percent to 65 percent of domestic production. For all goods, including mining and energy, liberalization will cover about 59 percent of production. According to the 1994 budget, the liberalization of textiles is supposed to be the last step of the reform process that started in 1987. Estimates show, however, that a significant share of domestic production will still be protected through import licensing.

The 1994 foreign trade law stated the principle of unrestricted import and export transactions for all goods except those in two categories. The first category included goods related to security, public order, health, the protection of species, and cultural endowment; the second category was not well defined. A decree in August 1994 of the products to remain temporarily or permanently under restriction exceeded the range of products mentioned in the March 1994 law. Permanently restricted products include cereals and cereal-based products, fruits and vegetables, olive oil, and luxury goods such as jewelry, watches, yachts, and passenger motor vehicles; temporarily restricted imports consist primarily of garments and passenger motor vehicles.

Tunisia's public cereal board has a monopoly on imports, and import restrictions in this sector were imposed to help subsidize domestic production. If the government removed these restrictions along with the cereal board's monopoly, private importers would be able to buy cereal abroad and sell it to the board at higher prices than the government now pays, which would increase the burden on the general subsidy fund and eventually displace domestic cereal production. This risk could be removed by adjusting duties on cereal imports in line with the support prices set by the government for local production, but the intervention of a public board will continue to be needed as long as the subsidy system remains in place.

The subsidy argument does not apply to cereal-based finished products, since subsidies intervene at early processing stages. Given that the import prices of these products are generally much higher than the prices of similar domestic products, imports cannot compete as long as subsidies remain. Liberalization would provide an incentive for local cereal producers to improve quality and reduce cost. Still, this move would not necessarily make prices more competitive.

Tariff barriers

With the easing of licensing since 1992, domestic production has relied increasingly on tariff protection. In addition to existing duties, additional temporary levies called provisional complementary duties have been collected since 1991 to protect local producers while they restructure to face foreign competition. These levies, varying between 10 and 30 percent, are not supposed to last for more than three years.

In addition to these temporary levies, the 1994 foreign trade law introduced compensatory or countervailing duties to offset prejudicial or threatening dumping practices or subsidies granted to exports by exporting countries. In accordance with GATT's definitions and conditions, this law states that dumping occurs when the export price of a good imported by Tunisia is lower than its normal value or the value of a similar product. Domestic production is also protected by countervailing duties against all kinds of direct and indirect subsidies, whether they are granted to production, exports, or transportation. These duties are allowed by GATT at levies equal to the estimated dumping margin, that is, the difference between a normal value and the actual price, or equal to the amount of the subsidy.

The Tunisian law stipulates that countervailing duties can be levied even after imported merchandise has entered the country, within a period not exceeding ninety days following customs declaration. This provision has been a source of uncertainty for importers since merchandise is often used in production or sold on the domestic market at prices based on duties already paid and before the government can establish a case of dumping or subsidization. The antidumping provision is a potentially powerful means of protecting domestic producers from foreign competition. In some cases, however, it may also induce capital flight through the overinvoicing of imports.

Since the beginning of the 1980s there have been significant cuts both in the average level of nominal tariff protection and in rate dispersion. Until structural adjustment customs duties were relatively high, exceeding on average 40 percent, and widely dispersed, ranging between 5 and 236 percent. Duties increased for all sectors during 1983–6, exceeding 60 percent for food processing and textiles and more than 40 percent for the total economy (Table 3.4). Under the

Table 3.4 Nominal domestic protection by sector, Tunisia, 1983–90 (percent)

Sector	1983	1986	1987	1988	1989	1990
Agriculture and fishing	22	41	39	25	23	23
Manufacturing	37	47	36	34	35	35
Food processing and agroindustries	30	63	38	35	33	33
Electrical and machinery	25	37	32	29	36	36
Chemicals	33	37	32	31	32	33
Textiles	58	67	46	40	38	37
Mining	11	13	15	17	17	17
Total economy	29	41	33	29	29	29

Source: IQE, 1992.

reforms implemented during 1987–90 average rates fell to 29 percent for the whole economy, with major cuts in agriculture, food processing, and textiles. Dispersion was also significantly reduced, with duties limited in 1990 to between 15 and 43 percent. However, the reduction of duties on food and textile imports during this period should not be interpreted as a significant step toward liberalization since import licensing continued to protect more than 90 percent of domestic textile production and about 85 percent of agriculture and processed food (see Table 3.3).

Effective protection shows a similar trend, declining for the whole economy from 70 percent in 1986 to 52 percent in 1987 and to 43 percent during 1988–90 (Table 3.5). Effective protection remained high for manufacturing, however, averaging 84 percent in 1990, with true protection probably much higher because of import licensing that was much more restrictive for finished than for intermediate goods.

Table 3.5 Effective domestic protection by sector, Tunisia, 1980–90 (percent)

Sector	1983	1986	1987	1988	1989	1990
Agriculture and fishing	33	46	43	25	22	24
Manufacturing	178	124	81	78	87	84
Food processing and agroindustries	191	421	120	134	110	100
Electrical and machinery	67	88	73	63	98	101
Chemicals	161	88	67	62	70	78
Textiles	175	194	107	82	76	73
Mining	24	9	14	16	17	18
Total economy	67	70	52	42	43	44

Source: IQE, 1994.

The gradual removal of licensing has been accompanied by an upward revision of duties for nonbound tariff lines as well as by the imposition of complementary provisional duties since 1991. In the middle of 1994 the simple average tariff rose to about 33 percent, including provisional duties. New provisional duties, on the order of 30 percent, were added in the beginning of 1995, especially on garments, so the average tariff has probably risen by two additional percentage points to an average of 35 percent for all imports. Because of the introduction of provisional duties rate dispersion has also increased; it now ranges between 0 and 73 percent.

Of all sectors agriculture and fishing have the highest rates of protection, at more than 40 percent inclusive of provisional duties, which have added an average of 6 percentage points to permanent duties. For many of these goods, though, nominal protection is not a good indicator of the degree of foreign competition faced by domestic production. For manufacturing the average rate was 33 percent in mid-1994, with provisional duties accounting for about 2.5 percentage points. Textiles, clothing, and leather products are the most protected of all manufactured goods, with an average rate of 43 percent. The new provisional duties of 30 percent on garments introduced in 1995 raised the average duty for the domestic garment industry to more than 70 percent. The footwear industry is protected at an average rate (including provisional duties) of more than 62 percent. Food, beverages, and tobacco are protected at an average tariff of more than 42 percent, but actual protection is higher because of the restrictive licensing that continues to be imposed on imported products. Finally, fabricated metal products, machinery, and equipment have tariffs averaging 28 percent (including provisional duties). Such low duties and the almost total removal of licensing make this the most liberalized sector.

The strategy of provisional complementary duties is to provide domestic producers with additional tariff protection during the three years following the removal of quantitative restrictions. However, provisional duties have been levied on goods that are still under import restrictions and even on goods, such as citrus fruit, that Tunisia exports. The rationale for such policy is not clear.

Tariff binding

In preparation for full membership in GATT in 1990, Tunisia reformed its trade classification system by adopting the so-called harmonized system with 6,052 tariff headings at the seven-digit level. As a member it committed itself to binding 909 headings at duties ranging between 17 and 52 percent, the upper bound being higher than the 43 percent of autonomous tariffs. Bindings were much lower for agricultural than for industrial products, the proportions in terms of their respective numbers of tariff lines being about 5 and 18 percent. In terms of value these bindings represented only 4.0 percent of 1992 imports of agricultural goods and 32.5 percent of imports of industrial goods.

During the Uruguay Round Tunisia made further concessions in tariff bindings for 2,900 lines. All agricultural items have been bound at tariff rates varying between 25 and 200 percent, a wide range. For industrial products bound duties lie in the range of 27–43 percent, excluding textiles. Total bindings represent about 63 percent of all items, comparable to the developing country average offered in the Uruguay Round (GATT, 1994). Still, bound tariffs remain too high for textiles and agricultural goods, both in absolute terms and compared with other developing countries (Jamel, 1995).

Because rates of effective protection are much higher than what nominal rates imply, and given the possibility of countervailing duties against dumping and subsidization, it is difficult to assess the extent of Tunisia's liberalization of textiles and leather products. While the removal of licensing will be a significant step toward liberalization, the binding of tariffs at such high rates may result in significant opposite effects.

INVESTMENT REGULATION AND INCENTIVES

Tunisia's system of investment incentives has grown out of the first code of 1969, which regulated both national and foreign investment. Major steps have been taken toward liberalizing investment, easing barriers to entry, and reducing distortion between activities, but further reforms are needed.

The old investment incentive system

Under the 1969 code any type of investment project had to obtain prior approval from the government. However, this code contained important fiscal and financial incentives that did not discriminate in principle between sectors. The main incentives were income tax holidays, investment tax credits, exemptions from import duties and other taxes on imported capital goods, and government guarantees for bank loans. The government could also grant other important advantages such as tax rebates, preferential interest rates, and even monopoly positions. These incentives lasted until 1987, giving rise to many inefficient and costly investment projects.

Since 1972 a specific incentives system has been applied to promote exports. Totally exporting or offshore firms were granted privileges, the most important of which were total exemptions from duties and other taxes on imports of equipment, raw materials, and intermediate inputs, as well as an income tax holiday of ten years, later made permanent.

The 1980s witnessed the proliferation of sectoral investment codes or incentive schemes that, in contrast to the code of 1969, discriminated between sectors. These codes contained incentives tied to the fulfillment of certain objectives, the most important of which were export promotion and the development of lagging regions. They all contained incentives similar to those in the 1969 code. In addition, tourism and agriculture benefited from access to credit at preferential interest rates.

These incentive schemes were expensive, costing more than 1 percent of gross domestic product (GDP) a year or more than 4 percent of total fiscal receipts (Institut d'Economic Quantitative, 1994). They also resulted in large distortions between activities, notably in favor of offshore firms, tourism, and agriculture. Such bias in favor of exports is no longer justifiable within the context of liberalization.

The discrimination between sectors resulted in highly dispersed marginal effective tax rates that differed wildly from the statutory corporate income tax rate of 35 percent. The preferential interest rates, income rebates, and exemptions granted to tourism and agriculture made the effective tax rates for these two sectors practically nil. Such distortions, bound to result in a misallocation of capital, have probably already induced excessive investment in tourism. Furthermore, despite tax exemptions on reinvested income, the granting of preferential interest rates to agriculture and tourism has created a bias in favor of debt as opposed to equity financing.

The new incentive system

The 1993 investment code (Law 93–120) replaced the sectoral codes of the 1980s as well as practically all other advantages granted to investors. The code applies to all activities and contains measures tied to the fulfillment of horizontal objectives, regardless of sector. Unlike the former codes, which favored export promotion and regional decentralization, the new code extends incentive measures to other objectives: agricultural development, which is a sectoral concern but which is associated with food security; environmental protection; the promotion of technology, research and development, energy conservation, and entrepreneurship; and the encouragement of institutions involved in support services and human capital formation, such as health, vocational training, and cultural activities.

One incentive common to all activities is a tax exemption on reinvested income for both individuals and companies. Companies benefit from this provided equity capital is not reduced during the five years following reinvestment. Another common incentive is accelerated depreciation of equipment with a fiscal amortization period exceeding seven years. And there are still other common incentives: the reduction of import duties to a rate of 10 percent; the suspension of the value-added tax and the consumption duty on imported equipment for which no similar local products exist; and the suspension of the value-added tax and the consumption duty on locally produced capital goods for which a list has been established. Most equipment is therefore taxed at the relatively moderate import duty of 10 percent, compared with the much higher average statutory rate averaging 25 percent.

Exporting Firms

Under the 1993 investment code totally exporting firms – defined as those that export at least 80 percent of their output if they produce manufactured goods or services and 70 percent of their output if they produce agricultural goods – are granted the following advantages: an income tax holiday for ten years after the first export operation, followed by a rate of 17.5 percent; an income tax exemption on personal or corporate income, provided a minimum tax rate (10 percent for most activities) is paid; and a total exemption from all taxes and duties on imported inputs.

Offshore firms are allowed to sell up to 20 percent of their output on the local market if they are producers of manufactured products or services, 30 percent if they are agricultural producers. However, these sales are unconditional only if they involve products for which there is no similar domestic production. If they compete with onshore production, sales allowed on the domestic market cannot exceed the amount of the firm's purchases of locally produced inputs and, in the case of textiles and footwear, only 50 percent of the value of such purchases.

These restrictions are meant to strengthen the linkages between offshore and domestic activities. But this approach has some drawbacks. For example, the 20 percent ceiling on companies producing goods with no onshore equivalents discriminates against these companies for no good reason. Because the activity of such companies does not compete with onshore production, it would make more sense to allow offshore companies and foreign investors to develop their exports and to have at the same time free access to the local market. With trade liberalization the Tunisian economy will greatly benefit from an equal treatment of sales of products coming from offshore companies and of imports. As stipulated in the investment code, this treatment should consist of levying on domestic sales exactly the same duties as those levied on similar imports, but with no restrictions on the share of output locally sold.

Tunisia is making important liberalization commitments within the framework of the free trade zone being established with the European Union, which accounts for about 80 percent of the country's foreign trade. All Tunisian tariff and nontariff barriers on goods exported by the European Union will have to be removed within twelve years, and this will have to be extended to at least 60 percent of Tunisia's imports from the European Union in the first five years following the agreement. If restrictions on domestic sales by offshore companies are maintained, it will clearly hinder local economic activity and favor foreign producers.

Partially exporting firms

The new incentive system grants partially exporting firms many but not all of the advantages given to offshore firms. They benefit from the same ten-year income tax holiday, followed by reductions in later periods, but only on profits earned from exports. They also get refunds of import duties paid on intermediate inputs and equipment, in proportions related to their exports. But earnings saved and reinvested in the expansion of export capacity do not receive any tax deduction or exemption beyond the 35 percent rate common to all activities. Furthermore, refunds of import duties on equipment are allowed only if there is no similar domestic equipment, a measure that puts partial exporters at a disadvantage with respect to sole exporters and discourages them from purchasing locally produced capital goods.

Given Tunisia's liberalization commitments under GATT and, more important, those that will soon be made with the European Union, the differentiation between sole and partial exporters must be rethought. With the projected removal of tariff and quantitative barriers on imports from the European Union, export incentives will no longer serve their purpose of compensating for the distortions resulting from protection. If these incentives are maintained, they will result in reverse discrimination against firms producing for the local market and adjusting to foreign competition. Furthermore, Tunisia's membership in GATT and the World Trade Organization (WTO) will require the removal within five years of trade-related investment measures (TRIMs), which include export incentives. Major revisions in the treatment of exporting and nonexporting firms are thus required in the medium term. In the meantime reforms should be undertaken to simplify the procedures related to handling and servicing the refunds of duties and other taxes levied on intermediate inputs used in the production of exported goods by partially exporting firms. In this transitional period it may even be possible to remove altogether the restrictions on domestic sales by offshore firms.

Other activities

The 1993 code grants important incentives to investment in first-stage processing of agricultural products and in other agriculture and fishing-related services. For all practical purposes these activities are exempted from personal and corporate income taxes. In addition to exempting reinvested income, the code grants them a ten-year holiday at the end of which they will be taxed at the flat rate of 10 percent – much less than the 35 percent rate applied to other sectors. Moreover, investment in agriculture can be subsidized by as much as 7 percent of the cost of investment. This measure is a significant improvement on the agricultural code of 1988, which gave investors access to credit at highly preferential interest rates. Preferential rates on loans to tourism have also been eliminated, a measure that is likely to reduce the capital intensity of this activity and its excessive attractiveness relative to other activities.

The removal of capacity licensing

As stated earlier, the 1969 investment code required prior government approval for any kind of investment and in some cases allowed for the granting of monopoly power to investors. This regulation hindered private investment and created an attitude of suspicion on the part of potential investors toward regulatory agencies, in particular the agency in charge of manufacturing investment. Entrepreneurs had to wait long periods for this agency to study investment applications and make its decisions. Furthermore, capacity licensing was very restrictive for activities such as textiles, the rationale being that they were saturated and that existing capacity had reached the optimal level. Regulatory agencies thus kept the market from playing its most important function: rewarding efficient projects and punishing inefficient ones.

The 1993 code reasserted the principle of freedom of investment, the only administrative requirement being an investment declaration made to the relevant agency or government department. Prior government approval was removed for all but certain activities listed in the 1994 decree as well as for other unspecified activities. Listed activities belong mainly but not solely to the service sector: fishing, tourism, handicrafts, transportation, telecommunications, education, vocational training, cultural production, health, and real estate. Investment in unlisted services is still highly regulated (cafés, for example). However, the code does not apply to financial services, mining, and energy, which continue to be regulated by relevant authorities and departments.

In terms of foreign investment, the 1993 code draws a distinction between offshore or totally exporting firms in all activities but agriculture, services other than those exported by offshore firms, and agricultural investment. Investment undertaken by offshore firms is unrestricted. For many service activities investment must receive prior approval of the Higher Investment Commission if foreign capital accounts for more than half of total capital. Foreign companies or individuals can invest in agriculture, but land ownership is strictly prohibited.

While the new regulation of foreign investment in agriculture is still somewhat restrictive, it represents significant liberalization since the time when foreign investment was shut out of the sector. However, the economic and strategic rationale behind investment restrictions in many service activities (such as software development, consulting, and auditing) is not clear. It is well known that other countries, such as India, have benefited from the opening of these activities to foreign companies.

PUBLIC PROCUREMENT POLICIES

Public procurement is regulated by Decree 89–442 of 1989, partially amended by decrees in 1990 and 1994. These decrees unified the legislation and rules applying to public enterprises and administrations.

Transparency of rules

To promote competition, the legislation adopted the following set of transparency rules:

- Procurement procedures must be followed for all purchases of goods and services costing above certain thresholds, with public enterprises allowed higher thresholds than other public entities.
- The nature, content, and technical characteristics of goods or services must be defined before any tendering is made.
- Procurement contracts can be broken down into several contracts if that is likely to produce technical or financial advantages. The terms of procurement have to specify the number, nature, and importance of each contract and eventually the maximum number of contracts any single bidder can bid for.
- Public entities, administrations, and enterprises are allowed to pool procurements in common contracts. This procedure strengthens the bargaining power of the public sector relative to the private sector.
- Contracts can stipulate fixed or revisable prices. Where prices are revisable, the contract should stipulate the period over which initially proposed prices will apply and the precise rules to be applied in case of revision.
- Bidders have to provide a temporary bail or deposit that is not to exceed 1 percent of the bid value. For the selected bidder a final bail or deposit amounting to 3 percent of the value of the contract may be required.

Differentiated treatment of firms

In principle, the system does not favor public entities over private firms, with the exception of the bails, deposits, or guarantees from which entities that are primarily public are exempted. In the case of international bidding, the system grants some advantages to domestic producers. First, foreign bids must subcontract primarily to local firms unless they cannot fulfill parts of the procurement. Second, products of Tunisian origin have to be preferred over same-quality foreign products as long as the prices of the Tunisian products do not exceed those of the foreign products by more than 20 percent. Third, unless it is impossible, a foreign consulting firm has to associate itself with a Tunisian consulting firm selected from a list held by the relevant public entity. This regulation, though discriminatory, is not very different from the legislation and practice in most countries, industrial and developing alike.

The restrictions are meant to tie the selection of foreign suppliers to some transfer of technology or know-how. However, the stipulation that domestic suppliers have to be selected even if their prices are as much as 20 percent higher than those of foreign suppliers represents excessive protection; foreign suppliers have to pay more or less the same taxes and import duties as domestic suppliers on the relevant goods. In principle, additional protection ought to be related to the value added during local production, not to the total value of the procurement.

PRICE REGULATION

The Tunisian economy has undergone major reforms in price regulation since 1986. Until then prices were regulated by a 1970 law that contained five regimes applying to different categories of goods and services: government price fixing for basic commodities and public utilities, price certification or prior government approval, price self-certification, a controlled or restricted free-price regime, and an unrestricted free-price regime.

Under the government price-fixing regime prices were set by the government and changed from time to time depending on cost increases, the weight of the subsidies incurred, and sociopolitical conditions. This regime was applied mainly to basic subsidized goods and inputs, products of mass consumption (such as tea, coffee, and black pepper), public utilities, and health services.

Under the prior approval regime firms submitted their accounts and other documents to the Price Regulatory Department when applying for price increases. This department made its decision on the basis of these documents and sectoral data. Firms were not allowed to change prices until the government announced its decision, in principle within forty-five days of receiving the request. Prices were set for each firm on the basis of average costs of production to which were added a net profit margin equal to 20 percent of equity and an additional margin to cover overhead costs. These two margins made up a total gross margin set for each firm. Thus prices could vary for the same product from one firm to another.

Whereas the prior approval regime applied to each set of products and to each firm, the self-certification regime applied to the same products across all firms, which were allowed to revise their prices forty-five days after notifying the government unless the proposed revisions were rejected. Price changes were based on average cost plus a gross margin set by the government in agreement with business representatives. These margins varied from one category of products to another. For example, they averaged 15 percent for food, 18 percent for construction materials, 20 percent for textile and clothing, and 22 percent for leather products.

Finally, the restricted free-price regime allowed firms to set their prices freely and to apply any changes fifteen days after notifying the Regulatory Department. Still, the government reserved for itself the right to influence firms' decisions and could even reject projected price modifications within fifteen days of being notified.

This complex system enabled the government to exercise some control over profit margins, especially in sectors where market power was concentrated in the hands of a few firms protected from foreign competition. Not only did the system generate distortions, but it was cumbersome and difficult to manage. The Regulatory Department did not have the capacity or the resources to run it efficiently. Of some 6,000 applications filed every year, the staff could not evaluate more than a third, resulting in long delays. In the meantime firms were able to lower the quality of their products, which was equivalent to increasing prices. Thus price control was ineffective.

Extent of price control

Until 1982 price control covered more than 80 percent of goods and services. Firms were free to set prices for just 17 percent of goods and services, mostly producer agricultural products. In 1982 the unrestricted regime was extended to another 18 percent of goods and services, bringing total coverage of this regime to about 35 percent. The self-certification regime was extended to about 26 percent of all products that had been under the fixed regime and marginally under the restricted free regime. The restricted free regime did not cover more than 2 percent of the total. A share of 37 percent was regulated through the other two regimes, government price fixing and certification (prior approval).

The 1991 law introduced the general principle of free price determination within limits, that is, depending on the protection of the purchasing power of low-income groups or, for some products, the degree of market concentration and the oligopolistic or monopolistic market structure. Free price determination was to be applied only to goods and services that did not fall under one of those two restrictions, the final objective being to liberalize pricing for about 85 percent of products at both the production and the distribution stages.

The 1991 law also fixed rules of competition and shielded the economy from abuses that might result from dominant market positions or collusion among firms in pricing, entry, production and capacity expansion, and market sharing. This law also required transparency of information regarding prices and sale conditions. However, the government reserves the right to intervene in price setting and to freeze prices for a period not exceeding six months, a provision that could be a source of uncertainty for firms and weaken the credibility of the whole policy of price deregulation.

For goods and services that are still regulated, two price regimes have been designed: prior approval and self-certification. Under the first regime, applicable to both production and distribution, the Regulatory Department sets prices on the basis of the applying firm's accounts or of sectoral data if price changes involve a whole sector or activity. The second regime, applicable only to distribution, sets distribution margins as rates, absolute amounts, or a combination of the two.

The liberalization achieved by the 1991 law accelerated in 1992 and 1993 when additional lists of unregulated products were added. By the end of 1993, 87 percent of products were liberalized at the production stage and 70 percent at the distribution stage. These estimates should be interpreted with caution, since they are calculated from lists of food and manufacturing products and exclude services and nonmanufacturing goods, whose prices generally continue to be regulated. In addition, cereal prices have been considered free even though they are fixed by the government, and until recently the public cereal board had a monopoly on grain purchases. Thus the 87 percent ratio is an overestimate.

Price control at the producer stage

In 1993 only 13 percent of products were still under the prior approval regime. The products still under regulation are:

- Cereal-based products (couscous and subsidized bread, flour, semolina, and pasta).
- Other food products (subsidized cooking oil, sugar, and powdered milk, as well as yeast, tea, coffee, hot beverages, beer, tobacco, matches, and alcohol).
- Subsidized paper, books, and notebooks.
- Chemicals (gasoline, cement, lime, compressed gas, medicine).
- Other manufactured products (metal containers and wrappings, motor vehicles).

- Public utilities (passenger transportation, water and electricity, telecommunications, port fees).
- Medical fees.

Regulation is thus concentrated in agroindustry and construction materials, which together account for more than 90 percent of total production still under regulation. Price control continues to hold sway over two subsidized categories of goods, cereal-based commodities and cooking oil, which combined account for 40 percent of total production of goods still under regulation. Control is also very restrictive for goods under monopoly or state production, such as tobacco, beer, pharmaceuticals, and cement, which together represent more than 40 percent of total regulated production.

For most of the goods and services still under price regulation the need for such control is likely to decrease as trade liberalization proceeds and consumer subsidies are reduced. For food products such as coffee and tea, however, the continuation of price restrictions can no longer be justified. The margins earned by the public trade board that holds a monopoly on coffee and tea are likely lower than what would have been earned on the same products by private importers. As with hot beverages in general, regulated prices vary widely from one product to another. Entry to this activity is restricted through licensing.

Price control at the distribution stage

Even though significant liberalization has been introduced, distribution margins are still regulated. Whereas in 1990 the unrestricted regime covered 47 percent of total absorption (domestic production *plus* imports *minus* exports), this regime rose to 70 percent in 1993. The government has set as a final objective the extension of this regime to 85 percent of all goods and services, implying that 15 percent of all goods and services will be liberalized at the distribution stage.

The most regulated sectors are agroindustry, mechanical and electrical industries, and agriculture and fishing. These three sectors represent about 28 percent, 31 percent, and 19 percent of total regulated absorption, respectively, or a total share of 78 percent. Chemicals and construction materials make up another 15 percent of total absorption.

For agriculture there is hardly any price control at the production stage, notwithstanding cereals and milk (for which the government guarantees minimum prices). By contrast, distribution margins are regulated for more than 80 percent of vegetables and 60 percent of fruits, sectors that qualify for liberalization according to the market structure criterion. Although the products involved are mostly basic commodities, their markets are competitive enough to eliminate fear of any significant increase in average margins if distribution is liberalized.

The regulation of distribution margins for motor vehicles will continue as long as imports are licensed. Importers and dealers have so far enjoyed oligopolistic positions; given the quantitative restrictions imposed on imports, they would have reaped high rents – despite the high tariffs levied on them – had consumer prices been deregulated. Until the end of 1994 dealers held monopolies for the representation of foreign car companies, which allowed them to earn handsome profits despite price regulation. With the end of exclusive representation in 1995, competition in the sector is likely to increase. The government has no plan to liberalize distribution margins in the near future and is unlikely to do so unless imports of these products are liberalized.

DEREGULATION OF THE BANKING SECTOR

Under structural adjustment significant progress was made toward financial liberalization and the deregulation of banking. Until 1986 practically all banking operations were regulated by Tunisia's Central Bank. A share of 20 percent of all deposits had to be held in government bonds called equipment bonds, which yielded interest rates far below the rates charged to the private sector. Another 5 percent had to be lent to the Housing Saving Fund, which in 1989 was converted into a deposit bank. Finally, 18 percent of deposits was allocated to medium-term loans for agriculture, exports, and small and medium-size enterprises. In addition to this credit earmarking, loan applications exceeding ceilings set by the Central Bank required its prior approval. Ceilings varied according to the type of loan, and though they were occasionally adjusted they remained relatively low.

Until 1987 interest rates were also set by the Central Bank for all types of loans (short- medium- and long-term) and differentiated by use. These rates were adjusted sporadically and implied low real rates, which were often negative. Between 1977 and 1984 rates changed only once, in 1981, increasing by 0.25 percent for subsidized activities and up to 1.5 percent for overdrafts. During this period the average annual rate of inflation stood at 9.6 percent, giving rise to negative interest rates for all loans except overdrafts, for which real rates were almost zero.

The Central Bank controlled liquidity through credit rediscount facilities. Banks were not allowed to rediscount at the base rate more than the equivalent of 15 percent of their deposits. Beyond 15 percent and 17.5 percent of deposits they were charged higher interest rates, and all rediscounting above 17.5 percent was subject to a penalty rate. Rediscounting of commercial paper involving exports and agricultural activities was granted at favorable rates and not included in the 15 percent ceiling. Thus until 1987 banks played a passive role and did not hold themselves responsible for their operations. The required approval of the Central Bank for the bulk of credit not only hindered economic activity but also freed commercial banks from risky lending.

The move toward financial liberalization has involved many aspects of banking. Prior approval of loans by the Central Bank was abolished in 1988. However, the Central Bank reserved the right to control lending operations *ex post*. It also issued detailed guidelines on lending and in 1992 established rules setting limits and equity ratios on risk exposure. The obligation for banks to hold 20 percent of their deposits in government bonds was abolished in 1992. Today the government issues treasury bills and bonds at market conditions, which will gradually increase the cost of government indebtedness while reducing financial repression.

In 1987 the government decided to liberalize borrowing and lending rates except for activities relating to priority activities (agriculture, exports, and handicrafts). For all other activities lending rates could vary within a margin of three points above the money market rate. The rate served on saving accounts was also liberalized, with a floor set at two points below the money market rate. For term deposits and other financial products rates were totally freed, leading to fierce competition between banks. The two largest banks, which are public and were hurt most by this competition, obtained an agreement from all deposit banks to harmonize borrowing rates. Concluded in March 1988, this agreement is still in effect. Thus the experience of free rates on deposits other than sight deposits and special savings accounts was short-lived.

Lending rates for activities other than agriculture, exports, and handicrafts were further liberalized in 1992, when the three-point margin above the market rate was set in terms of an average margin. This new regulation, which gave banks more freedom to differentiate between borrowers, was loose and its compliance was difficult to check. In 1994 the Central Bank decided to abolish the margin system and free lending rates altogether. In response banks have agreed to minimum lending rates and uniform fees for some services. This collusion, which has met with the silent approval of the Central Bank, provided banks with new opportunities to differentiate among borrowers. Furthermore, there has been a progressive upward adjustment of rates charged to priority activities, from 6 percent to 8 percent in 1987 and 10 percent to 11 percent in 1992. These rates, close to money market rates, have resulted in positive real rates. Activities qualifying for this subsidized credit have been narrowed considerably, the objective being the total elimination of such credit.

The money market rate now plays a leading role in determining lending and borrowing rates. Although created in 1964, the money market rate started to function effectively only in 1987, when large firms were allowed to issue and sell treasury paper on the money market, banks began to issue relatively large certificates of deposit, and interbank operations developed. With liquidity no longer provided through rediscounting, this market is the only way the Central Bank exerts its authority in this area. The money market and its interest rates, however, tend to be dominated by the monetary authority. Interbank liquidity flows have been much smaller than the funds injected by the Central Bank. Furthermore, the monetary authority uses its discretionary power in lending to banks more than half of the funds injected. The money market rate thus results almost exclusively from Central Bank policy, and the influence of interbank transactions is minor.

With the reforms already achieved, banks have been asked to play a much more active role than in the past. Today banks are responsible for assessing loan applications and observing prudential rules, functions that far exceed their old processing role with loans submitted for approval of the Central Bank. Furthermore, the monetary authorities have granted tax incentives for adequate provisioning, deducting as much as 50 percent of provisions from taxable corporate income. Restrictions and interest rate distortions have been significantly reduced, although the Central Bank continues to exert a strong influence on their formation through the money market.

CONCLUSION

Given the size of the Tunisian economy, competition cannot be enhanced unless foreign trade is further liberalized. Actions have been taken to gradually remove import licensing as well as to reduce tariff dispersion, but protection by tariff as well as nontariff barriers remains high. Trade policy has been rationalized through tariff reduction and the tariffication of remaining licensing. This licensing measure, however, has been accompanied by an upward revision of duties for nonbound tariff lines as well as by the imposition of excessive complementary provisional duties since 1991. Serious restrictions and distortions have been removed from Tunisia's investment incentive and regulatory system, but remaining distortions – such as differentiated treatment of offshore firms exclusively devoted to exporting – should also be eliminated.

The Tunisian economy will greatly benefit from the equal treatment of sales of imports and products from offshore companies. As the investment code stipulates, the same duties should be levied on domestic sales as on similar imports, but with no restrictions on the share of output locally sold. With the projected removal of tariff and quantitative barriers on imports from the European Union, which make up the bulk of Tunisia's imports, export incentives will no longer serve the purpose of compensating for the distortions resulting from protection. Rather, they will result in reverse discrimination against firms producing for the local market and adjusting to foreign competition.

Barriers to entry still exist for some foreign investment activities. While the regulation of investment in agriculture is understandable for strategic reasons, the economic and strategic rationale behind the restrictions imposed on investment in support services (such as software development, consulting, and auditing) is less obvious. The opening to foreign investment of auditing and consulting services, notably in the area of international marketing and quality and technological improvements, would benefit Tunisian firms that need to restructure to enhance competitiveness.

Other innovations include the removal of price controls and privatization of public enterprises. Although price controls have been eased considerably since 1986, these changes have taken place more at the production than at the distribution stage, where significant human and material resources continue to be devoted to regulation that is no longer needed. The deregulation of important services such as transportation and telecommunications as well as the privatization of state-owned enterprises has been proceeding sluggishly, incurring needless losses for the state. Meanwhile, the deregulation of banking – particularly a shift of operational responsibilities from the Central Bank to individual banks – should help Tunisia move closer to its ultimate goal of enhancing economic performance through competition.

Note

1 The author is grateful to Bouaziz Rached and Naccache Sonia for their helpful assistance in preparing this chapter.

References

GATT (General Agreement on Tariffs and Trade), 1994. 'Trade Policy Review, Tunisia,' Geneva: GATT.

Institut d'Economie Quantitative, 1994 'Investment Incentives in Tunisia,' mimeograph, Ministry of Economic Development, Tunisia.

IQE (Institute of Quantitative Economics), 1994. 'Etude sur la Réforme du Système des Incitations à l'Investissement en Tunisie,' Ministry of Planning and Regional Development.

Jamel, Zarrouk, 1995. 'Policy Implications of the Uruguay Round Results for the Arab Countries,' paper presented at the Arab Joint Seminar on the Uruguay Round and the Arab Countries sponsored by the Arab Fund for Economic and Social Development, Kuwait.

Lahouel, Mohamed Hedi, 1994a. 'Trade and Exchange Rate Policies and the Performance of the Tunisian Economy in the Eighties,' paper presented at the African Development Bank Development Policy Seminar (forthcoming in *African Development Review*).

———— 1994b. 'Tunisia's Economic Profile,' paper prepared for the *African Development Report 1995*, Abidjan, Côte d'Ivoire: African Development Bank.

Nsouli, Saleh M., Sena Eken, Paul Duran, Gerwin Bell, and Zühtü Yücelik, 1993. 'The Path to Convertibility and Growth,' *Occasional Paper* 109, Washington, D.C.: International Monetary Fund.

Republic of Tunisia, 1994. 'Politique Commerciale de la Tunisie.'

Part II

Perspectives from the Mashreq

4 A Vision for Egypt in 2012

Heba Handoussa and Hanaa Kheir-El-Din

Egypt faces a number of challenges as the twenty-first century approaches. Long-term projections indicate that the population and labor force will continue to grow rapidly, requiring 11 million new jobs and significant expansion of physical and social infrastructures. Globally, trade liberalization, technological change, and environmental concerns demand adjustments in production structures and institutional frameworks as competition mounts from countries in South and Southeast Asia and Eastern Europe. To meet these challenges, Egypt must integrate its economy with the world system by achieving a balanced macroeconomy, increasing competitiveness, reducing protection, and adopting free market policies.

This chapter presents the preliminary results of a modeling exercise that targets an ambitious but achievable program of economic and social progress over the next seventeen years. It calls for a consistent menu of public investment in infrastructure, the environment, science and technology, human resource development, and social safety nets, while forecasting growth in private investment across the production sectors. The focus here is on one best-case scenario in which the state focuses its resources on the social sectors, with a vigorous assault on all aspects of human deprivation.

Egypt's history since the 1952 revolution has been one of political struggle for independence, economic struggle for better living standards, and social struggle for equality of opportunity. Even though the ideological stance of the ruling regime has shifted twice–first toward socialism, nationalization, and a closed economy in the 1960s and then back to an open-door policy in the mid-1970s–some features are common to the entire period. Successive governments have relied on centralized administration, public sector dominance over economic activity, import-substituting growth strategies, and an overly generous social contract that provides open-ended subsidies and guarantees employment for educated citizens.

Each decade has had a different focus and different achievements. During the 1950s the country was able to overcome social inequality and reduce disparities in income and wealth. During the 1960s education and health services expanded significantly and jobs in the public sector became guaranteed to college graduates. During the 1970s subsidies became an important tool in providing a social safety net. Efforts also began to make better use of the desert and to reduce urban spread and industrial pollution. During the 1980s the focus was on upgrading and expanding the country's infrastructure. In addition, a new population policy brought down runaway population growth and gave priority to basic health care for women and children.

The cost of these achievements has been high, however, and the growth path has proved unsustainable. Too often planners and policy-makers have lost sight of the tradeoffs involved in these achievements. An early emphasis on university education neglected primary education, leaving nearly half of the adult population illiterate. Too much emphasis on subsidies left too few resources for investment and led to growing indebtedness. The drive toward job creation in the government and public sector lowered real wages and reduced productivity. If Egypt is to achieve sustainable growth, a better balance must be struck between equity and efficiency, the resource base must be better used, and the country's most important asset–its people–must play a larger role in the process, both as producers and consumers of progress. These objectives require a reformed institutional framework that allows people to participate at every stage of development. While public spending must be used to prioritize human development, decentralization and democratization must be accelerated if the promise of development is to devolve from government and be shared by civil society.

In 1991 Egypt adopted a bold economic reform and structural adjustment program to address a problematic social and economic situation, manifested in rising structural unemployment, mounting external debt, double-digit inflation, and an increasingly negative balance of payments. Stabilization and liberalization have been achieved, significantly raising the country's creditworthiness. Although macroeconomic indicators have improved, stabilization has had a number of negative impacts–sluggish (gross domestic products) growth, increased unemployment, and increased poverty–that must be addressed if development is to be sustained. A resumption of high levels of investment is essential, boosted by private sector confidence and by donor support for a balanced, well-focused public program for developing social and physical infrastructure. Egypt is poised to launch a second reform program–one that creates an equitable and self-reliant society, promotes sustained growth, and allows its citizens to achieve living standards commensurate with those of middle-income countries and beyond.

THE STRATEGY

A vision for Egypt in 2012 that aims at higher living standards, improved efficiency, and a self-reliant economy with sustained, long-term growth is being designed by a team of Egyptian economists in consultation with relevant government departments. The plan's key targets over the two decades that began with the Third Five-Year Plan (fiscal 1992 to fiscal 1997) are:

- Average annual growth in gross domestic product (GDP) of 6.5 percent, with national savings rising to 21.5 percent of GDP and investment to 24.0 percent.
- Growth in agricultural value added of 4–5 percent a year and manufacturing value added of 10–11 percent a year.
- Accelerated annual growth of exports from manufacturing (averaging 12.4 percent), agriculture (6.0 percent), and tourism (9.8 percent).
- Consistent productivity growth, with the incremental capital–output ratio falling to 4.3 and labor productivity rising by 2.4 percent a year.
- Full employment of a growing labor force, rising wage levels, and acceptable minimum wages.
- An institutional framework that eliminates unnecessary bureaucracy, promotes decentralization, and raises the returns to productive activity.
- Free and universal access to high-quality basic education and health services.
- Vocational training systems that provide appropriate skills compatible with the needs of formal and informal enterprises.
- Continued decline in the birth rate through better family planning services, maternal and child care facilities, and programs to accelerate demographic transition. Annual population growth is projected to decline from 2.4 percent to 1.4 percent by 2012.
- Poverty alleviation through a well targeted system of transfers, ultimately leading to the gradual elimination of poverty.

- Elimination of all disparities resulting from regional or gender biases.
- Arresting environmental degradation and improving the coverage and quality of infrastructure services.

These ambitious targets can be met if Egypt's macroeconomic framework is sound, competitiveness and market efficiency are increased, and a holistic strategy is adopted that places human development at the heart of economic development. Political stability, social justice, a shift toward higher value-added activities, the development of domestic and regional markets, and economic, financial, and price stability are prerequisites for self-sustained development.

ADAPTING THE MACROECONOMY

Most of the elements needed for rapid, sustained economic recovery are now in place. Over the past four years significant adjustments have been made in fiscal, exchange rate, and monetary policies – three crucial policy areas. As a result Egypt has overcome its main macroeconomic imbalances. The fiscal deficit is less than 3 percent of GDP, mainly due to increased government revenue. The general sales tax raised the proceeds from the former consumption tax from 3 billion Egyptian pounds (£E) to more than £E 12 billion a year. The reformulation of income taxes toward a unified tax increased revenue. Stamp duties have been raised and the sales tax has been extended to capital goods. Many analysts, however, believe that the increased tax burden is one of the main causes of continued recession in the Egyptian economy. And although the annual inflation rate has fallen to about 11 percent as a result of the lower deficit and its financing through real sources – treasury bill auctions – the stock of treasury bills outstanding at the end of 1994 was £E 40 billion.

Still, a number of developments have significantly improved creditworthiness and donor confidence. By the end of fiscal 1994 external indebtedness had fallen to about $32 billion and the debt service–exports ratio to about 19 percent. The balance of payments on the current account has been positive since fiscal 1992. The Central Bank's foreign reserves were $17.5 billion at the end of 1994, about three times the safe level of six months' worth of imports. The exchange rate has been unified and stabilized within the range of £E 3.3–3.4 to the U.S. dollar. The economy is no longer dollarized. Real interest rates have risen to positive levels, while the nominal interest rate on treasury bills has dropped from more than 20 percent to about 10.5 percent. Based on these indicators, conditions are ripe for the resumption of high levels of investment, boosted by private sector confidence and donor support.

Nevertheless, stabilization has had negative impacts that must be addressed. Inflationary pressures are again building up. The tax burden hinders investment and discourages entrepreneurial activity. Open unemployment exceeds 14 percent, mainly because of new entrants to the labor force with intermediate and university degrees. Although the current account balance (including transfers) has been positive, growth of industrial exports has declined and imports have stagnated. As a result the current account balance (excluding transfers) is increasingly negative and threatens to erode accumulated reserves.

The stabilization effort has lasted too long, resulting in continued economic recession. This situation calls for a strong drive toward enhancing economic growth. The proposed policy package encompasses three broad classes of growth-promoting economic measures:

- The *macroeconomic* – combining fiscal and monetary policies in order to attain the desired growth rate without causing inflation or other destabilizing phenomenon.
- The *microeconomic* – promoting the productive efficiency of economic agents. These measures will reform industrial organization; raise domestic, regional, and international competitiveness; and improve training, management, incentive systems, and employer-worker relations.
- The *socio–ethical* – dealing with human values, behavior, and preferences. This area encompasses such elements as attitudes toward work and discipline, consumption patterns and thrift, appreciation of quality and precision, and so on. These values will be developed through education and media campaigns and thorough incentive structures in the workplace.

Given the drastic shift in the policy framework toward a more open, less distorted structure of incentives, it is difficult to forecast macroeconomic variables based on the dismal trends of the past decade. Targeted average GDP growth through 2012 is 6.5 percent, rising from 4.0 percent to reach 7.0 percent by the end of the period. This growth is based on an increase in the national savings rate to 26 percent of GDP, an increase of investment to 30 percent of GDP, and a reduction in the incremental capital–output ratio from the peak of 6 reached during the 1980s to 4 by 2012.

These targets will require the government to contribute significantly to national savings by continuing to manage current revenue and spending. They will also require an enabling macroeconomic and institutional framework that encourages domestic and foreign investment. Growth-promoting macroeconomic policies involving fiscal and monetary measures and price and wage determination mechanisms must be pursued. Finally, the transition from inward-looking, import-substituting strategies to export-led growth will be completed by liberalizing the trade and exchange regime and lowering protection, which is still high in certain manufacturing subsectors (such as consumer goods).

Public spending must be revised toward areas that have an impact on growth. With privatization and peace on the rise, public spending should emphasize health, education, infrastructure, and the development of science and technology. On the revenue side, taxation should not be used solely as a revenue-generating device; rather, it should be used as a means of promoting equity, providing incentives, and stimulating growth. The tax system should be drastically reformed to achieve vertical and horizontal equity. Income tax rates must be lowered. The general sales tax should be converted into a value-added tax that promotes output, exports, and investment – a move that focuses on limiting final consumption rather than increasing government revenue. Other indirect taxation that constrains investment also should be revised. Finally, tax exemptions should be confined to certain vital activities.

Real interest rates must be kept positive and, eventually, nominal interest rates will be determined in the capital market. Prices and wages should be freed from government controls and allowed to adjust to market forces. Wages should be flexible and respond to productivity increases. The exchange rate should gradually be allowed to float in the exchange market to maintain export competitiveness.

Under the strategy the state's role in production, finance, and trade will decline substantially, allowing it to assume greater responsibility as an arbitrator and regulator in the marketplace. The state should focus on ensuring economic stability in order to promote full employment, prevent inflation, and avoid unsustainable internal and external deficits. In its role as regulator, the state must promote competition by fully liberalizing the trade and investment regimes and by revising the legal and administrative framework governing market entry and exit. Moreover, providing public goods that enhance the functioning of markets and that foster sustained growth should be a major concern of the state and be upgraded considerably. These include access to information, research and development, technology transfer, human capital formation, and environmental protection.

Education, science, and industrial policies should promote change and innovation. While investment in infrastructure and utilities requires substantial resources and has traditionally been the responsibility of the state, experience elsewhere shows that there is substantial room for private investment in utilities, particularly in telecommunications and electricity. The state should also continue to play an important redistributional role, with an emphasis on a well-targeted social security system.

Administrative reform is also essential, since the Egyptian civil service hinders production and investment. Reform will require simplification and modernization of laws and regulations, particularly those relating to economic activity. The size of the civil service, which employs 3.5 million people, also must be reduced. In the short term this could be achieved by not recruiting new entrants unless an equal number withdraws from government employment. The basic salary scale must be revised to bring it in line with realistic living standards and to minimize corruption. Tying promotions and remunerations to actual performance will also ensure a competitive civil service and attract qualified people. Finally, civil servants should continuously be provided with training opportunities.

ACHIEVING EXTERNAL COMPETITIVENESS

The impact of trade liberalization—within the Uruguay Round framework—on the Egyptian economy depends on the degree of economic openness achieved, the level of change in customs tariffs imposed, the degree of change in preferential treatment, and the sensitivity of the Egyptian economy to these changes.

Forming trade alliances

Egypt enjoys preferential treatment in European Union (EU) countries under the Mashreq–EU agreements. Most tariff lines exported from Egypt to the European Union enjoy complete tariff exemptions; the rest are granted partial tariff reductions. They are, however, subject to quantitative quotas and seasonal restrictions.[1] These preferences are likely to be eroded once the Uruguay Round agreements are implemented. Thus it is imperative that Egypt negotiate with major importing nations – particularly with the European Union within the framework of the proposed association agreement – to increase market access for Egypt's main exports (textiles, clothing, and agricultural products) in return for privileged access of European products into the Egyptian economy.

The Uruguay Round's removal of quantitative restrictions on agricultural commodities, gradual phasing out of restrictions on textiles and clothing (over ten years), and eventual removal of nontariff barriers on industrial products will improve market access for developing countries in general. But Egypt's competitiveness relative to South Asian countries will be negatively impacted. The percentage of Egyptian exports facing quantitative restrictions in industrial markets will be reduced by less than the percentage of exports from other developing countries, particularly those in South Asia. This factor should be taken into consideration during Egypt's negotiations with its main industrial trading partners. The degree of tariff escalation also has been reduced as a result of the Uruguay Round. This development should encourage Egypt to move toward higher value-added exports, particularly in metals and food processing.

The tariffication of nontariff barriers and the reduction of tariffs on industrial imports from developing countries (by an average of 40 percent) imply both improved market access to industrial countries and a potential diversion away from Egyptian exports as preferential treatment erodes. Egypt's gains from the Round are projected to be $21.2 million. Since the total gains to developing countries are expected to be $80 billion, Egypt's 0.023 percent share appears quite dismal. Static gains should not, however, eclipse the importance of dynamic gains, which are more significant and will depend on the efficiency gains from increased competition, greater innovation, and the supply response of the Egyptian tradables sector. The negotiations for a free trade agreement with the European Union present a real opportunity for export expansion in this market. Eastern Europe, for example, at one time (1970–72) received 57 percent of Egypt's exports. Egypt must strive to increase its competitiveness and enlarge its share of the most likely markets – the European Union, Eastern Europe, and the Arab countries, particularly the Gulf states.

The Arab market is another area that could absorb Egyptian manufactured exports. Low transport costs, a common language, and similar tastes, business practices, laws, and conventions make this region a natural destination for Egypt's exports. A regional Arab common market–to which Egypt could be a major contributor–is in the interest of Arab countries. Such a market would rationalize the allocation of resources, avoid wasteful duplication of investment, stimulate competition, enhance productivity, and accelerate industrial restructuring. In 1992 Arab countries imported $83.0 billion worth of manufactured goods, with food accounting for $10.0 billion, textiles and clothing for $7.4 billion, and iron and steel for $5.4 billion. Although Egypt enjoys comparative advantages in these three sectors, as well as many others, its intraregional exports did not exceed $188 million in 1992 (excluding petroleum). Given the size of the region's manufactures imports, Egypt should look to the Arab states and reap the potential gains of a market of 240 million inhabitants.

Reforming the trade framework

Achieving export competitiveness by 2012 will require implementing structural economic transformation, moving away from agricultural and petroleum exports and toward exports of manufactures and services, and shifting production structures toward higher value-added products, higher skills, and more technology-intensive activities. Since production is becoming globalized, success in attracting multinational corporations and foreign direct investment will depend on creating an enabling environment. In addition, moving along complementary lines of action is essential, namely, by providing adequate incentives through policy and institutional reforms that reduce the anti-export bias and by increasing quality and price competitiveness by upgrading the production process through technological change.

Reforming the trade regime involves providing nonactionable forms of support to exporters along the lines permitted under Uruguay Round agreements, moving the structure of exports toward higher value-added products, and encouraging a more diversified geographic destination. Direct and indirect priority measures for achieving these goals include:

- Reducing tariffs and indirect taxation on inputs to enhance the competitiveness of domestic firms by reducing the cost of inputs.
- Improving the customs regime for exports, including temporary admission and duty systems.
- Providing exporters with credit and guarantee facilities.
- Revising the tariffication of water, electricity, telecommunications, and transportation to ensure their competitiveness with international equivalents.

- Adopting supportive employment and industrial relations policies by revising labor laws, improving worker skills and knowledge, and promoting positive and progressive attitudes among the labor force.
- Developing export processing zones and converting free zones into export processing zones.
- Increasing the availability of air and maritime transport to overseas markets and of ground transport to regional markets.
- Eliminating impediments to exports, paying special attention to demonopolizing public sector shipping and other port-related services.
- Encouraging alliances with foreign trading companies.
- Identifying activities with a comparative advantage and focusing on policies that promote products, product design, process improvement, and market development. Doing so will require government and private sector participation.

Augmenting domestic technology

Of equal importance is a focus on Egypt's science and technology policies. Egypt's industry is based on imported technology; very little technology is adapted to local conditions. Developing an alternative approach is a relatively long-term process that warrants developing human capital and technology institutions and promoting activities to acquire, adapt, develop, and diffuse technology at the national and firm levels. Enhancing the capacity to receive and benefit from science and technology requires integrating science and technology policies with long-term strategies for economic, social, and political development; increasing public awareness of the role of science and technology in improving living standards, and increasing the population's ability to use and contribute to science and technology; creating awareness in the private sector of the potential benefits of science and technology; and increasing the share of gross national product (GNP) devoted to research and development, particularity for industrial purposes.

ENHANCING SECTORAL GROWTH

The potential for GDP growth will heavily depend on the growth of three pivotal economic sectors: agriculture, manufacturing, and human resources.

Agriculture

Agriculture has traditionally been the main source for growth, with the government providing basic infrastructure, irrigation, and drainage services and the private sector owning and farming the land. However, more than three decades of pervasive government intervention in pricing, marketing, input delivery, crop area fixing, and crop rotation determination have had a detrimental impact on agricultural performance. The sector now generates about 15 percent of GDP (from 30 percent in 1973) and 12 percent of export proceeds (from 50 percent), and provides about 36 percent of employment (from 51 percent). The decline in agriculture also reflects the accelerated growth in other sectors, particularly petroleum, construction, and services.

With the government's increasing awareness of the limits of its useful intervention and of the need to stimulate private participation to ensure growth, far-reaching policy reforms have been implemented since 1986. These include liberalization of input and output prices and elimination of compulsory delivery, crop area controls, and intervention in crop rotation. Cotton and sugar cane are the only two crops in which the government continues to intervene. Farmer responses to these reforms indicate their sensitivity to markets forces and their ability to react to growth stimuli. Production of field crops (wheat, maize, beans) and fruits and vegetables has increased significantly, while cotton has declined. Still, the growth potential of agriculture remains constrained by the availability of water and arable land.

Per capita area of cultivable land has fallen below 0.13 feddan. Future growth in agricultural output will require enhancing the efficiency of cultivated land and water resource use, as well as increasing the land reclamation effort. The objective is to achieve 4–5 percent annual growth in agricultural output, permitting increased exports and contributing to food security. Furthermore, agriculture will provide agroindustries with required inputs. This will warrant raising the productivity of land and water resources, thus increasing national output and farmer incomes.

The key elements of the agricultural strategy include:

- Improving the management of water resources by applying water-conserving irrigation techniques and encouraging the efficient use of water by imposing water charges that cover the costs of operating and maintaining the irrigation network and by improving water management at the farm level.

- Increasing the productivity of old lands by changing the product mix, using high-yielding varieties, emphasizing soil conservation measures, reducing salinity and waterlogging, and rationalizing the use of fertilizers and pesticides.
- Maximizing returns from newly reclaimed land by improving support services to the newly settled farmers, and improving production and irrigation technology through continued research in desert agriculture techniques.
- Carefully examining additional land reclamation from technical, financial, and economic perspectives because it requires sizable investments with long gestation periods and uncertain returns. Over the long run Egypt will have to spread its population over a larger area to absorb the projected population growth.
- Increasing exports by removing impediments to trade. For example, the government should liberalize the production and marketing of cotton, liberalize imports of agricultural inputs, disseminate timely information on trade opportunities among exporters, and focus research activities on exportable crops other that cotton. Developing adequate infrastructure for exports is also essential, including improving the domestic and international transport system, developing storage facilities (including refrigerated storage for perishables), and improving packaging. It will also be necessary to remove obstacles to private sector participation in domestic marketing and agricultural commodity exports.
- Achieving rural development by diversifying rural activities, including developing cottage and agroindustries and providing education and health care services with an emphasis on care for women.
- Upgrading institutions that serve the agricultural sector, strengthening the cooperative system among farmers (and away from government control), extending financing to rural activities other than agriculture, and encouraging private banks to participate in agricultural financing.
- Increasing the share of agriculture in the public investment program and focusing it – along with improved water use and new land development – on agricultural research and extension and agricultural export promotion and marketing. Private investment in developing new lands, agricultural marketing, and export promotion also should be encouraged by removing regulatory and institutional barriers.

Manufacturing

The manufacturing sector has been at the center of Egypt's growth strategy since the 1950s, receiving the lion's share of public investment with an emphasis on import substitution and diversification. Although annual growth rates in the sector have been impressive–averaging 8.9 percent during 1975-92 – the sector's contribution to GDP has remained at 17 percent, its growth having been superseded by that of petroleum, utilities, and services. The share of manufacturing in total employment also has been stable, at 12 percent, accounting for about 1.9 million jobs in fiscal 1992.

Three important features make the manufacturing sector a leading candidate for export-oriented, accelerated economic growth. First, it enjoys a highly diversified production base with substantial installed capacity in upstream processing along a wide horizontal spectrum.[2] Second, the labor force is abundant, experienced, and highly competitive in terms of wages.[3] Third, a wide range of labor-intensive industries is based on sales to a large and protected domestic market – and now shows signs of being profitable in export marketing, even if on a small scale.[4]

The target annual growth rate for industry is 10–11 percent, which will allow for accelerated exports and significant absorption of labor. Certain strategies are essential to maximizing the potential of both the large, formal manufacturing sector and the traditional small sector. First, the sector must shift from an inward to an outward orientation to allow for more rapid growth that utilizes existing capacities, accelerates the move toward higher value-added products, and encourages specialization among producers of goods and auxiliary services.

Second, foreign direct investment must come in at a much faster pace. Establishing strong links between domestic firms and transnational corporations would generate employment and promote the adoption of modern technology and managerial practices. It is hoped that reforms in trade, investment, and fiscal regimes will allow Egypt to serve as the locus of transnational industrial activities for European and Middle East markets.

Third, high-tech industries should be developed that better utilize Egypt's pool of highly skilled engineers, technicians, and other professional. Such industries pay extremely competitive wages. Obvious candidates include microelectronics, telecommunications, and computers.

Finally, the traditional microenterprises (211,000 manufacturing establishments have fewer than fifty employees) should be developed so that they can modernize their production processes and be integrated with the modern industrial complex. Doing so would eliminate the constraints that have maintained the dualistic structure of manufacturing and forced small firms to lag behind in terms of access to technology and skills formation.

In order for these objectives to be achieved, a number of policy and institutional changes are required to complete the process of liberalization that was started with the economic reform and structural adjustment program. Although prices are no longer controlled for more than 80 percent of industrial output, some sectors suffer from direct or indirect controls or from monopoly behavior that prevents competition and constrains the transition toward an export orientation. Examples on the input side include the production and import of cotton yarn, the major intermediate for the textiles sector, with $1 billion worth of output (£E 3,954 million) and $564 million of exports. On the output side are pharmaceuticals, with a domestic market of $370 million and a projected regional market of $5.6 billion by 1997.

Tariff levels and structures are another major constraint to competition. With few exceptions, nontariff barriers have been removed and the tariff range has been reduced to 5–70 percent. Further liberalization of trade and the tariffication of nontariff barriers are expected to move industrial production along the lines of comparative advantage, with gradual elimination of industries that were only able to produce behind high tariff walls. Tariffication of nontariff barriers will enhance the transparency of the trade regime, with textiles as the only item that remains a prohibited import.

The government has taken a major step toward the liberalization of investment licensing by abolishing licensing for all but a negative list of activities. Further steps should be taken to streamline investment approval, especially at the local level.

Human resource development

A well-designed human resource strategy is a key component of the vision for Egypt in 2012. Two shifts in focus are necessary for success. First, national priorities should be restructured and government resources reallocated in favor of basic services. Second, welfare programs should move away from universal provision of subsidies toward well targeted programs that reach the truly needy.

Education

Egypt is committed to prioritizing education as a primary area for human resource development, and has defined the achievement of specific educational targets by 2000 as the "National Project of the 1990s." These targets include universal primary and preparatory school enrollment (students aged six to fourteen years), school enrollment and the eradication of illiteracy, as well as raising the quality of basic education by reforming curriculums, institutionalizing educational evaluations, upgrading teacher training, reducing the average number of students per classroom (from forty-seven to forty), eliminating double shifts, overhauling school buildings, and creating multiple delivery systems to reach all groups, especially girls and women in remote areas. The literacy campaign is being spearheaded by the newly created Specialized Agency and its regional branches, which provided 33,112 classes in fiscal 1994 for a two-year curriculum benefiting adults between the ages of fifteen and thirty-five. The program is designed to expand rapidly to cover the 9.8 million citizens in this age group.

The vision for 2012 incorporates these medium-term targets as well as longer-term goals, including the addition of two years of kindergarten (for four- and five-year olds) to compulsory education, further reducing class sizes to thirty students per classroom, addressing the needs of handicapped and gifted children, ensuring the availability of school playgrounds and libraries, and providing nutritional supplements for primary school children in rural and poor urban communities. At the secondary level schools are to be equipped with computer rooms, science laboratories, and specialized technical buildings. Curriculum reform and teacher training will eliminate rote memorization teaching methods, encourage creativity, promote the development of transferable skills, contribute to awareness of such issues as the environment and health, and give priority to science, mathematics, and languages.

If this ambitious program is to succeed, it will require a significant increase in compensation for teachers. The projected wage bill (on current account) for the Ministry of Education will need to increase by 350 percent by 2012 to accommodate a gradual 200 percent increase in the average wage and a 50 percent increase in teaching staff. The significant expansion in school buildings (more than doubling by 2012 for the primary and preparatory levels) will improve considerably the balance between teachers, classrooms, and students, and will end the practice of double shifts, which has long hindered educational quality.

Health

The health sector has achieved impressive results in improving the health profile of Egypt's population, especially children. Between 1982 and 1992 infant mortality dropped by 43 percent, from 108 to 62 per 1,000 live births. Child mortality fell by 55 percent during the same period. Vaccination coverage increased from 30 percent in 1984 to 90 percent in 1991. Proper oral rehydration therapy use also increased, from 66 percent in 1983 to 98 percent in 1991. Significant improvements have also been recorded for infectious and endemic diseases, with the prevalence of bilharzia falling from 36 percent in 1981 to 10 percent in 1991. These achievements are reflected in the significant decline in deaths attributable to infectious and parasitic diseases, from 17 percent in 1982 to less than 10 percent in 1989. Life expectancy increased from fifty-seven years in 1982 to sixty-three years in 1992.

The targets for 2000 are to further improve maternal and child health (including universal vaccination coverage), eliminate several diseases, and reduce the incidence of others. Over the medium term the target is to raise the quality of primary health care and to improve existing health clinics, especially in rural areas. Although secondary and tertiary health facilities are adequate, public hospitals suffer from low occupancy rates, largely as a result of inadequate medicine supplies, poor maintenance, and inadequate remuneration for doctors, nurses, and technicians. In order to improve the quality of health services that are provided by the government and to raise the occupancy rate of public hospitals, the Ministry of Health's current budget should be immediately raised to increase annual spending on medicine (to £E 400 million, or 40 percent of total drug consumption), maintenance (to £E 100 million), and salaries (to be doubled from current levels, which were £E 606 million in 1992).

Investment spending will maintain the current level of hospital coverage – one Ministry of Health hospital bed per 700 citizens – over the Third and Fourth Five-Year Plans (fiscal 1992 to fiscal 2002). Under the Fifth and Sixth plans coverage will improve to 500 citizens per bed. The number of dental clinics will also increase, reducing the number of citizens per clinic from the current 37,000 to 5,000 by 2012. Expansion is also foreseen in the number of specialized institutes and hospitals (training, geriatric, diabetic, ophthalmic, skin, speech and hearing, paralysis, heart and kidney). In order to rehabilitate existing hospitals, the investment budget will also include an allocation for renovation.

CHALLENGES

The human resource strategy is designed to move immediately on four parallel fronts:

- Providing free, universal access to basic education and health services by 2000.
- Improving the quality of all social services while ensuring their cost-effectiveness and sustainability.
- Providing a transparent and well-targeted welfare system for the ultrapoor. and
- Implementing investments and programs that reinforce and complement human development strategies, namely in the areas of infrastructure (especially sanitation) and the environment.

The main challenges facing the government involve making the necessary adjustments to macroeconomic policies, structural measures, and the public investment program in order to maximize growth while minimizing the adverse impacts of development on the country's vulnerable groups. These challenges are made more complex by population growth, the extent of poverty, the state of the environment, the need for more advanced infrastructure, and extensive unemployment.

Population growth

Egypt's rapid population growth rate may be the most important factor contributing to the high growth of the labor force and thus to extensive unemployment, urban problems, environmental degradation, and aggravation of poverty.

Now that Egypt has entered the stage of demographic transition, the vicious circle of poverty, population growth, and environmental degradation can finally be broken. Yet this goal cannot be achieved unless adjustments are made to fertility rates. According to a slow-decline scenario (population growth declining from 2.4 percent in 1994 to 1.9 percent by 2010), the population will reach about 84 million people by 2012. A more recent model, however, estimates that population growth could fall to 1.4 percent, for a population of 74 million by 2012. The difference between the two scenarios over the next seventeen years could amount to as many as ten million additional young people who will require education, employment, housing, and other services. For example, the slow-decline scenario adds four million children to the basic school age category (five to fourteen years old); the second scenario adds only 600,000. Thus Egypt must strive to achieve the rapid-decline scenario. Doing so will require far more effort in order to maintain the momentum of recent successes in family planning and to reach less accessible segments of the population, especially in rural areas.

Even the rapid-decline target population of 74 million people will add significant annual additions to the population – an average of one million people a year through 2012 – and require that all basic services and infrastructure be expanded. Better coverage and higher-quality services will require large public investments as well as increased current budget spending to pay better salaries, purchase adequate supplies of intermediates, and perform proper maintenance of the capital stock of social services and utilities.

Current spending on family planning is considered adequate, at £E 17 a couple, and the program's costs are included in the overall health sector budget. But even though contraceptives are almost universally available (with an access rate of 95 percent since 1992) and media campaigns have an extensive reach, levels of use still vary tremendously across regions, with contraceptive use ranging from 20–62 percent. This variation underscores the vital importance of providing basic education and health services – especially to women – and promoting employment in poor areas in order to achieve the targeted rate of decline in fertility.

Poverty alleviation

The living standards of the poor and ultrapoor deteriorated substantially as a result of the structural adjustment program and elimination of most subsidies in 1991. More than 40 percent of poor families' spending went toward subsidized foods in 1990, and the price index for food increased by 52 percent for controlled food and 686 percent for decontrolled food during 1990–3. The poor also suffer because their households are larger than average (6.5 people per household compared with an average of 5.3 people in urban areas and 7.8 people compared with 6.7 people in rural areas). In addition, more than 20 percent of poor households are headed by women, adding to the problems that these families face in earning an adequate income.

The government is finalizing a program of social welfare transfers to benefit the estimated 4 million ultrapoor, who receive less than a quarter of the average per capita income. Total cash transfers to the ultrapoor were only £E 164 million in 1991, but subsidies provided several multiples of this figure in income support to vulnerable segments of the population. For the new social safety net to be effective, it must provide sufficient income to purchase a least-cost but healthy diet and other basic necessities and ensure a strict screening process that limits beneficiaries to ultrapoor citizens who are unable to work and have no other source of income. The total annual cost of the welfare program is estimated at £E 2.9 billion (£E 60 a month per beneficiary) and will be introduced over the next two years.

The government envisages three models of intervention to alleviate poverty among the working poor. The first is a program to create jobs in the vast small enterprise sector by extending credit, improving vocational training, providing technical assistance in marketing and management, and selling serviced land at concessional prices for the establishment of new enterprises. The second is a program designed to help nongovernmental organizations (NGOs) that work toward community development expand their activities, especially as they relate to income-generating projects and human resource development. The third is a review of all civil service wages and salaries and an increase in minimum wages.

Prevailing social programs and transfer mechanisms (pension schemes for widows, the elderly, and the disabled) do not provide an adequate safety net to protect the most vulnerable groups from the effects of adjustment, nor are there any employment adjustment services, unemployment benefits, or retraining programs to assist the unemployed or those displaced by public enterprise reform, privatization, and the proposed administrative reform. The social safety net should be designed to benefit both the poor and those who are hurt by adjustment but not necessarily poor. Cost-effective targeting should be developed by setting clear objectives for the social safety net. Targeting should also be directed at easily identifiable groups and at regions with a high concentration of the poor, particularly in rural Upper Egypt (where more than 45 percent of the population is poor).

Environment

Egypt's Environment Action Plan was created in 1992 by ten national, multisectoral, and multidisciplinary working groups – representing relevant ministries, agencies, and NGOs – who identified the major environmental problems facing or likely to face the country over the coming decades and who together elaborated the policies and strategies needed to overcome them. Specific projects were recommended for implementation, and others are being evaluated.

According to the action plan, the requirements for environmental investment over the ten years starting in 1992 are £E 4.7 billion (1992 prices). Other projects costing about £E 1 billion have since been identified by the Egyptian Environment Affairs Agency. These figures do not include infrastructure investments in drainage programs (for agriculture) or water and sewerage networks. Priority investments are those that strengthen environmental institutions and that implement projects to reduce water and air pollution from industry and vehicles. Projects for water treatment, energy conservation, dust control, and waste disposal have been evaluated for about 300 large industrial plants. In addition, efforts will be made over the medium term to improve air quality by reducing the lead content of gasoline from 0.90 to 0.15 grams per liter, and to produce and encourage the use of unleaded gasoline.

Water pollution

The Nile river is the nation's lifeline, providing more than 95 percent of its water supply. Yet water scarcity is threatening the balance between population growth and natural resources, requiring more conservation and better management. Water pollution, a rising water table, and salinization are on the rise because sewerage and drainage system development have not kept pace with the growth in housing settlements and the increased use of water, fertilizers, and pesticides in agriculture. Industrial pollution is also causing serious damage to riverbeds and to aquatic life in major lakes and canals. Land reclamation (2.1 million feddans to date, with another 1.3 million feddans before 2012) and tourism also threaten the water quality of underground aquifers and require stronger environmental institutions and proper water management.

Land use

Land use is another key element of Egypt's environmental strategy. The scarcity of fertile agricultural land in the Delta and Nile Valley (5.7 million feddans) makes it imperative to avoid any further encroachment from urbanization (0.4 million feddans have been lost since 1950) or decline in long-term productivity from water pollution and from improper use of water and other inputs. Land use plans that accommodate the growing population and provide the necessary infrastructure in the most viable areas for human settlement are therefore an essential part of the program to conserve agricultural land. The current ratio of population per feddan is 7.0 people (up from 3.0 people in 1952) and is expected to reach 7.8 people by 2012 under the rapid-decline population growth scenario and on the assumption that no further losses are made to existing lands or to those that are planned for reclamation. The target is to reduce annual losses to urbanization from 5,000 to 1,000 feddans, and to add 10,000 feddans of public parks by 2000 in order to double the ratio of parks to population, from 0.7 to 1.4 square meters per capita.

Air pollution

Air pollution, especially in urban areas, threatens both human health and the country's wealth of antiquities. The heaviest industrial polluters are cement, fertilizer, chemical, and metal-producing firms. A rehabilitation program that introduces pollution control techniques and closes down some plants is under way. Heavy use of leaded gasoline by an aged transport fleet and increasingly congested traffic are also a major source of air pollution and will require the introduction of unleaded gasoline, better traffic management, and a shift toward higher occupancy and cleaner modes of transport. One of the environmental action plan's main strategies is to promote a shift from high-sulfur to low-sulfur oil and natural gas, especially for power generation.

Infrastructure

Major expansions have been achieved in Egypt's infrastructure over the past fifteen years. The per capita increase in the production of electricity, the extension of telephone lines, and the coverage of sewerage networks far surpassed those of other developing countries – at both higher and lower levels of income – during the 1980s. Donor assistance in this field has been highly beneficial, and these achievements have had a significant impact on productivity and health indicators. Electricity now reaches more than 85 percent of rural households, and 82 percent of rural inhabitants have access to clean water. By 2012 rural access to electricity and clean water will have reached 95 percent.

Sewage disposal, however, continues to be a serious problem in both urban and rural areas – only 51 percent of the population has proper sanitation. Such inadequate coverage has grave repercussions on health and the environment. Sufficient investment must be earmarked to provide urban sewerage and rural sanitation facilities to 95 percent of the population by 2012. Rural roads also need improvement–the current length of paved road per inhabitant is less than half that for countries at Egypt's level of development. Such investment has high returns in terms of reduced maintenance costs for road vehicles and increased access to markets.

Another priority concerns planning for urban expansion. The urban population is expected to grow by more than 10 million people by 2012. To discourage urbanization and to avoid further encroachment on agricultural land and the spread of informal settlements, urban planning and development must be immediately undertaken in areas away from the Nile Valley and Delta. A number of sites have been identified for this purpose, and these areas require significant investment in basic infrastructure. Given appropriate incentives, private developers would assume a significant part of the responsibility for implementation of land development projects. The government is currently promoting private involvement in the provision of electricity in an effort to ease public investment in this vital area.

Employment

The most daunting challenge facing Egypt is the restructuring of the economy and the acceleration of growth in order to support productive employment for the labor force, which will reach 30 million people by 2012 (under the rapid-decline population growth scenario). The strategy is to promote high levels of investment in three major areas of private sector activity with high employment multipliers: export-oriented manufacturing by domestic and foreign firms, small-scale enterprises in the nonagricultural production sectors, and high-growth service subsectors including information, finance, transport, tourism, and personal services. The goal is to create an enabling environment that attracts foreign capital and technology and Egyptian private savings from abroad (estimated at more than $40 billion) and to provide institutional support for the enhancement of micro-enterprise activity. Reforms of the financial sector and capital markets are already in place and, together with continued macroeconomic stability, these will ensure that rapid growth in national savings is channeled into productive investment.

Egypt's labor force is growing by 2 percent a year and the total increase in its size by 2012 is projected at 11 million people (based on a target participation rate of 40 percent for that year). About 20 percent of these jobs will be in the public sector, mostly in social services, while the private sector will be the major provider of jobs in the dynamic manufacturing and service sectors. Economic growth is predicated on significant structural change in favor of the productive commodity and service sectors that enjoy high levels of productivity, especially manufacturing. Within the manufacturing sector growth will be concentrated in high value-added, labor-intensive downstream industries that use skilled labor and enjoy strong links with the world market.

CONCLUSION

The vision presented for Egypt in 2012 entails a significant improvement in material welfare and the quality of life for all segments of society. Within twenty years it foresees the elimination of illiteracy, extreme poverty, and endemic diseases. It predicts full employment and a standard of living that allows families to acquire decent housing and enjoy effective social and infrastructure services. It also envisages a vastly improved environment and the sustained protection of Egypt's natural resources and cultural heritage.

This ambitious program requires political will. What is needed is a dramatic reorientation in the role of the state and a new approach to development. Such a transition will require a major transformation in the role of the state – handing over a major portion of its former responsibilities to the private sector (especially those of providing employment and operating productive assets) and strengthening its role as arbitrator and regulator. Government intervention should be focused on the redistribution of income and the provision of public and merit goods, with a significant reallocation of resources toward basic social services. In addition, the private sector should be invited to share in the cost and management of tertiary services in education and health. The state must also reform education, industrial, and science and technology policies to promote the rapid transfer of modern skills and technologies that the economy needs to be globally competitive.

The challenge is to adopt a development paradigm that ensures both a significant improvement in economic performance and an equitable and sustainable growth path that makes better use of the county's most important asset, its people. Meeting this challenge will require a fundamental shift toward an export orientation and the manipulation of incentives and institutional structures to promote rapid growth in savings, productive investment, employment, and real incomes. More important, the reformed institutional framework must promote rapid decentralization, democratization, and participation to engender the consensus and confidence that come from a shared national effort.

For this proposed scenario to materialize, the vision it describes must become a focal point among politicians, policymakers, and citizens, so that all agents in society understand their newly assigned rights and responsibilities. The vision should respond to the aspirations of society as a whole and provide a set of targets that reflects a consensus on priorities. This approach would be best achieved by decentralizing the system of governance, facilitating democratic participation, increasing transparency and accountability, compensating losers, and, above all, ensuring that fiscal and regulatory systems are reformed to reduce rent-seeking behavior and ensure that national self-interest translates into productive employment growth. A vision is inspired by the collective conscience of those who establish the new rules of the game. It is no less than a new social contract.

Notes

1. Some Egyptian exports enjoy Generalized System of Preferences (GSP) treatment in Japan and the United States. The United States does not, however, allow preferential treatment for textiles and clothing, which are Egypt's main exports.
2. Upstream industries include petrochemicals, steel, aluminum, industrial and nonindustrial chemicals, and spinning and weaving. Downstream processing includes food, clothing, engineering, metal working, building materials, clay and refractory products, glass, fertilizers, plastics, and paper.
3. Egypt's hourly cost of labor in the textile industry (almost 500,000 workers) is one-third of that in Eastern Europe, 25 percent of that in Turkey, 5 percent of that in the United States, and close to that in India and China.
4. These include processed food, beverages and tobacco, cotton textiles and clothing, hand-made and machine-made carpets, paper and publishing,

pharmaceuticals, perfumes and cosmetics, ceramics and tiles, glassware, sanitary ware, furniture, leather products, iron and steel shapes, metal household equipment, cutlery, and electrical distribution equipment.

References

Fergany, Nader, 1994a. "Access to Primary Education in Egypt: Patterns and Determinants," *Research Note*, 5, Al-Mishkat Center for Research and Training, Cairo.

——— 1994b. "Poverty and Unemployment Profiles on the Level of Administrative Units (Kism and Markaz) by Urban–Rural Classification and Implied Allocation of Funds," *Research Note*, Al-Mishkat Center for Research and Training, Cairo.

Handoussa, Heba, 1989. "The Burden of Public Service Employment and Remuneration: A Case Study of Egypt," in Wouter Van Gineken (ed.), *Government and Its Employees*, Geneva: International Labor Office.

——— 1995. "The Role of the State: The Case of Egypt." in J. Harris, J. Hunter, and C. M. Lewis, (eds.), *The New Institutional Economics and Third World Development*. London: Routledge.

Handoussa, Heba, and Gillian Potter (eds.), 1991. *Employment and Structural Adjustment: Egypt in the 1990s*, International Labour Office, Cairo: American University in Cairo Press.

Institute of National Planning, 1994. *Egypt Human Development Report*, Cairo.

Kheir-El-Din, Hanaa, and A. El-Dersh, 1992. "Foreign Trade Policy of Egypt 1986–1991," In Said El-Naggar (ed.), *Foreign and Intratrade Policies of the Arab Countries*. Washington, D.C.: International Monetary Fund.

UNDP (United Nations Development Programme). 1994. *Human Development Report*. New York: Oxford University Press.

UNIDO (United Nations Industrial Development Organization). 1993. *Industry and Development, Global Report 1993/94*. Vienna: UNIDO.

UNIDO (United Nations Industrial Development Organization) and The Economist Intelligence Unit. 1994. *Egypt Industrial Development Review*, London.

World Bank, 1993. *Arab Republic of Egypt: An Agricultural Strategy for the 1990s*, A World Bank Country Study, Washington, D.C. : World Bank.

——— 1994. "Private Sector Development in Egypt: The Status and The Challenges," Paper presented at a conference on the private sector in Egypt: Investing in the future (October 9–10), Cairo.

5 The State and the Private Sector in Jordan

Taher H. Kanaan

This chapter reviews the role of the public sector in the Jordanian economy and the response of economic policy to the changing wisdom regarding the state's role in sustainable development. The study advocates the principle that activities whose output and inputs are traded in open markets are plausible candidates for privatization. To the extent that output or input markets are imperfect, however, and market forces are unable to deliver the efficient resource use or optimal welfare benefits expected from privatization, commercialization is recommended. The study also relates the Jordanian case to the political economy of public governance, emphasizing the relevance of the new institutional economics to that case.

The declared economic policy orientation of the Jordanian government could be characterized as a moderate, market-friendly approach that calls for government to do less in the production sectors – where markets work – and more in areas where markets are unreliable, such as education, health, poverty alleviation, macroeconomic stability, regulatory and legal infrastructure, and environmental protection. In practice, however, few of the privatization measures that have been considered in recent years have been implemented. This is partly because of the vested interests and resistance to change of government bureaucrats and partly because of the lingering impact of the ideological beliefs of the 1950s and 1960s, which defined a more interventionist role for government. Yet a narrow focus that deals only with the elimination of market distortions caused by price controls and with transferring productive assets to the private sector will not be sufficient to induce economic vitality and sustainable growth.

What is needed is a vision of the economic role of the state that accommodates the interactions between markets and social, political, and economic institutions. That means developing the values and institutions associated with "civil society," such as equality before the law and equal access to opportunity. Building up a productivity-oriented civil society that can survive the increasingly competitive environment in the region will require political reform, a deeper process of democratization, and a clear vision of the role of public governance.

SIZE AND COMPOSITION OF THE PUBLIC SECTOR

Jordan's economy has a basic private sector orientation. Most of the country's productive assets are privately owned, and the legal system, both in its secular form and its Moslem Shari'a origins, expressly protects private property. Accordingly, direct state ownership is relatively small, significant only in mining (phosphates and potash) and public utilities (electricity, water, communications, and bus and air transport). The share of gross domestic product (GDP) originating in public sector establishments, excluding government services (as defined in the United Nations System of National Accounts), was about 14 percent in 1992. The private sector dominated construction (100 percent of sectoral GDP), manufacturing (94 percent), and financial, business, community, and personal services (95 percent, Table 5.1).

Still, general government activity, including government services, accounts for more than 30 percent of GDP. The government is the country's largest employer, accounting for more than half of the total economically active labor force and total employee compensation (Table 5.2).

The public sector dominates the economy in many other ways as well. The government is perhaps the largest single purchaser of goods and services – excluding wages and salaries. In 1993 the central government's outlay for goods and services amounted to 72 million Jordan dinars (JD) in the current budget and JD 220 million in the capital budget. Commodity imports by the government amounted to JD 383 million, or 15.6 percent of total commodity imports, in 1993. In terms of its financial weight, the Jordanian government appears to be one of the largest in the world, matched only by Egypt and Oman (Table 5.3).

Through its ownership of state enterprises, the public sector accounts for an estimated 14 percent of the aggregate value 4 added (GDP) generated by public utilities and corporations.[1] Entities wholly owned by the government include the Electricity Authority, the Telecommunications Corporation, the Public Transport Corporation, the Water Authority, the Industrial Estates Corporation, the Housing and Urban Development Corporation, and the Agricultural Credit

Table 5.1 Gross domestic product in the public and private sectors by economic activity, Jordan, 1990–92
(millions of Jordanian dinars)

Economic activity	1990		1991		1992	
	Public	*Private*	*Public*	*Private*	*Public*	*Private*
Industry	361	1,518	394	1,651	401	2,001
Agriculture, hunting, forestry, and fishing	0	188	0	214	0	247
Mining and quarrying	142	7	108	17	117	14
Manufacturing	31	315	32	312	23	384
Electricity and water	36	18	48	14	51	16
Construction	0	106	0	126	0	215
Wholesale and retail trade, restaurants, and hotels	−69	286	−26	281	−47	326
Transport, storage, and communications	221	141	233	150	263	188
Financial, insurance, real estate, and business services	−4	411	−5	478	−9	530
Community, social, and personal services	4	48	5	61	4	83
Producers of government services	449	0	474	0	555	0
Producers of private nonprofit services to households	0	31	0	34	0	39
Domestic services of households	0	6	0	5	0	7
Total	810	1,555	869	1,691	956	2,047
Less imputed bank service charges	0	−40	0	−54	0	−42
Gross domestic product at factor cost	810	1,515	869	1,637	956	2,005
Indirect taxes less subsidies	39	305	27	323	30	502
Gross domestic product at producers' prices	849	1,819	896	1,960	986	2,507

Table 5.2 Value added in the public and private sectors, Jordan, 1985–90
(millions of current Jordanian dinars)

Indicator	1985	1986	1987	1988	1989	1990
Gross output	3,752.0	3,751.3	3,933.6	4,133.2	4,705.7	5,195.3
Public sector	892.4	936.9	958.9	982.0	1,018.5	1,196.7
Private sector	2,859.6	2,814.4	2,974.7	3,151.2	3,687.2	3,998.6
Intermediate consumption	1,782.2	1,636.7	1,770.9	1,914.8	2,394.9	2,605.7
Public sector	414.4	403.2	400.3	397.9	442.0	540.9
Private sector	1,367.8	1,233.5	1,370.6	1,516.9	1,952.9	2,064.8
Value added	1,969.8	2,114.6	2,162.7	2,218.4	2,310.8	2,589.6
Public sector	478.0	533.7	558.6	584.1	576.5	655.8
Private sector	1,491.8	1,580.9	1,604.1	1,634.3	1,734.3	1,933.8
Compensation of employees	758.8	809.8	844.7	900.0	934.6	986.7
Public sector	364.2	410.7	431.6	469.5	484.3	508.6
Private sector	394.6	399.1	413.1	430.5	450.3	478.1
Consumption of fixed capital	197.3	187.7	193.8	209.2	226.9	219.8
Public sector	57.7	57.3	68.8	67.8	68.2	68.7
Private sector	139.6	130.4	125.0	141.4	158.7	151.1
Indirect taxes less subsidies	237.3	342.4	330.3	317.0	261.8	337.2
Public sector	3.4	1.6	2.2	−4.6	−8.2	−5.7
Private sector	233.9	340.8	328.1	321.6	270.0	342.9
Operating surplus	776.4	774.7	793.9	792.2	887.5	1,045.9
Public sector	52.7	64.1	56.0	51.4	32.2	84.2
Private sector	723.7	710.6	737.9	740.8	855.3	961.7

Corporation. In addition, the government has almost virtual control over a number of other enterprises in which it shares equity with the private sector. These include the Jordan Electric Power Company, the Irbid District Electricity Company, the Housing Bank, and the Industrial Development Bank.

The government also holds sizable equity in shareholding companies that are formally part of the private sector. This equity is held by the Jordan Investment Corporation, which is the government's official investment agency, and by the Social Security Corporation, which manages the mandatory social security program. At the end of 1994 the Jordan Investment Corporation had holdings in forty-three public shareholding companies listed in the Amman Financial Market (18 percent of the market's capitalization) and in twenty-eight unlisted companies. Of the listed companies, the corporation had management

Table 5.3 Public financing, various countries, 1991
(percentage of GDP)

Country or country group	Tax revenue	Central government spending	Government consumption
Industrial countries	24	30	17
East Asia (excluding China)	16	17	10
Southeast Asia	19	21	10
Medium-income developing countries (excluding China)	19	30	12
Egypt	23	40	10
Iran	15	23	13
Israel	24	36	28
Jordan	22	41	23
Morocco	—	—	15
Oman	9	45	35
Syria	19	24	—
Tunisia	25	35	16
Turkey	18	30	17

— Not available.
Source: UNDP, 1994.

control (more than half of equity) over at least seven, and held 10–50 percent of equity in seventeen others. Of the unlisted companies, the corporation had management control over six and 10–50 percent of equity in eleven. At the end of 1994 the Social Security Corporation had equity investments in sixty-six listed and twenty-four unlisted companies. It held more than 30 percent of equity in only three of these companies, entitling it to management board membership.

The proportion of public enterprise ownership has declined some-what in recent years, however. Between 1987 and 1992 the number of registered private companies increased by 118 percent (from 1,990 to 4,349 companies), while the number of companies in which the public sector held equity fell from 115 to 112.

IMPACT OF STATE ENTERPRISES ON CORPORATE GROWTH AND PERFORMANCE

What has the public sector done with its power to influence corporate regimes directly through its management control and indirectly through its policies governing investment, human resources, marketing, and other management practices? While this influence could, in theory, be exercised constructively to promote the state's strategic development objectives, it is at least as likely that corporate policies will be subjected to such noncommercial considerations as giving preference to employment over efficiency.

The evidence points to little constructive influence of public officials on corporate boards. A recent study of the performance of government-controlled companies (defined as those in which government equity exceeds 15 percent of a company's stock), compared with the performance of companies with little or no public interest, finds a positive correlation between government ownership or control and inferior financial performance (World Bank, 1994). The study concludes that companies in which the government has invested heavily appear to have experienced lower growth in sales, lower average pretax returns on investment, and significantly lower productivity gains. These trends are evident across sectors, in declining industries (steel, for example), as well as in emerging sectors (such as telecommunications). This indicates that either ownership or control, or both, and not some other variable, is responsible. Companies in which the government had no ownership interest grew faster, invested more, earned higher returns, achieved larger productivity gains, and generated more employment for each dinar of investment than did public enterprises or public shareholding companies with sizable government equity. (Further details on the findings of the study are given in appendix 5.1, p. 97.)

Whether the blame for the inferior efficiency of government-associated enterprises lies with the ownership itself or with the control and management pattern associated with the ownership remains an open question. It may be true that government representation on company boards opens the way for noncommercial considerations to influence corporate policies. More likely, however, the main drawback of this representation is that government representatives are less engaged and less active than other board members. The representatives are often civil servants, appointed to board membership primarily to reward them for services rendered elsewhere rather than to contribute dynamic managerial skills to the company. This is not to imply that private sector board members are necessarily more skillful or dynamic. The motives and attitudes of private sector representatives can be as remote from the objective interests of the company as those of the least competent government representatives. Moreover, abusive behavior resulting from conflicts of interest tends to be more rampant among private sector board members than among government representatives.

A STRATEGY FOR THE FUTURE

Evidence such as that presented above has convinced some analysts that reliance on the private sector's unlimited dynamism and initiative is the secret to the miraculous growth performance of the newly industrialized countries (NICs) – particularly those of East Asia. Though some aspects of the recent economic history of the NICs seem to support this thesis, the theory suffers from considerable inexactitude. True, excessive government intervention and regulation often stifle private initiative and handicap growth. Similarly, fiddling with the price system will lead to inefficient allocation of resources and investments. Accordingly, limiting government functions to the strictly justifiable spheres of governance and regulation appears to be a necessary condition for sound and growth-oriented economic policy. Equally necessary, however, is the sound configuration by the government of governance and regulation of private markets, to prevent monopolistic and oligopolistic practices that distort the price system.

Efficient and effective government is necessary for successful growth policies – a thesis that has been researched and verified in the economies of East Asia. The governments of these high-performing economies were better than others in pursuing policies defined by neoclassical economics as the essence of good governance. These policies include:

- Providing a stable macroeconomic environment and a reliable legal framework to promote domestic and international competition.
- Orienting the economy toward international trade by eliminating or minimizing price controls and other policies leading to price distortions.
- Investing in people through quality education and health (World Bank, 1993).

The governments of the East Asian economies also intervened systematically to promote development objectives or to support specific industries. Among the many policy instruments used were:

- Targeting specific industries and subsidizing credit to them.
- Keeping deposit rates low and maintaining ceilings on borrowing rates to increase profits and retain earnings.
- Protecting domestic import substitutes, subsidizing declining industries, establishing and financially supporting government banks, and investing in applied research.
- Establishing firm- and industry-specific export targets, developing marketing institutions, and sharing information between public and private sectors (World Bank, 1993).

Weighing the evidence, the World Bank and others come down somewhere between the neoclassical strategy, which assigns center stage to market forces and a minimal role for government intervention, and the revisionist strategy, which views market failures as pervasive and requiring government intervention in prices and incentives to accelerate growth in startup industries.

Between these is a strategy often labeled the market-friendly strategy. The central premise of this strategy is that sustained growth results from the positive interaction of four aspects of economic policy: macroeconomic stability, human capital formation, openness to international trade, and an environment conducive to private investment and competition. The attainment and convergence of these policies depend on effective but carefully limited government activity. Thus, governments need to do less in the production sectors, where markets work or can be made to work, while doing more in areas where markets are unreliable. Governments should be required to invest in education, health, nutrition, family planning, and poverty alleviation; to build social, physical, administrative, regulatory, and legal infrastructure; to protect the environment through the proper pricing of resources; to define and enforce property rights; and to ensure macroeconomic stability (World Bank, 1991).

JORDAN'S STRATEGY FOR THE ROLE OF GOVERNMENT

Jordan's declared economic policy orientation is close to the moderate, market-friendly strategy described above. The government's Economic and Social Development Plan for 1993–97 defined four basic principles. The first of these involves liberalizing the economy and its institutions, eliminating distortions that obstruct sound economic performance, and developing an appropriate business climate. This principle is to be realized by:

- Enhancing the regulatory and supervisory role of the government and initiating legislation to encourage saving, maintain capital assets, and curb conspicuous consumption; increase opportunities for fair competition; prevent monopolies; protect consumers through the development and enforcement of standards and specifications; raise export capacity and reduce excessive protection of domestic products; promote the use of domestic factors of production; conserve natural resources and protect the environment; and protect intellectual property rights.
- Reducing the government's role in direct production, enhancing the role of the private sector by improving incentives for domestic and foreign investment, and discouraging government competition with the private sector.
- Encouraging private provision of infrastructure and basic services and increasing private sector participation in the management and ownership of public sector institutions on an equitable basis.
- Developing financial markets with the aim of ensuring the free movement of capital and increasing saving and investment.
- Restructuring public sector institutions undergoing financial difficulties, improving their efficiency, and gradually implementing measures to eliminate subsidies, recover costs, free prices, and adopt commercial performance criteria.

The second principle is to reduce direct government involvement in production and enhance the role of the private sector in this respect. The third involves making room for active private sector participation in investment in infrastructure and basic services and for private sector participation in the equity and management of public corporations. Finally, the plan calls for reform of the financial system and markets toward freer movement of capital and higher rates of saving.

Jordan's Economic and Social Development Plan is a document of government policy intentions and was not submitted to Parliament for enactment into law. Parts of the plan may be drafted into legislation and passed by Parliament (the government investment budget is an example), but otherwise the plan is not mandatory. And despite the government's declared intentions of reducing the public sector role in direct production and the market, actual implementation has been limited. Since the mid-1980s the government has been considering various measures to encourage the private sector, including:

- Encouraging the Jordan Investment Corporation to gradually sell its equity in companies it helped establish and using the funds to stimulate new ventures.
- Privatizing public transport.
- Commercializing the Telecommunications Corporation and the Jordan Electricity Authority.
- Privatizing the national airline.
- Gradually liberalizing the financial system by floating the exchange rate, limiting interest rate regulation, and declaring the free convertibility of the dinar in current account transactions.
- Abolishing discretion in licensing industrial establishments, so that the Ministry of Industry and Trade cannot deny an operating license to a legitimate industrial enterprise.
- Revising the Encouragement of Industry Law to improve the range of incentives and concessions to encourage local and foreign capital investment.

Significant progress has been made on most of these measures. For those relating to privatization, however, movement has been both more recent and more modest. In 1995 the Directorate of Petroleum in the Ministry of Energy's Natural Resources Authority was reformed into a public shareholding company owned jointly by the Jordan Investment Corporation and the Industrial Development Bank. Similarly, the Center for Vaccines in the Ministry of Health was reformed into a public shareholding company owned jointly by the Jordan Investment Corporation and private investors. The commercialization of the Telecommunications Corporation, pending since 1988, is nearing completion, and a start has been made on commercializing the Jordan Electricity Authority. A new Law of Telecommunications was enacted that limits the duties of the Ministry of Post and Telecommunications to regulatory and policymaking functions. The law established a legally and financially independent entity called the Organization for Regulating the Telecommunications Sector to make recommendations to the Council of Ministers on the granting of licenses to private parties for the construction and operation of public telecommunications networks and the provision of telecommunications services to beneficiaries on a fair, competitive basis.

There has also been some progress in transferring the Jordan Investment Corporation's holdings in public companies to the private sector. In 1995 the corporation sold 29 percent of its 27 percent ownership in the Paper and Cardboard Company and 88 percent of its 88 percent equity in the Hotels and Tourism Company, for a total of JD 16.2 million. The slow progress in privatization is largely the result of inertia, resistance to change, and the vested interests of the government machinery. Privatization decisions are delegated mainly to the governing bodies in charge of the corporations and enterprises slated for privatization – bodies that are not eager to liquidate themselves or reduce their domain of control. The government is also highly sensitive to the political repercussions of the large numbers of layoffs that will inevitably result from privatizing the highly over-staffed corporations. Many members of Parliament are sensitive to this issue, as well as to the idea of giving up public control of so-called strategic industries. And the current generation of politicians and civil servants came of age during the 1950s and 1960s, when ideological precepts were quite different.

THE POLITICAL ECONOMY OF PUBLIC GOVERNANCE

The success or failure of a particular strategy of public governance depends on much more than the strategy's conceptual validity and theoretical merits. It is possible, for example, to transfer ownership of a public corporation to the private sector and to end up replacing a public monopoly with a worse and no less abusive private monopoly.

Realigning and streamlining the role of government may not require a reduction in the size of public service, but it does require a redefinition of government's duties and functions. Institutional reform should bring the state closer to the embodiment of civil society and away from the tribal and patriarchal tradition that has characterized Jordanian and other Arab societies since the Middle Ages. A sound assessment of the challenges facing the Jordanian economy in the years ahead requires a consideration of several important conceptual considerations.

The state and its institutions do not function independently of the many other forces operating and interacting in a society. These social forces express themselves, exercise their influence, and seek their material interests not only through the political system and political institutions, but also through the economic system and its institutions. These include the legal framework of the system, in particular laws on property rights and other laws affecting the distribution and enforce-ment of economic rights and entitlements.

An economy will function effectively to generate income and accu-mulate wealth only when the struggle for power and material gain among the dominant social forces encourages the efficient functioning of the economy and the various markets that generate economic development. Both factor and goods markets must do more than function efficiently in the short run. To ensure sustainable growth and development, they should also function in ways that will not upset the social balance or create social tensions in the long run. Such problems could lead ultimately to an institutional upheaval, and thus arrest the momentum of economic growth and development.

The market-friendly strategy partly recognizes the inadequacy of a narrow focus that ignores the interaction between market and economic and social institutions. This strategy recognizes that focusing solely on the elimination of price controls and subsidies and on turning over public enterprise ownership to the private sector will not by itself be sufficient to revitalize the economy and set it on the path to self-sustained growth. The strategy instead stresses the importance of effective government performance in appropriate areas. These government functions should include maintaining law and order; investing in physical, human, and social infrastructure; and regulating the protection of disadvantaged segments of society and country, the conservation of natural resources, the protection of the environment, and the safeguarding against monopolistic and monopsonistic practices. Often lacking in the market-friendly strategy, however, is an adequate appreciation of the social and political conditions necessary for successful and enduring public sector reform.

An important prerequisite is social cohesion among the people constituting the body politic, which is what constitutes a civil society. In a civil society personal merit or behavior is the only standard – neither public nor private institutions discriminate against individuals or groups of citizens for other reasons. In Jordan and many other Arab countries the social structure still lacks these attributes of a civil society. A long and complicated historical process has maintained primary social allegiance to the family, the tribe, or the local community. State and country remain abstract and distant.[2]

The tribal tenets of society may prevent the evolution of development-oriented governance regardless of the legal and regulatory reforms undertaken. Tribal bias reduces the chances of forming a civil service based on merit and competence. These features are important to the high performers in East Asia. The aspiring high performers in Southeast Asia – Indonesia, Malaysia, and Thailand – have gradually introduced measures to upgrade their bureaucracies, with Malaysia at the forefront (World Bank, 1993).

Regrettably, some civil servants, journalists, and leaders of public opinion in Jordan and other Arab countries tend to support policies based on faulty economic thinking. One fallacy underlying much of the muddle in current economic and political policy is the assumption that a country's level of income and wealth is a zero-sum game – a pie of fixed size, so that if one side gets a larger share other sides must get smaller shares. This fallacy is fed by the fact that many people with vast wealth and high incomes do not know how a modern productive system works and grows.[3] As the political economist North (1994: 4) states:

> If the institutional framework made the highest payoff for piracy, then organizational success and survival dictated that learning would take the form of being better pirates. If, on the other hand, productivity-raising activities had the highest payoff, then the economy would grow.

Exposing the fallacies mentioned above and building a civil society depend on political reform directed toward deepening the process of democratization. Such reform had a good start in Jordan in 1989 but is proceeding slowly now. Such political reform is also needed to strengthen economic performance, to enable the economy to compete in increasingly competitive regional and global markets.

A highly skilled and educated work force and highly motivated entrepreneurs, high saving and investment rates, and high rates of technological change and innovation are important for economic competitiveness and comparative advantage, but they are not sufficient for sustainable growth and development.

Saving, investment, and technological change are essential for increasing productivity and specialization in the production of goods and services. But as the inputs and outputs from that production are traded among economic agents, both within the domestic market and between the domestic and foreign markets, these agents incur costs. Costs arise from complying with or attempting to evade various regulations and institutions in the course of those transactions. The nature of the prevailing institutions and their methods of operating determine the transaction costs of such activities as processing business documents, negotiating and concluding contracts, litigating violated contracts, and getting timely information on the institutions and their vulnerability to influence from third parties. Institutions are not independent of the influence and negotiating power of economic agents. But the power of economic agents is itself a function of the prevailing institutional setup, that is, the laws and regulations in force, particularly those concerning property rights and the distribution of material entitlements and access to social utilities and infrastructure.

An economy's efficiency, level of performance, and comparative advantage and international competitiveness are affected by transaction costs and their relation to institutions and institutional change. This phenomenon, once explored through Marxist analysis, has been rediscovered recently and studied within the framework known as the new institutional economics. The Nobel prize in economics was awarded to one of the leading proponents of this new discipline, Douglass North.

The new institutional economics modifies the rationality postulate of neoclassical economic theory by adding institutions as a critical constraint and, according to North (1994: 15–16), by analyzing

> the role of transaction costs as the connection between institutions and the costs of production. It extends economic theory by incorporating ideas and ideologies into the analysis, modeling the political process as a critical factor in the performance of economies, as the source of the diverse performance of economies, and as the explanation for "inefficient" markets ... Institutions are not necessarily or even usually created to be socially efficient; rather they, or at least the formal rules, are created to serve the interests of those with the bargaining power to create new rules. In a zero transaction cost world, bargaining strength does not affect the efficiency of outcomes; but in a world of positive transaction costs, it does – and it thus shapes the direction of long-run economic change.

Institutional reform is needed throughout the entire polity and society. It can be achieved through an irrevocable commitment to civil and democratic society and to the appropriate institutions – a commitment that should be positive and active. Passive commitment, at best, will discourage deviation from the democratic path. Active commitment goes beyond that: it strives to create the institutions that protect and consolidate the democratic process. Such institutions include modern-style political parties, an enlightened and critical free press, an effective judicial system, and cultural and intellectual non-governmental organizations dedicated to educating the public about democratic values and practices.

ELEMENTS OF PUBLIC SECTOR REFORM

The elements of reform constitute a list too long to be adequately surveyed in this brief study. A few illustrative, if not representative, examples may be cited here, however.

Privatization

Any activity that can market its output and procure its inputs in open markets should be – in principle – a prime candidate for privatization. The underlying assumption here is that the price mechanism is more efficient than any discretionary human decisions in ensuring the best prices for output, the greatest satisfaction for users of that output, and the lowest input costs in its production.

If either the output (product) market or the input (costs) market of the activity is imperfect – for example, because of constraints on information or freedom of entry, or because of other distortions arising from monopoly – then the price mechanism is not likely to deliver the efficient resource use or optimal user welfare expected from privatization.

The market principles outlined above lead to three conclusions on privatization. First, the transfer of public enterprise ownership to the private sector should be conditional on freeing the market from any monopolistic and similar imperfections or distortions. The most serious adverse results in this respect are likely to arise from the privatization of public utilities such as telecommunications. Privatizing such enterprises as the Housing Bank and the Industrial Development Bank is a safer bet, however. The highly competitive market in banking services and the high cost to taxpayers of the explicit and implicit subsidies and privileges enjoyed by these institutions justify privatization.

Second, in cases where markets are not open, but where the public sector activity is "productive" – that is, it can still be governed by the price mechanism – commercialization rather than privatization should be the rule. In addition to the public corporations already run on a commercial basis, we have identified eighteen government entities, with 16,000 employees, that would benefit from·commercialization (Appendix 5.2, p. 99). If, because of their social orientation, some of these commercialized public activities are not able to generate profits, running them on a commercial basis will still bring gains. An acceptable level of losses can be defined and management can be made transparent and accountable.

Third, privatizing infrastructure provision through build, operate, and transfer arrangements offers several advantages. It can ease the financial and managerial burdens of the government, attract the most efficient contractors, and shift the cost burden from the general tax-payers to those who benefit more directly from the infrastructure improvement. Some argue that these advantages can be secured within the traditional system by combining international finance and compe-titive contracting. The way to settle the issue is to proceed with care-fully selected test cases.

Reform of public universities

Market forces and the interaction of supply and demand can be applied as well to the reform of government activities that are not market-oriented. A good example is government-run universities, which suffer from chronic financial difficulties.

Government universities are in the business of providing a service, higher education, that is highly valued by consumers (the students and their parents) as well as by the state. The state considers spending on higher education to be an investment in social overhead capital. Both sides are willing to pay a price for this service. The problem is the large gap between the cost of providing the service and the revenue received from fees and government subsidies.

Enrollment is growing much faster than revenues, and student–teacher ratios are rising continuously. The result is a deterioration in the quality of education and a mushrooming of private universities. Private universities, which are able to command higher fees from students and thus pay higher salaries to teachers, are successfully drawing better instructors away from public universities.

Furthermore, the gap between costs and revenues distorts the sys-tem of accountability and makes it impossible to detect cases of waste and inefficiency. The quality of education is also largely concealed by the supply-determined value of education. Degrees from Jordan's universities are marketed in the public sector and in much of the private sector at their nominal value on a par with degrees from the best universities in the world. A market-supportive reform of the university system, one that is also sensitive to social objectives, would involve two primary changes. One is to set university fees per student on the basis of the minimum actual costs of delivering educational service of a specified quality. The university management can be held accountable for efficient performance through audits of this direct link between costs and revenue. In addition to such quantitative and financial efficiency controls, qualitative controls can be established by requiring general competitive examinations for job applicants in the public and private sectors, a practice that will gradually deflate the nominal value of university degrees.

Second, to make hidden subsidies transparent and so to improve public accountability and general government efficiency, a system of partial and complete scholarships should be set up by the government, independent of the management of the universities. The scholarships should subsidize university fees for well-defined categories of students according to clearly specified social and political criteria under an investment budget established for this purpose.

Reform of the legal and regulatory framework

In addition to the broad principles laid out above to improve public sector performance, there are several specific areas of Jordan's legal system and regulatory framework in need of reform. Those presented here illustrate the kinds of reforms needed to bring down transaction costs in the Jordan economy and thereby improve private sector performance.[4]

Company law

Provisions are needed for new organizational forms to accommodate professional service companies, mutual investments funds, and the like. In addition, the discretionary powers of company controllers should be limited, and the market pricing of shares and bonds by underwriters should be facilitated.

Civil law

The law should be modified to give a clear security interest in movables (machines and equipment), to permit security interest to continue in the proceeds of collateral, and to permit floating security interests. Efforts should be made to improve and expand the use of legal registries, to improve the legal enforcement mechanism's capacity to provide streamlined judicial and nonjudicial procedures, and to establish and maintain standards to encourage investment in services. Finally, a law protecting intellectual property should be enacted.

Procurement laws

The 1993 Supplies Act and 1994 Regulation 1 restrict new entry and limit competition to a few large, well connected firms. Reform should facilitate the entry of competitors, reduce centralized government purchasing, reduce contract size and financial performance requirements (but with better monitoring of procurement regulations), and lift the requirement for large guarantees in service contracts.

Investment law

The current investment law (no.11, 1987) lacks transparency, adequate monitoring, and provisions for automatic processing. Instead of encouraging investment, the law has frequently been used as a way to avoid taxation. Simplification of tax laws and tax administration would be the single best overall investment incentive. Any incentives should be uniform, based on performance, offered for short periods, and received automatically. Dropping or relaxing current government instructions that prohibit international arbitration where foreigners are party to contracts involving the government will also help encourage foreign investment.

Amman Financial Market law

The regulatory and operational functions of the stock exchange need to be separated. The Amman Financial Market should be split into two separate entities, one to regulate and one to manage the exchange. This would require amendment of the law to establish a securities commission to handle the regulatory functions associated with the exchange. Left with only the operational functions, the Amman Financial Market could be turned into a private institution.

Income tax law and administration

Tax settlement procedures are too discretionary and result in inequities, loss of revenue, and high costs of doing business. Reforms are needed to streamline procedures, reduce discretion, and improve coverage.

Import–export law

Under Law 14 (1992) businesses must obtain a product-specific license to import or export. Ministry of Industry and Trade regulations require that, to obtain a license, a business must be on the importers register, have a vocation license, and hold an import card. Such procedures unnecessarily raise the costs of doing business, discourage trade, and reduce competition. Overdue reforms to streamline and expedite import and export transactions include the following:

- Abolish the importers register and import card system, retaining only a negative list of goods that, for health or security reasons, require an import license.
- Simplify customs inspection and consider contracting out the inspection function, especially preshipment inspection; install a modern computerized system of inspection, valuation, collection, and clearance.
- Reduce the number of steps and signatures required for customs clearance.
- Eliminate the practice of giving customs officials a share of the fines they impose.

Appendix 5.1 The Comparative Performance of Public Shareholding Companies with and without Significant Government Interest*

ASSET PERFORMANCE

In 1991 government-controlled shareholding companies accounted for more than 85 percent of listed service companies' assets and more than 60 percent of listed manufactures assets. When the assets of Royal Jordanian are added, the total assets of government-owned or government-controlled firms amount to three times the assets of non-financial shareholding companies. The government-controlled firms, however, lost more than JD 54 million during 1984–88, while privately owned firms recorded profits of more than JD 22 million (the equivalent of a 21 percent return on the assets they owned). Moreover, the performance of private manufacturing companies improved during the recession, while those of government-controlled firms worsened substantially.

RATES OF RETURN

The rate of return on investments in public and quasi-public enterprises was an average of 2.0 percent, strikingly below the average rate of return of 6.8 percent for companies without major government investment. The low rates for public enterprises are surprising given the preferential access to credit and the variety of tax benefits and concessions they enjoy. The productivity of labor and investment, measured as a ratio of the number of employees per JD 1 million of investment, is also markedly lower in government-controlled firms (7.9 percent against 29.0 percent for privately owned firms), as is the

---

* This annex draws on World Bank (1994: 63–4).

ratio of output to labor growth for 1981–90 (35 percent compared with 83 percent; Table A5.1).

GROWTH IN SALES AND IN FIXED ASSETS

Companies with significant government ownership reported a 94 percent growth in sales for 1981–90, or roughly one-half the growth in sales of companies with no significant government ownership.

Table A5.1 Performance of public shareholding companies listed in the Amman Financial Market, 1981–90 (percent)

Indicator	Firms with significant government ownership	Firms without significant government ownership
Sales growth	94	188
Fixed asset growth	39	87
Average annual pretax return on assets	3.6	7.1
Ratio of output to labor growth	35	83

Source: Bataineh, 1992.

Appendix 5.2 Public Entities Suitable for Commercialization

Table A5.2 Public entitites and employment

Entity	No.
Agricultural Marketing Corporation	136
Aqaba Railways Corporation	7
Civilian Consumers Corporation	853
Free Zones Corporation	446
Hijaz–Jordan Railways	107
Jordan Investment Corporation	75
The Judiciary Institute	34
Natural Resources Authority	521
Ports Authority	2,667
Post Office Savings Fund	80
Public Administration Institute	71
Public Corporation for Housing and Urban Development	320
Public Transport Corporation	39
Royal Geographic Center	270
Telecommunications Corporation	3,891
Vocational Training Corporation	1,095
Water Authority	5,183
Total employees	15,795

Notes

1. Information on government ownership is based on reports of the corporations concerned and other material obtained from the Ministry of Planning.
2. A body of interesting literature explains the geo-historical reasons for this phenomenon and its implications for the formation of modern Arab states. For a survey of this literature, see Al-Ansari, 1994.
3. For many this wealth came from the rent accrued on the value of real estate. Property values appreciated greatly with the large inflow of remittances from citizens working abroad, and the smaller, but substantial, inflow of Arab and other external financial assistance during the 1970s and early 1980s.

4.   These examples come from a survey of Jordanian entrepreneurs conducted by a World Bank mission in November–December 1994.

References

Al-Ansari, Muhammad Jaber, 1994. *Arab Political Formation and the Significance of the Sub-Nation State*. Beirut: Center for Arab Unity Studies (in Arabic).

Bataineh, Safwan, 1992. "The Case for Privatization in Jordan," mimeograph Amman, Jordon.

North, Douglass C., 1990. *Institutions, Institutional Change, and Economic Performance*. Cambridge: Cambridge University Press.

————. 1994. "The New Institutional Economics and Development," *Newsletter of the Economic Research Forum for the Arab Countries, Iran, and Turkey*, 1 (May).

UNDP (United Nations Development Programme). 1994. *Human Development Report 1994*, New York: Oxford University Press.

Wade, Robert, 1990. *Governing the Market, Economic Theory, and the Role of the Government in East Asian Industrialization*, Princeton: Princeton University Press.

World Bank. 1991. *World Development Report 1991: The Challenge of Development*, New York: Oxford University Press.

———— 1993. *The East Asian Miracle: Economic Growth and Public Policy*, A World Bank Policy Research Report, New York: Oxford University Press.

———— 1994. "Jordan: Consolidating Economic Adjustment and Establishing the Base for Sustainable Growth," Middle East and North Africa Region, Country Department II, Washington, D.C. : World Bank.

6 The Palestinian Economy: Alternative Futures

George T. Abed

The 1993 Oslo Declaration of Principles and subsequent agreements between the leaders of the Palestinian Liberation Organization (PLO) and Israel have led to the establishment of a Palestinian Authority in the West Bank and Gaza Strip with limited powers of self-rule. The Palestinian–Israeli accords, based on a negotiated and gradual transfer of civil authority over large areas of the West Bank and Gaza Strip, also attracted the political and financial support of the world community, which pledged large amounts of aid for the reconstruction and development of the Palestinian economy. However, the slow disbursement of external aid, combined with setbacks in the implementation of the various agreements, has delayed the realization of the economic benefits of peace. Indeed, at its current pace the peace process may lack sufficient momentum to generate sustainability. This chapter assesses the present situation and proposes an alternative, more promising approach based on an acceleration and deepening of Palestinian empowerment leading to self-determination and statehood. Such a strategy, when combined with institutional and policy reforms in the Palestinian Authority, and when supported by greater flexibility on the part of Israel, carries the potential for launching the Palestinian economy on a path of self-sustained growth over the medium- to long-term.

In my last treatment of the subject of the economic viability and long-term development of a Palestinian state (Abed, 1990), I felt an obligation to state clearly the central assumptions for such an inquiry. Except in the imagination of the Palestinians (and dare I say, in the nightmares of the Israelis), such a state did not exist then, and in order to examine this virtual entity's viability and long-term development, it had to be given some corporal dimension. The key assumptions I made then were:

- Complete Israeli withdrawal from all lands occupied in the 1967 war (including, of course, East Jerusalem).

- The early exercise by the Palestinians of the right to self-determination, including the right to establish a sovereign and independent state in the West Bank and Gaza Strip (WBGS).
- The exercise by Palestinian refugees of the right of return or compensation.
- The restoration of Palestinian rights over land, water, and borders as defined by the boundaries of the agreed Palestinian state.
- Equitable resolution of all other outstanding issues by mutual agreement with Israel.

Clearly, these assumptions still do not obtain, and although a Palestinian state is no longer a distant fantasy, it has not fully materialized either. In the meantime, a number of changes have intervened since that first inquiry.

THE OSLO FRAMEWORK

The Oslo Declaration of Principles, much more so than even the negotiations framework established in Madrid, completely negated the concept of Palestinian sovereignty on any portion of Palestine. Indeed, the declaration can be read to mean that the leadership of the PLO has ceded sovereignty over all of Palestine to the Israelis and has accepted the logic of receiving from Israel (which by this logic is now recognized as the sovereign state) certain essentially administrative powers under a Palestinian Authority established and empowered legally by the terms of the declaration, but in effect by Israel. This arrangement represents the most important historic concession ever made by a Palestinian (or, for that matter, by an Arabic) leadership to Israel on the question of Palestine. Everything else that has taken place or will take place since the Declaration of Principles was signed on September 13 1993, is essentially a further elaboration of this fundamental premise.

Thus the declaration and subsequent agreements between Israel and the Palestinian leadership have established the following:

- A regime of limited autonomy for Palestinians over about two-thirds of the Gaza Strip and the Jericho area (about 270 square kilometers, equivalent to a little more than 1 percent of the total area of historic Palestine), with a gradual expansion of autonomy over areas in the West Bank as determined by Israel.[1]

- Except in the Gaza and Jericho areas and, eventually, in the Palestinian Arab population centers in the West Bank (but probably not in East Jerusalem), the Palestinian Authority's control over the natural resource base (for example, land and water use, border posts) of the areas under its jurisdiction will likely remain circumscribed over the short- to medium-term.
- The Palestinian Authority's capacity to repatriate and absorb large numbers of Palestinians will also be limited, a process considered essential if the WBGS economy is to make use of the rich experience and vast resources of the expatriate Palestinian communities.
- Israel's annexation and extensive colonization of East Jerusalem, together with the ascendancy of the trend toward physical separation, has severely limited the ability of the Palestinian Authority to exercise full economic and commercial rights or to develop significant activities in tourism and related sectors.

One salutary aspect of the Oslo accord is that it focused the attention of the international community on the development needs of the Palestinian society in the WBGS and elicited pledges of aid, mostly grants and concessional loans, of about $2.3 billion over five years (1994–98).

Thus, in contrast to the two-state solution envisaged in the pre-Oslo political and economic discourse, emerging arrangements between Israel and the Palestinian leadership point to a much more restricted expression of Palestinian authority in the WBGS. This arrangement imposes severe constraints on the capacity of the WBGS economy to rid itself of the legacy of twenty-seven years of occupation and repression, and to effect the rapid recovery and growth that are necessary for long-term economic viability.

Implementing the agreements

The record of implementation of the autonomy agreements by the two signatories has not been reassuring. One central reason for this is that the last word in the interpretation of these agreements belongs to Israel and, in this regard, Israel's interpretation on all key issues has been more restrictive than even a neutral reading of the agreements would indicate.

A stalemate develops

On the Palestinian side, the Palestinian Authority has failed to develop the necessary institutional capacity to attract and invest the development assistance funds pledged by the donor community.[2] Of the $2.3 billion pledged, less than 5 percent had been disbursed for development projects through mid-1995, while an equal amount has been used for funding current rather than development expenditures – essentially the salaries of the burgeoning security and civil service apparatus. Incomes declined by nearly 15 percent in 1993–4, and unemployment remains high (more than 40 percent in the Gaza Strip and 25 percent in the West Bank), while the Palestinian economy is more dependent on Israel and more isolated from neighboring Arab countries than ever before. Palestinian and, to a much lesser extent, other investors have made some cautious moves but have run up against a confused and confusing regulatory environment that has slowed private sector activity. The inflated and creaky political machinery of the PLO has been grafted onto a feeble governmental structure in the WBGS and, with most of the available funds redirected to satisfy this machinery's considerable consumption appetite, the Palestinian Authority has transformed itself into a unproductive, rent-seeking regime, impeding genuine social and economic development in the WBGS.

As for the Israelis, they have shown neither the needed flexibility in interpreting the terms of the transfer of authority nor the required political commitment to proceed with speed and efficiency. Largely because of domestic political considerations but also because of undue deliberation and indecisiveness on the part of the Israeli leadership, the implementation of the agreements has been hopelessly behind schedule. Full empowerment in the West Bank, due to have taken place by July 1994, will likely be delayed by at least a year.[3] Israel's redeployment of forces and evacuation of most of the West Bank to allow Palestinian elections are being increasingly complicated and circumscribed by the pervasive presence of the settlements and by Israel's insistence on protecting the settlers and all routes prescribing their movement. Arrangements for clearing the border posts and for dismantling the Israeli Civil Administration remain a distant possibility. Israel continues to block most Palestinian workers from working in Israel, to prepare for quasi-permanent checkpoints separating the two areas, to extract a fiscal surplus from its extended presence in the West Bank, and to hinder Palestinian access to Israeli and world markets for the movements of goods.

BREAKING THE STALEMATE: THE ALTERNATIVES

The stalemate in the Israeli – Palestinian peace process cannot persist because the approaching deadline for elections in Israel and the deteriorating economic situation in the WBGS are exerting pressure on Israeli and Palestinian leaders to find solutions to current impediments and to accelerate the pace of progress. In this connection, there are two possibilities for proceeding forward: an incremental approach and a more radical or fundamental approach.

The incremental approach

The incremental approach has characterized the current style of negotiations between Israel and the Palestinians as well as the speed of implementation of agreements reached between them. It is detailed, arduous, time-consuming, and yields only gradual and usually meager results. Against the grand vision of peace in Palestine engendered by the initial breakthrough at Madrid and, to optimists, at Oslo, this approach concerns itself, in a tedious and sequential manner, with such details as the number of permits for Palestinians to work in Israel; which sectors to transfer to the Palestinian Authority in the West Bank and when, and with what specific financial arrangements; what procedures to institute at border posts for the processing of visitors and goods; how many truckloads of produce from Gaza to allow into Israel during any given period; and so on. Furthermore, these drawn-out discussions and agreements are frequently subject to the vicissitudes of unpredictable events, most notably security-related incidents, causing discussions to be interrupted, agreements to be suspended, and delays in implementation to accumulate.

In general, this approach implies a measure of disingenuousness – if not outright dishonesty – on both sides. Thus Israel has permitted the use of certain code words in the agreements that, while engendering an expectation of sovereignty and statehood among the Palestinians, also allow the Israeli leadership to deny that it has made any concessions. Similarly, the Palestinian leadership continues to agree to language that clearly denies Palestinian sovereignty, yet makes constant pretensions to being a sovereign entity. And so the deception on both sides persists.

From a practical standpoint, the incremental approach has also been too slow and too feeble to generate the thrust behind the peace process needed to render it self-sustaining. Hence the repeated setbacks, the rancor, the disappointments, and the frustrations.

The fundamental approach

A more fundamental approach to breaking the current stalemate is to recognize, *a priori*, that the only viable outcome in Palestine is its partition into two distinct, sovereign states and to move to achieve such an outcome as rapidly as possible. Such an approach would be more honest and forthright because it would restore the widely accepted notion of a two-state solution (with the Palestinian state extending over nearly all of the territories occupied by Israel in the 1967 war – including East Jerusalem – and allowing for mutually agreed border adjustments for security or demographic reasons), restore Palestinian sovereignty over these territories, repatriate refugees in the Palestinian state in accordance with demographic and economic possibilities, and establish close economic links (perhaps a free trade area or a customs union) among the three contiguous states – Israel, Palestine, and Jordan.

These features encapsulate what most peace proposals sought to achieve prior to the Oslo agreement between PLO Chairman Arafat and the Israeli leadership. In fact, these principles were more or less embodied in the understandings reached by the Palestinians with the cosponsors of the Madrid Peace Conference.

To arrive at an outcome incorporating these features, the strategy of the peace process would need to:

- Accelerate the transfer of authority.
- Broaden the interpretation of the Oslo Declaration of Principles to explicitly allow the Palestinians to establish full sovereignty over nearly the entire WBGS according to an agreed schedule.
- Schedule final negotiations on such issues as refugees, Jerusalem, borders, and the settlements and set a tighter deadline for completing them.

Such an approach may appear somewhat quixotic until one contemplates the consequences of the current course of events. Furthermore, the key characteristics of this approach have been almost universally accepted as a basis for a just and durable settlement of the Palestinian–Israeli problem.

ECONOMIC POSSIBILITIES

Each of these two approaches implies a different scenario for the future development of the Palestinian economy. The key assumptions underlying each scenario and the outcomes associated with them may be summarized as follows.

The incremental scenario

Assumptions

Under the slower pace of the incremental scenario events would proceed as follows:

- The Palestinian Authority would proceed from early empowerment in the West Bank (authority over five sectors) to full empowerment by the end of 1996 or early 1997.
- By then the Palestinian Authority would gain control of some areas in the West Bank but not over the entire area; East Jerusalem and its surroundings would remain outside the jurisdiction of the Palestinian Authority.
- Palestinian elections in the WBGS would take place in late 1995 or early 1996 and would, with the election of the Council (powers unknown) and further technical work on domestic regulations, begin to clarify the legislative and regulatory environment. This would sustain private sector investment for a period and could help repatriate external capital for direct investment. However, initial increases in private sector activity would soon taper off because of the confusion about sovereignty, property rights, and continued controls on border crossings.
- The number of Palestinian workers in Israel could increase from the current 30,000 but would fluctuate up to 40,000 over the next five years.
- Restrictions on Palestinian exports from Gaza and from the West Bank would gradually be eased, permitting export receipts to grow by 10–12 percent a year (from current depressed levels) over the next five years.
- Trade agreements between the Palestinian Authority and Jordan and agreements between the Palestinian Authority and Israel on border crossings (envisaged within twelve to eighteen months) would permit modest growth of trade with Jordan and the beginning of trade with the Arab countries.
- Because of the slow buildup of administrative capacity in the Palestinian Authority, the public sector investment program (all foreign financed) would proceed gradually, with utilization rates rising from about $150 million in 1995 to about $300 million by 1998.[4]

Outcomes

Assuming reasonable incremental capital–output ratios, and without going into the fine details of the underlying macroeconomic calculations, the principal outcomes of the incremental scenario can be characterized as:

- Output growth would range between 3 and 5 percent a year over the next five years, barely exceeding population growth and causing per capita incomes to stagnate and per capita consumption to decline marginally. GDP growth would be buoyed by improved private sector saving and investment, but public sector dissaving and a trade deficit would cause a drag on the economy.
- Unemployment and underemployment would decrease somewhat, mainly because of expanded opportunities for work in Israel and only marginally as a result of job creation in the domestic economy, but they would remain near current rates.
- Public sector finances would continue to show a deficit on the current account for most and possibly all of the five-year period, thus requiring continued dependence on foreign financing of a current budget deficit[5] or, failing this, the accumulation of arrears or public debt.
- The balance of payments would continue to show a deficit on the current account ranging from 7 to 10 percent of GDP, and would be financed by external official transfers and foreign direct investment (and possibly by accumulation of external debt). However, the deficit could widen toward the end of the period and may become unsustainable.

Assessment

It is evident that if the Palestinian–Israeli peace process continues to unfold at the current pace, it will not produce a viable solution in Palestine. The Palestinian economy would essentially remain severely handicapped and underdeveloped, its infrastructure in a state of disrepair or at least inadequacy, with high unemployment and minimal growth. The economy would remain dependent on Israel and only moderately open to the rest of the world. It could conceivably slide into an unsustainable external debt and arrears situation. Private sector investment would be sustained for a while but would eventually decline.

Indeed, the outcomes of such a scenario would not only be untenable over the medium term, but the unfolding of such a scenario may bring about its own demise even sooner, by possibly causing the peace process to unravel over the next twelve to eighteen months.

A more promising scenario

This scenario derives from the enlargement of the concept of full autonomy and from the acceleration of the process leading to statehood in the WBGS.

Assumptions

The fundamental approach rests on the following assumptions:

- Full empowerment of the Palestinian Authority in the West Bank would be completed by the fall or winter of 1995 leading, as in the Oslo Declaration of Principles, to the dismantlement of the Israeli Civil Administration.
- Following an early redeployment of Israeli forces, the Palestinian Authority would extend its authority over all areas of the West Bank with the exception of limited zones around Jewish settlements, where mutual security arrangements would be agreed.
- Elections for a Palestinian Council with broad legislative powers would take place in late 1995, to be followed shortly by elections for all local authorities (village and municipal councils).
- Restrictions on work in Israel would be greatly eased or gradually eliminated (as was the case prior to the *intifada*), leading to an increase in the number of workers in Israel, initially to more than 80,000 (this figure would gradually decline as employment opportunities in the local economy improve). At the same time restrictions on Palestinian exports to Israel would be lifted (except for the few agricultural commodities set by the Paris Protocol of April 29 1994).
- Border crossings between the Gaza Strip and Egypt and between the West Bank and Jordan would be opened for freer trade (in accordance with recent agreements between the Palestinian Authority and Jordan), with the supporting infrastructure expanded to handle the larger volume of trade. An open land corridor linking Gaza to the West Bank would be established. Movement of people between Jordan and the WBGS (and Israel if it wishes) would also be greatly liberalized to facilitate tourism, commerce, or family reunions.

- Given the improved opportunities for employment in Israel and the rapidly expanding private sector, public sector employment (which has been used as employment of last resort) would stabilize and possible decline, reducing the burden on public finances.
- A more credible transitional arrangement leading to full statehood within an agreed timeframe would attract Palestinian expatriates, leading to a rapid increase in foreign direct investment and a pronounced improvement in the Palestinian Authority's administrative capacity.

Prerequisites

There is no doubt that, for a while at least, a more accommodating political environment would greatly facilitate the rapid development of the Palestinian economy, but it may not be sufficient for securing long-term viability. Certain prerequisites must also be present, summarized as follows.

Governance and institutional reform is essential, since the current structure of governance in the WBGS is untenable. It is primitive, cumbersome, confusing, and revolves around the personal authority of a single leader. The heavy weight of the repatriated PLO bureaucracy drags down the level of efficiency and hinders reform.

The Palestinian Authority's relations with the PLO structure and with the Palestinian population outside the WBGS have been seriously compromised. With Chairman Arafat at the head of what is essentially a local authority, the question of who represents the Palestinians at large (about 6.5 million people living not only in the WBGS but also in Israel, the neighboring Arab countries, and elsewhere) and how they are to be represented has been complicated. Levels of authority within the PLO have been confused by Arafat's plunge into the autonomy process, while accountability has been lost.

In the meantime, the most basic features of a modern system of governance are absent. No attempt has been made to establish a system of laws by which the Palestinian society is to govern itself. The judicial system remains in a state of disarray, while administrative systems are primitive, ambiguous, contradictory, and leave wide margins of discretion to the personal whims of those in charge, inviting malfeasance and corruption. Citizens have no established legal recourse for venting their grievances. Moreover, Palestinians in the WBGS have to cope with the dual weight of two systems of control: a Palestinian as well as an Israeli one.

The challenge here is to reconstitute the Palestinian society on the basis of certain organizing principles that are rational, modern, and resilient. In this regard the Palestinian leadership, with the participation and help of the Palestinian intelligentsia, needs to articulate a vision of an open and democratic society and a relatively free and liberal economic system. This vision then needs to be translated into the specific legal, political, economic, and administrative structures that constitute a modern state – even if this state, during the transition, lacks full political sovereignty.

In the socioeconomic domain, the economic, financial, and monetary organs of the Palestinian Authority must be reconstituted to render them open and efficient, Palestinian expatriates must be mobilized to serve in a reconstituted national authority, and the economic reconstruction and development program must be revitalized with the help and support of multinational and regional institutions and the international donor community.

An appropriate *development strategy* for this scenario would consist, initially at least, of two tracks: one emphasizing employment creation to help raise incomes in the short- to medium-term, with a second emphasizing investment in human capital as a basis for export-oriented, technology-driven development in the long term.

In the immediate period ahead the priority is for employment creation to help absorb the unemployed, integrate the repatriated Palestinians, relieve poverty, and improve living conditions. This emphasis would coincide with widening opportunities for work in Israel, considerable labor absorption in infrastructure construction (especially housing), and the expanding trade and transport sectors. All these sectors have excess capacity, and with a lax and flexible labor market, prospects for rapid expansion of economic activity over the next two to three years are quite good.

At the same time a second track aimed at long-term needs must be activated. This track would focus on the following key components of development policy:

- Rapidly developing basic infrastructure facilities to help the Palestinian economy escape dependency on Israel.
- Reforming the education system and shifting priorities (and resources) to basic, universal education, supplemented by rapid expansion of technical education, both formal (through schools and training centers and institutes) and informal (on the job training).

- Allocating a greater share of resources to the social sectors, especially basic and environmental health, education and integration of women into the labor force, eradication of poverty, and provisions for a social safety net.
- Accelerating technological development by directing resources to applied research, improving information infrastructure, providing intensive training in special fields (through careful but phased interventions), and piggy-backing on Israeli technological industries.
- Rapidly developing and modernizing the financial sector, especially banking.
- Maintaining flexible labor markets, controlling the size of the public sector, keeping open borders for the movement of labor goods and capital, and maintaining a stable macroeconomic environment.
- Developing a modernized agricultural sector, centered on high-value agriculture, and a technologically deepened industrial sector oriented toward export markets and using low-cost skilled labor. In later stages, however, greater value-added must be drawn from the modernized and knowledge-based services sector, especially banking and finance, information processing, and so on.

While the general principle underlying the WBGS's *external economic relations* (with Israel, Jordan, and the rest of the world) would be that of relatively free movement of goods, labor, and capital, a more nuanced elaboration of this principle needs to be spelled out. This essentially requires freeing the Palestinian economy from the distorted dependency and repressed growth that characterized it during the preceding twenty-seven years of Israeli occupation. It is therefore urgent that external trade outside Israel be expanded as rapidly as possible and that immediate steps be taken to renegotiate new and enlarged economic and trade arrangements to help transcend current constraints and limitations.

The Palestinian Authority also needs to choose the trade regime that will govern its relations with its immediate neighbors – especially Israel, with whom the WBGS has an inequitable and one-sided customs union. Eliminating the option of autarky, the choice is essentially between a free trade area and a customs union, with the long-term interests of the Palestinian economy favoring a free trade area. Establishing a free trade area, however, would require extensive preparations and lengthy negotiations, and these would need to commence soon.

Finally, a number of key issues affecting fiscal and monetary policies need to be closely coordinated with Jordan and renegotiated with

Israel. These include harmonization of systems of indirect taxation to reduce distortions in production and exchange, arrangements for compatible regimes of investment incentives, agreements for avoidance of undertaxation or double taxation, regulation of property rights associated with foreign direct investment, coordination of monetary policies and exchange regimes, and harmonization of policies on capital movements.

Outcomes

Under this more credible and hence more hopeful scenario, the main outcomes would be:

- Early establishment of a clear and investment-friendly regulatory environment would stimulate private sector activity and expedite implementation of the public sector development program. Accordingly, foreign direct investment would rise sharply to about 25 percent of GDP and, together with increased private domestic investment, could raise total private investment to about 35 percent of GDP by the third year. Implementation of the development program would commence earlier and disbursement could average $500–$750 million a year for the first two years, rising to nearly $1 billion by the third year.
- Output growth would range between 10 and 12 percent in real terms over the next several years,6 indicating improvements in real per capita income and consumption of 5–7 percent a year and causing per capita income to rise from about $1,500 now to more than $2,200 in 2000 (at 1994 prices).
- Unemployment would decline sharply and the economy could reach full employment by the beginning of the fifth year.
- As the resurgence in economic activity gave rise to improved tax receipts and a healthier fiscal stance, public sector finances (except perhaps for the first year) would tend toward balance and would show a surplus by the third year, allowing the Palestinian Authority to free itself of reliance on foreign grants for financing the budget and to build up some reserves.
- The balance of payments would fare less well because of the heavy import content of investment expenditures and the rapid rise in consumption against a narrow domestic production base. However, after an initial period of deficit on the current account, the deficit could taper off and become less important over the medium term.

Assessment

The outcome of this scenario, which would develop in the context of an enlarged political framework for the Palestinian Authority and a more liberal economic regime in the immediately surrounding region, could provide the Palestinian economy with the needed momentum to ensure self-sustained growth. Such an outcome would provide the Palestinians with a more hopeful future – thereby reinforcing their commitment to an enduring peaceful settlement – and, by achieving economic success in the WBGS, enhance the credibility of the peace process, with considerable potential implications for the entire region.

The long-term outlook

Beyond the critical five-year period ahead, and if the political situation in the region begins to improve with a movement toward democracy and liberalism, the Palestinian economy, with thriving trade and invest-ment relations with the neighboring countries in the region, would continue to grow at fairly rapid rates. On the political front, the Palestinian Authority would consolidate the remaining attributes of a modern state by completing the buildup of its institutional infrastruc-ture. As political and economic prospects improve, Palestinian exiles would return and be steadily absorbed in the new society, increasing its demographic weight and further improving its long-term viability. Over the next decade – or possibly even sooner – as many as 600,000 Palestinians could return to their homeland. By then the population of Palestine would approach 3.75 million people and, if good economic growth is maintained, per capita income could rise to $2,800 by 2005 (at 1994 prices). Given the high educational achievement of Palestinians and the progress that will have been made in the key social sectors, and if the pattern of economic growth proceeds as outlined in the second scenario, Palestine could easily join the group of reasonably developed, middle-income countries by the middle of the next decade.

CONCLUSION

Having started my chapter with a reference to an earlier work of mine, let me close by quoting the concluding statement from that work:

> In conclusion, a Palestinian state established within the framework of an equitable and comprehensive peace settlement in the Middle

East can indeed be economically viable, provided certain fundamental conditions are fulfilled. Moreover, and this is probably an
equally important point, the establishment of a Palestinian state as
a homeland in which the majority of Palestinians may reside and to
which all Palestinians may belong would afford the Palestinian
people, with the help of other Arab states and the world community
at large, a unique opportunity to build a modern, healthy and
progressive society that would contribute materially to the future
peace and prosperity of the entire region. (Abed, 1990)

Notes

1. The area of the West Bank (including East Jerusalem) is 5,560 square
   kilometers, or about 20 percent of Mandatory Palestine. According to
   the Oslo agreement, it is unlikely that the Palestinian Authority will
   extend its autonomy over more than a portion of this area during the
   interim period (1997–99).
2. This chapter was prepared in June 1995, before agreement was reached
   on the transfer of authority in the major cities of the West Bank and the
   scheduling of elections for January 20 1996. These developments, as well
   as the succession of Shimon Peres as Israeli prime minister following the
   assassination of Prime Minister Rabin on November 4 1995, may have
   altered the prospects for peace in Palestine, probably in the direction
   indicated by the alternative strategy proposed in the chapter. However,
   the chapter was not revised to take these developments and their implications into account.
3. The term 'full empowerment' refers to the Palestinian Authority's
   assumption of full authority over all civilian functions in the West Bank,
   as distinct from early empowerment, whereby the Palestinian Authority
   took control of five sectors in the West Bank: domestic taxation, education, health, social welfare, and tourism.
4. By contrast, of the $2.3 billion in pledges mentioned earlier, available
   commitments for 1994 (the first year of the envisaged five-year public
   investment program) amounted to $722 million.
5. As has been the case to date, this would entail the reallocation of pledged
   development assistance funds to finance current budgetary expenditures.
6. These rates would duplicate those achieved during 1967–75, when
   restrictions on trade and movement of labor between the WBGS and
   Israel were relatively relaxed.

Reference

Abed, George T., 1990. *The Economic Viability of a Palestinian State*,
Washington, D.C.: Institute for Palestinian Studies.

7 Reconstructing Lebanon's Economy

Georges Corm

This chapter analyzes the issues associated with reconstructing the Lebanese economy after fifteen years of violence (1975–90). An ambitious $11.7 billion reconstruction plan launched in 1992 seeks to restore Beirut to its former position as an important regional banking and services center. The analysis here focuses on the implementation of this plan, particularly its shortcomings. Two issues are paramount. The first pertains to the huge fiscal and monetary imbalances that threaten Lebanon's economy in the postwar era; the second concerns the huge social needs of the poor segments of the population. The plan, the chapter concludes, is not addressing either issue effectively.

For some three decades after its independence from France in 1943, Lebanon was one of the economic and social darlings of the Middle East. In fact, economic liberalism and the development of a strong middle class were key elements of the broad political consensus that led to the country's independence.

On the economic front political leaders, buoyed by affluent families of traders and real estate developers who resented the regulatory constraints imposed by France, were eager to open up the economy. Economic restructuring reached its peak during the presidency of General Fouad Chehab (1958–64), who established the Central Bank of Lebanon and the Ministry of Planning. Within the ministry a Central Directorate of Statistics quickly consolidated the production of fundamental economic data that had previously been supplied by outsiders.

Lebanon's open economy blossomed early on, and the country soon became one of the most advanced economies in the Arab world. Functioning as a deregulated, decentralized economy, the country also developed some of the best telecommunications, tourism, education, and health infrastructures in the region. Similarly, Lebanon had a high per capita income (about $1,250) and its currency (the Lebanese pound, or L£) was among the strongest in the world, appreciating

116

from L£3.2 to L£2.5 to the U.S. dollar between 1964 and 1974. The country had no external debt and an insignificant amount of domestic debt. For the most part the Central Bank functioned independently of government; it did not engage in credit administration and – in contrast to other developing countries – was not used to refinance a fragmented credit market or to monetize the treasury deficit. Lebanon was once called the Switzerland of the Arab world, hinting not only at its economic and financial performance but also at its natural beauty and relatively equitable distribution of political power among the leaders of its different religious communities.

On the social front Lebanese economists immediately promoted reconstruction and state reform on the heels of independence. Some of the most prominent economists and reformers called for, in particular, taxation and social justice reform (Menassa, 1946; Corm, 1994b). But social and human development had to wait until the 1960s after the political disruptions endured in 1958.[1] General Chehab proved to be a devoted reformer, and with the assistance of a French team of experts headed by Abbé Louis Lebret dedicated himself to balanced economic and social development. A new generation of Lebanese economists seized on the opportunity afforded by the environment of reform and immediately began collecting extensive data on socioeconomic conditions throughout the country. The data revealed large discrepancies between central Lebanon and Beirut and the rest of the country. Within Beirut the data revealed economic and social imbalances between prosperous parts of the capital and the emerging shanty towns (Ministry of Planning and Institute de Recherches et de Formation en vue du Développement, 1961; Corm, 1964).

ECONOMIC AND SOCIAL PROGRESS FALTERS

During 1964–74 Lebanon's economic growth was remarkable.[2] Yet as violence escalated in the 1960s and 1970s – triggered by the first massive Israeli attack on Lebanon in December 1968 and growing tensions between the Lebanese army and Palestinian resistance movements – the political climate deteriorated, threatening economic and social development.

Still, the economy remained strong even as late as April 1975, when full-scale war erupted between Lebanese and Palestinian factions. Despite heavy casualties and property losses, the banking sector was buoyant and consumption levels remained high. Fueled by the influx of income from Lebanese citizens who had migrated to the oil-booming economies of the Arabian peninsula or Iraq, an uncontrolled real estate boom took place as commercial activities moved from downtown Beirut to its eastern and southern peripheries and to provincial capitals like Saïda, Tripoli, and Zahlé. The infusion of money strengthened the Lebanese pound and increased the assets of the banking sector.[3]

A turning point came in 1977, when a wholly centralized agency – the Council for Reconstruction and Development – was created to rebuild the basic infrastructure that had been destroyed by the war. The council was granted extensive administrative power over technical ministries and autonomous public services in water, electricity, and telephones. As such, it supplanted the Ministry of Planning and its statistical directorate, whose data, archives, and equipment had in any case been destroyed by the war. Thus the country was deprived of the capacity to produce accurate official statistics. Because hostilities resumed in 1978 and lasted until 1990, the council was unable to implement its reconstruction plans, including those for the historical district of Beirut, heavily damaged by the fighting in 1975–6 (Iskandar and Baroudi, 1994). The council also abstained from formulating an institutional and policy framework to guide reconstruction under a three-year World Bank program prepared in 1982/83 (Sbaiti, 1994).

The violence during 1983–90 was extremely disruptive. The Lebanese pound fell sharply, from L£5.5 to L£842.0 to the U.S. dollar. Total deposits in the banking system dropped from the equivalent of $11.5 billion in 1982 to $3.1 billion in 1987. The resulting loss of confidence in the traditionally strong Lebanese pound spurred the dollarization of private sector activities and most domestic savings. Deposits in Lebanese pounds fell from 71 percent of total deposits in 1982 to 8 percent in 1987, although they recovered to 33 percent in 1989. The violence between the official Lebanese army (under the command of General Aoun), the Christian militia of Lebanese forces, and the Syrian army came to end in 1990. Once General Aoun was finally subdued (and later exiled to Paris), the Taïeff agreement of 1989 could begin to be implemented. Under this constitutional agreement the distribution of power between the three largest communities (Maronite, Sunni, and Chia) was made more equal because the power of the prime minister (a Sunni) and the Parliament speaker (a Chia) were reinforced relative to the president of the republic (a Maronite). The agreement also provided for militia leaders to form a government of National Unity.

The governments of National Unity that have been in power since the end of 1990 have forged an economic alliance between wealthy Lebanese contractors, whose fortune originated in the Gulf countries, and the new wealthy political establishment, whose fortune originated in the economic hegemony achieved by Lebanese militia leaders between 1975 and 1990. This alliance of influential contractors and business and community leaders is imposing the new approach to reconstruction and reform (Corm, 1993b, 1994a).

THE RECONSTRUCTION PLAN

Prompted by the implementation of the Taïeff agreement, the new administration has totally changed the focus of economic thinking in Lebanon. The reconstruction plan deviates from long-held economic principles in four important ways:

- Despite fifteen war-induced years of dramatic social distortions, the plan does not embody the sustainable growth and regionally balanced development policies that characterized prewar planning (Charif 1994). As mentioned earlier, this shift away from progressive development was initiated by the Council for Reconstruction and Development's first reconstruction program in 1977.
- The reconstruction plan does not provide sufficient resources for the country's pressing social needs. In particular, the new governing elite is ignoring the magnitude of environmental pollution generated by fifteen years of war – the tons of waste accumulated in Beirut and throughout the country and the thousands of barrels of toxic waste that came from Italy during the last years of the war.
- Economic reform is oriented toward privatizing state enterprises and limiting the government's role in promoting and regulating reconstruction activities – a role that was already quite modest before the war. Given the new business elite's strong influence on and considerable participation in the government, there is now minimal control over whether the large and powerful private sector distorts to dangerous levels the distribution of income across society. In addition, a strategy for downsizing the bloated and unproductive civil service and for infusing it with professional ethics and standards has not yet been developed.[4]
- The main advisers to the Council for Reconstruction and Development – still the sole state institution in charge of reconstruction

policy – will be the private engineering firms of Bechtel and Dar Al
Handassah. The new governing elite is not seeking consultation
from independent, nonprofit institutions with experience in development issues, as during the Chehab era.

Despite these shortcomings and weaknesses, the new reconstruction
plan and its economic policies have received unqualified support both
within and outside Lebanon. Much of this support can be explained
by the formal coherence of the reconstruction plan and its broadly
based economic appeal.

The basic goal of the reconstruction plan is to restore the commercial and financial importance of Beirut in the new Middle Eastern
economy.[5] The plan includes three elements geared toward attaining
this goal. The first is the creation of the largest real estate company in
the Arab world – Solidere – entrusted with reconstructing Beirut's
historical and commercial downtown district. Solidere will operate as
a private entity; neither the government nor the Beirut municipality
will have any control over company operations. With a capital of $1.6
billion, trading in the company's shares will be the cornerstone of a
capital market that is designed to play a regional role. Solidere is
empowered to design the physical layout of the new town, execute
the rehabilitation of the infrastructure, carry out real estate promotion
and maintenance activities, reclaim several thousand square meters of
land on the sea, and expropriate land from 120,000 property holders,
making them compulsory shareholders of the company.

The second element is the implementation of a massive transportation and telecommunications infrastructure program that includes:

- An airport that can accommodate 6–7 million passengers a year;
- A highway network linking Beirut to Damascus and other regional
  capitals;
- A seafront international conference center with a luxury hotel of
  1,000 rooms, to be built in the Ras Beirut area; and
- A one-million-line telephone network and a complementary cellular telephone system.

The third element is a sharp reduction in direct taxation to attract
Arab and international capital to Lebanon and to reactivate Beirut's
role as a regional financial center.

The reconstruction plan will be implemented over a ten-year period
(1992–2002) at a total cost of $11.7 billion (in constant dollars). Of
this, $10.5 billion will be used for physical reconstruction and $1.2

billion will go to the private sector in the form of grants and credit support. An initial three-year plan (1992–4) prepared by Dar Al Handassah and Bechtel directed $3.9 billion toward removing bottle-necks in electricity, water, and telephone supply and to rehabilitating roads, public schools, hospitals, and other basic infrastructure (such as the port of Beirut) but was superseded in 1993 by the $11.7 billion plan. By the end of 1993 Solidere had issued $600 million in shares to raise liquid funds – a move that strengthened Beirut's image as a revived financial center and an emerging market.

The reconstruction plan is grounded in two basic documents: the law on the creation of Solidere adopted by Parliament in December 1991 and the *Horizon 2000 Plan* for infrastructure adopted by the Council of Ministers and managed by the Council for Reconstruction and Development. Both documents have been the subject of intense debate inside Lebanon, but they have received little attention at the regional or international levels (see the self-published collective work of ten Lebanese experts – engineers, urban planners, lawyers, socio-logists, and economists – published in Beirut in 1992, "Beirut Recon-struction: A Lost Opportunity"; Corm, 1993a, Kabbani, 1982; Beyhum, 1993; Khalaf and Khoury, 1993). Moreover, in-depth inter-nal discussions of the technical constraints and shortcomings of the new economic policies have not been reported by the media.

Although the Mexican peso crisis in December 1994 has made international investors more cautious about emerging markets, and despite a growing social crisis in Lebanon, the new governing elite has not in any way amended its reconstruction and reform strategies. To the contrary, its belief in the soundness of the basic assumptions governing reconstruction is more solid than ever. In particular, it believes that as the regional peace process proceeds, Lebanon should accelerate implementation of the reconstruction plan so that Beirut can return to its prewar status as the most attractive tourism, com-mercial, and financial center of the Arab world. No consideration has been given to the major changes that have taken place in the region over the past twenty years, or to the urgent domestic social needs after fifteen years of violence and destruction.

WHAT THE PLAN OVERLOOKS

Six issues are pertinent to any debate about the potential success of Lebanon's reconstruction plan. They cover a spectrum of technical, fiscal, financing, and social constraints that militate against the wisdom of implementing the plan in its current form.

The lack of basic economic data

A fundamental issue in any debate about Lebanon's economic policy is the paucity of basic data derived from census and sampling. Since the Directorate of Statistics stopped functioning in 1975, no population census has taken place, and the number of buildings damaged and new square meters constructed during the war are unknown. The absence of information on the precise level of gross domestic product (GDP) precludes deriving the main ratios needed to analyze the economic assumptions underlying the reconstruction plan. Only at the end of 1994 did the Council of Ministers reestablish the Directorate of Statistics, although with a reduced budget. The directorate has not yet published official figures for the macroeconomic aggregates underlying the formation of GDP.

The only reliable GDP estimates come from a 1988 survey financed by the United Nations Development Programme (UNDP). The survey, compiled by the most reputable Lebanese economists, arrived at an estimate of $3.3 billion, or $1,160 per capita, for 1988. Other sources, however, indicate a GDP of $2.6 billion for 1988 (RDCL, 1993; Iskandar and Baroudi 1994). GDP estimates for 1992 range from $3.8 billion (Lebanese Banks' Association 1992) to $6.5 billion (Banque Audi, 1993). A recently published International Monetary Fund (IMF) paper states a figure of $5.1 billion for 1992, jumping to $7.7 billion in 1993 (Eken et al., 1995). The government's most recent economic scenario for 1995–2007, as presented to Parliament with the 1995 budget law, assumes a GDP of $8.5 billion for 1994 (Ministry of Finance, 1995).

Given this confusion about GDP figures, any economic policy could be justified or criticized when considered in relation to the most contested economic issue in Lebanon today – the level of affordable indebtedness given the size of the economy and its low productive capacity. In fact, the confusion about GDP figures stems from the dollarization of the economy, which has not yet been properly analyzed.

Based on discussions with several Lebanese economists, my estimate of 1994 GDP is $6.8 billion, derived according to the following assumptions:

- A 1988 GDP of $3.7 billion, representing a 16 percent increase over UNDP estimates to correct for an undervalued GDP at that time.
- An average annual domestic inflation rate of 10 percent (in U.S. dollar terms) during 1988–94.
- An annual percentage change in GDP as indicated by the official figures and the IMF figures.

The dollarization of the economy

No objective discussion has taken place on the harm done to the economy by allowing its dollarization to the point where:

- U.S. dollar bank note are a basic component of M1, yet are not included in official figures of circulated currency.
- The public and private sectors conduct transactions in different currencies – the public sector in Lebanese pounds (including the issuance of treasury bills) and the private sector in dollars (including more than 90 percent of credit extended by banks).
- The largest part of domestic savings (70 percent) is still held in U.S. dollars despite the stability of the exchange rate over the past two-and-a-half years.

Given the complexity of the issues, there are a number of reasons to doubt the commonly held view that the dollarization of the economy is a positive macroeconomic development that does not impede economic growth. One is that since the steep decline of the Lebanese pound during 1985–87, the authorities have not made any effort to preserve the value of financial assets or liabilities that are held in domestic currency – in contrast to Israel and several Latin American countries. This laissez faire policy has allowed pound debtors to avoid reimbursement and pound savers and wage earners to be ruined by the crumbling pound.

In fact, with the restoration of political stability and security at the end of 1990, the Central Bank adopted an administered exchange rate policy to prevent a sharp appreciation of the Lebanese pound relative to the U.S. dollar – a phenomenon that would have taken place had market forces been left free. Then in 1992, when speculation against the pound began, the Central Bank tried to control the market and administer the exchange rate to prevent a depreciating pound, which fell to its lowest level since 1987 – L£2,560 to the U.S. dollar. Since then the administered rate has both prevented a substantial appreciation of the pound against positive market forces and prevented depreciation in the face of a changing market.

Table 7.1 Inflation rates and exchange rates, Lebanon, 1989–94
(percent)

Year	Inflation rate	Exchange rate (end of period)	Exchange rate fluctuation (annual average)
1989	72.2	5	−81
1990	68.8	−67	−41
1991	51.5	−4	−32
1992	120.0	−109	−85
1993	29.1	7	2
1994	8.0	4	1

Sources: Eken *et al.* 1995; Bank of Lebanon.

Another constraint is that since fiscal 1987 inflation measurements have not accounted for the dollarization of private sector activities. Price increases in domestic currency might not have the same impact on revenue and consumption in a dollarized economy that they would in an economy whose transactions are made in domestic currency. This two-currency structure might explain the inconsistent relationship between inflation and variations in the exchange rate (Table 7.1). If it does, exchange rate variations reflect either speculation against the Lebanese pound or artificial exchange rate administration by the Bank of Lebanon when speculators are dormant. Given that the formation of local value added depends heavily on imported inputs and that Lebanon's economy is open, with no domestic bottlenecks, there should be a strong causal relationship between the depreciation of the exchange rate and the domestic inflation rate. But although the inflation rate shows some correlation with the annual average exchange rate, the relationship between inflation and the end-of-period rate is inconsistent except for 1990 and 1992 (Khalaf and Munla 1984; Khalaf, 1985).

A third constraint is that in the past ten years the balance of payment has shown a net surplus (except in 1992) ranging from $32 million in 1987 to $1.0 billion in 1991, to more than $1.1 billion in 1993 and 1994. These figures confirm our analysis of the successive phases of speculation against the Lebanese pound and exchange rate administration that bears no relationship to economic fundamentals.

Where should the Lebanese pound stand in relation to the U.S. dollar? This question is open to debate. One could argue that the pound is grossly overvalued and has remained artificially high since

1992 because of the overly generous interest rates granted on treasury bills that have attracted Lebanese and Arab savings from abroad. But the opposite argument could also be made. After all, the exchange rate stood at L£450–500 to the dollar in 1989 and L£500–700 to the dollar in 1990 despite the violence and political strife that were paralyzing the economy. Today Lebanon is essentially free of violence (except in the border area with Israel) and has a strong economic and political leadership that is devoted to reconstruction, in addition to a continuous inflow of Lebanese capital that helps cover the huge deficit in the current account balance. Why, then, is the exchange rate standing at L 1,625 to the U.S. dollar? Is the budget deficit responsible for the demise of the pound? The answers to these questions are essential to Lebanon's future.

The budget deficit and taxation policy

The budget deficit is clouding the prospects for solid economic recovery, yet it is an issue that is not being addressed properly. The government's economic scenario envisages that the 1995 public deficit (that is, including reconstruction expenditures) of $2.4 billion will decline sharply by 2003, reaching a surplus in 2005 (in constant dollars). The scenario projects that the ordinary budget deficit (that is, excluding reconstruction expenditures) will achieve a surplus of $160 million by 2000, increasing to $600 million by 2002. According to this scenario total budget operations, including development expenditures, will reach a surplus by 2004.[6]

In fact, the financing constraint is one of the central issues in the debate over the reconstruction plan.[7] In its various progress reports the Council for Reconstruction and Development sounds confident about the availability of various types of financing, including build-operate-transfer schemes (which have already been implemented in the cellular telephone system). To date, about $2 billion of foreign financing has been contracted ($1.6 billion in loans and $0.4 billion in grants). In addition, the government's economic scenario envisages development spending of more than $10.7 billion (in constant dollars) between 1995 and 2005, financed almost entirely by domestic and foreign borrowing.

In actuality, however, the total budget deficit climbed from L£1,260 billion in 1992 to L£2,800 billion in 1994 (or from $736 million to $1,600 million based on the yearly average exchange rate), representing more than 55 percent of total expenditures (Ministry of Finance,

1995). Consequently, the amount of treasury bills quadrupled in terms of Lebanese pounds, from L 2,333 billion at the end of 1991 to L£9,339 by September 1994 (or from $2.6 billion to $5.6 billion: Bank of Lebanon, various issues). Yet the percentage of projects in the reconstruction plan implemented by the Council for Reconstruction and Development in May 1994 ranged from a low of 0.6 percent in health and social affairs to a high of 37.0 percent in solid waste disposal, with an average of 8–12 percent (CRD, 1995). At the same time the ordinary budget deficit jumped from L£452 billion in 1992 to L£1,450 in 1994.

The authorities have not formulated an overall strategy for redressing these increasingly dramatic fiscal imbalances. Deficit financing has come at a very high cost – in 1993 the average yield offered to subscribers of treasury bills was about 20 percent (16 percent higher than the U.S. dollar interest rate for three-month deposits) while the currency was stable and appreciated by 7.24 percent; in 1994 the average yield was about 19 percent while currency appreciation continued at a rate of 3.88 percent.

Curiously, the authorities borrowed more than the treasury needs in 1993 and 1994, as evidenced by the sharp increase in public sector deposits with the Bank of Lebanon, from L£927 billion ($500 million) at the end of 1992 to 2,749 billion ($1.65 billion) by September 1994 (Bank of Lebanon, various issues). It is not clear whether this policy originated from a desire to attract a greater inflow of foreign capital and so strengthen the Central Bank's foreign currency reserves, or to capture liquid reserves for the government and the Council for Reconstruction and Development to spend on reconstruction programs to meet expected shortfalls in foreign funding.

Whatever the reason, the burden of servicing domestic debt is by far the largest item in the budget, costing about L£1,600 billion in 1994, or the equivalent of $1 billion (against total expenditures of $2.5 billion). To this should be added the more than L£1,300 ($0.7 billion) of unbudgeted expenditures disbursed through treasury advances.

Another puzzling aspect of the government's fiscal policy is the drastic cut in direct taxation in an effort to attract foreign investment and promote private sector activity. In effect, the private sector pays a 10 percent flat tax on all types of activities and 5 percent on share dividends. However, the share of direct taxation of total public receipts was already low when Lebanon was enjoying a booming economy (1960–74), standing at about 22 percent of total receipts, with the income tax representing only about 10 percent of such receipts. In 1972 the total tax burden as a share of GDP was 12 percent.

Because the precise level of GDP is unknown, it is difficult to estimate the current tax burden as a share of GDP. Detailed figures on the collection of various taxes are also unavailable. According to the most recent report from the Bank of Lebanon for 1990–2, direct taxes (including registration taxes) amounted to 17.8 percent of total public receipts in 1992 (L£183 billion against total tax receipts of L£1,031 billion).[8]

According to the 1995 budget presented to Parliament, however, total tax receipts were L£982 billion in 1992, L£1,855 billion in 1993, and L£2,200 billion in 1994. Using the International Monetary Fund's estimate of 1993 GDP (L£13,122 billion), the tax burden that year would have been just 14.1 percent. In 1995, assuming an increase in current GDP of 14 percent (9 percent inflation and 6 percent growth), taxes as a share of GDP would have increased slightly, to 14.7 percent.

Because the level of public indebtedness is already very high, the real issue here is whether the reconstruction plan can be financed in the absence of a significant increase in taxation – particularly direct taxes, given the already high rate of indirect taxation. As of September 1994 the commercial banking sector was already financing 75 percent of the treasury bills issued, with an additional 6 percent financed by the Bank of Lebanon. Although Lebanon's banking sector has traditionally financed the private sector exclusively, its ratio of public lending increased from 31 percent of total domestic lending in 1990 to 46 percent in September 1994. Treasury bill subscriptions by Lebanese banks now represent 87 percent of their resources in Lebanese pounds, a very high ratio given the volatility of pound deposits in the banking system should a new wave of speculation against the domestic currency occur. It should also be noted that the average maturity for deposits in the banking system ranges from 30 to 40 days. By contrast, the average maturity for treasury bills has increased over the past two years, reaching 316 days by the end of 1994 (Lebanese Banks' Association, 1995).

The real estate boom and its link to savings

During 1977–83 a large share of savings went toward investment in real estate. Between 1984 and 1990 the market declined dramatically; it has since revived and is now booming despite inflated prices and the fact that an estimated 30 percent of the buildings constructed since

1977 are empty. Renting has become practically nonexistent as a result of a series of laws that froze rents in favor of tenants. Despite new laws that allow for a gradual increase in formerly frozen rents, real estate owners continue to prefer selling apartments or offices to renting them. Given the high level of savings among the wealthiest part of the population – and their ability to self-finance new construction – Lebanon does not have a market for regulating real estate prices.[9] As in many Arab countries, real estate is considered the best local investment because it safeguards the value of money invested in the middle term and grants economic prestige to building owners. Rather than selling at a lower profit level than envisaged, self-financing owners prefer to keep buildings empty, waiting for the market to reach the desired level and deliver the highest possible amount of profit, which normally ranges from 30–50 percent (in constant terms) of initial investment. In addition, the construction of luxury apartments is a predominant feature of the real estate sector in Lebanon, despite the huge need for low-cost housing. Given the current boom in construction activities, some concern has been expressed about the fate of new buildings that will soon be constructed by Solidere in the large downtown area, as well as of all the new buildings constructed during the war years in the Beirut suburbs, where most companies relocated after the destruction of the center of Beirut.

An in-depth study has not yet been undertaken of how the real estate market in Lebanon functions and whether it is adequate for addressing the country's needs. In this context it is difficult to envisage an efficient mobilization of savings as long as the real estate market continues to be inelastic and to freeze a large part of savings in the luxury segment of the market. The larger issue here is that of helping the economy develop an effective financial market.

The domestic financial market and the status of the currency

One of the key constraints facing the government's goal of making Beirut one of the important financial markets in the Arab world is the absence of an effective domestic market that supplies the needs of the economy through properly structured financial instruments. Although prewar Beirut was the commercial banking center of the Middle East, it was never able to develop a domestic capital market. Its stock exchange was limited by the small number of companies whose shares were registered and by the small number of transactions that took place. Indeed, most companies were owned by a few families that were unwilling to raise additional equity capital through the stock exchange.

Little has changed that would indicate the promise of the ambitious plans to turn Beirut into a full-fledged financial center. Solidere is the only actively traded share on the stock exchange; the price of the mammoth real estate company, which jumped from an initial offering of $100 to $170 within a few months, is now down to a more realistic level of $120-130. Byblos Bank, owned by a single Lebanese family, is proceeding with an equity capital increase through the services of a newly established financing company. Similarly, Ciment Libanais has proceeded with an offering of $100 million in bonds and equity. In spring 1994 a $400 million Eurobond issue for Lebanon was also issued for three years at $10^1/_8$ percent – a very high cost.

There is no doubt that there is great potential for developing a capital market, but many preliminary steps must be taken before this market can be considered solid. One prerequisite is modernization of the laws and regulations that support a mutual fund industry. Another is the securitization of banking and real estate assets, together with efforts to train judges in modern financial issues and improve their salary structure. Without the proper set of modern laws and a well-trained judiciary, a sound and long-term capital market cannot develop.

Another obstacle is the low level of income tax, which makes it difficult for the government to offer tax incentives (as has been done elsewhere) that direct savings toward capital markets and away from short-term banking deposits and real estate investment. Thus the Central Bank should adopt regulations that encourage commercial banks with an effective branch network to participate in developing capital markets and to gradually transform themselves into global banking institutions. This process would require completely redrafting the current banking law to promote investment banking activities.

One final prerequisite for the development of a domestic capital market is a clarification of the status of the Lebanese pound. The main objective of the government's current policy is still unclear: is the dollar going to continue to be encouraged as the main currency outside the payment of state expenditures and subscriptions to treasury bills? The denomination of Solidere shares in U.S. dollars, and the fact that the Bank of Lebanon is operating a system that compensates checks in U.S. dollars and other foreign currencies, and that the bank is attracting U.S. dollars deposits from Lebanese banks at a premium over LIBOR – these moves could be interpreted as supporting dollarization of the economy, restricting the Lebanese pound to public domestic payments and financing the deficit at a very high cost.

The ambiguity of government policies will in the long run preclude establishing a solid domestic capital market. Rather than obscuring the fate of the Lebanese pound, the government should seek either to develop a more coherent policy for reestablishing the pound (implying that the state deficit would have to reduced drastically) or to adapt a transparent link between the U.S. dollar and the pound, encouraging savings to remain in pounds.

The social climate

A sharp contrast between an affluent, prosperous Lebanon and misery belts around Beirut was already emerging before the war, as were unemployment and deprivation in eastern, northern, and southern peripheral areas.

Migration to the Gulf countries and Africa has brought dramatic social changes to Lebanon, as it has in other parts of the Arab world. New wealth has been diffused. But with fifteen years of war and the crumbling of the Lebanese pound, the social and economic dislocation in Lebanon has been particularly severe:

- Between 600,000 and 800,000 people were displaced by force inside their own country, and only a small percentage of these populations have returned to their original locations (Labaki, 1993; Kasparian, 1995).
- The war maimed 50,000–60,000 people.
- Public health and education systems have almost disappeared, private schools and hospitals are too expensive for ordinary citizens, and the social security system is limited to regular wage earners.
- Income inequality is greater than before the war, and the middle class is suffering to such a degree that many are seeking to migrate to OECD countries.
- The lack of a public transportation system and an increase in the aging vehicle fleet has created a terrible bottleneck in the transportation system, exacerbating air pollution.
- The influx of unskilled migrant workers from East Asia and Syria is exerting downward pressure on salary scales. Salaries range between the equivalent of $150 and $600 a month, with the average salary at $250–300. Given the high cost of living, this wage is

totally inadequate. Many Lebanese also are unemployed or under-employed. Although no unemployment figures are available, a large segment of the population – possibly 30 percent – lives below the poverty line (Hamdane, 1995).

The reconstruction plan does not address these social issues directly, nor does it recognize the links between these social bottlenecks, distortions, and imbalances and the generally low levels of productivity and high production costs that hinder competitiveness. The plan's exclusive emphasis on physical infrastructure seeks to ensure that Lebanon can reestablish its position of prominence in the new Middle Eastern economy. In the eyes of the new governing elite, only if Lebanon regains its position will economic growth become sustainable and social progress become achievable for a large part of the population. The current wisdom is that only through private sector expansion and services can social problems be redressed. Thus the government will play only a small role in the process of economic development. Its high level of indebtedness, denominated largely in the unstable domestic currency, does not seem to strike policymakers as a significant obstacle to establishing a sound financial market.

CONCLUSION

In the absence of reliable economic data it is difficult to appraise the reconstruction plan or to assess its chances of success. Even if regional development proceeds smoothly – a big if – the country must first develop a serious and coherent policy of institution building, improve mechanisms for economic and political governance, and implement policies that retrain workers and create jobs. The low level of economic productivity and the high costs of the productive sector, primarily services, will not be cured by focusing exclusively on building major infrastructure.

Lebanon's huge infrastructure scheme must be downsized, both to contain the treasury deficit and to support greater spending in areas of crucial social and educational importance. Pollution, in particular, also must be addressed. In any case it unrealistic to believe that the reconstruction plan can be financed adequately without a serious review of the tax policy. This review should seek to increase the tax burden for a few years (particularly by raising income taxes) and to remedy the unfair balance between direct and indirect taxation.

Without such a review the deficit will continue to increase, further endangering financial stability and the status of the Lebanese pound. Any increase in the already heavy domestic indebtedness will also crowd out the financing needs of the private sector.

The overall tax burden should be raised to at least 30 percent of GDP just to put a brake on the alarming increase in domestic debt. Total state spending increased from $1.3 billion in 1992 to $1.7 billion in 1993, to $2.6 billion in 1994, while receipts remained stable at about $1.0 billion in 1993 and 1994. If current fiscal policies are not reformed immediately, Lebanon will find it difficult to emerge from the spiraling budget deficit and fiscal imbalances will continue to fuel domestic inflation, increase social unrest, and threaten the stability of the financial system and the development of an efficient capital market.

To make the reconstruction plan more efficient, the government should:

- Reduce its overly ambitious infrastructure schemes, or at least phase them in more gradually.
- Devote more resources to fighting pollution, developing a strong public transportation system, improving the public health and education system, providing more worker rehabilitation and training, and supporting the agricultural and industrial sectors (through marketing, research and development, and export promotion).
- Adopt a fiscal stabilization plan that lowers domestic debt and its huge interest costs, thus strengthening the Lebanese pound and starting to de-dollarize the economy.
- Allow the Lebanese pound to float freely on the domestic foreign exchange market, leaving it to find its adequate level within an improved macroeconomic framework, a fiscal stabilization plan, and a properly refocused reconstruction plan.

However realistic and urgent these objectives are, the most fundamental obstacle to economic restructuring is the absence of real dialogue between the new governing elite and those who are trying to introduce flexibility and rationality into the reconstruction plan. By using its financial influence to prevent any serious and thoughtful debate on the difficult issues of reconstruction, the authorities are contributing to the demise of democracy in Lebanon and to impoverished economic and social thinking. These were among the country's strongest comparative advantages before the war.

Notes

1. In 1958 an acute crisis erupted in the wake of President Chamoun's (1952–58) alignment with Western policies against a wave of anticolonial Arab nationalism in Egypt, Iraq, and Syria. This push toward nationalism started in 1956 with the nationalization of the Suez canal in Egypt and the subsequent invasion of Sinai by Israeli, British, and French troops.
2. Except in 1967, when the intrabank crisis of 1966 and the Arab–Israeli war of 1967 combined to produce a decline in GDP.
3. By the time Israel invaded Lebanon in 1982 total bank assets had jumped from the equivalent of $5.0 billion in 1977 to $14.6 billion despite seven years of violence and political instability (Iskandar and Baroudi, 1994; Corm, 1988).
4. The World Bank has provided a $25 million loan for a public administration rehabilitation project, the content of which has not yet been made public. The project will probably consist of financing for hardware equipment and related training needs.
5. Fundamental to this goal is the resolution of the Arab–Israeli conflict, the opening of Arab economies, and efforts to create a Middle East trade zone that includes Israel and its Arab neighbors.
6. A previous scenario elaborated by the Council for Reconstruction and Development and submitted to Parliament in 1992 envisaged that ordinary budget operations would reach a surplus by 1996, allowing up to 60 percent of the reconstruction program to be financed.
7. In a 1994 article Professor Elias Gannag , a highly respected and well-known Lebanese economist, expresses doubt that the reconstruction plan is realistic, not only in terms of funding but also in terms of the high annual rate of investment implied by the plan (38 percent of GDP, on average, for the first five years).
8. Note, however, that this was before the 1994 tax reform lowered the income tax to the flat rate of 10 percent.
9. Banking sector credits for construction accounts for just 9 percent of total credit granted to the private sector (Bank of Lebanon, various issues).

References

Bank of Lebanon, various issues. *Quarterly Bulletin*. Beirut.

Banque Audi, Secretariat for Planning and Development, 1993. *Major Economic Indicators in 1992*, Beirut.

Beyhum, N., 1993, "Les Trois Plans de Reconstruction de Beyrouth ou la Crise de la Citadinité," *Cahiers de l'IRMAC* 2, Université Lumière, Lyon II.

Charif, H., 1994. "Regional Development and Integration," in D. Collings(ed.) *Peace for Lebanon? From War to Reconstruction*. Boulder, Col.: Canadian Institute for International Peace and Security.

Corm, Georges, 1964. *Politique, Economique et Planification au Liban, 1954–1964*. Beirut: Imprimerie Universelle.

————— 1988. "Current Economic and Social Conditions in Lebanon," in H. Barakat(ed.), *Toward a Viable Lebanon*, London: Croom Helm.

————— 1993a. "La Reconstruction du Centre de Beyrouth, Un Exemple de Fièvre Immobilière au Liban,"in *Revue d'Economie Financière*, numéro hors-sèrie, sur le théme "La Crise Financière de l'immobilier: Réflexions sur un Phénomène Mondial" (December). Paris.

————— 1993b "La Reconstruction: Idéologie et Paradoxes," *Les Cahiers de l'Orient* (Fourth quartes), Paris.

—————1994a. "Militia Hegemony and the Reestablishment of the State." in D. Collings(ed.), *Peace for Lebanon? From War to Reconstruction*, Boulder, Col.: Canadian Institute for International Peace and Security.

————— 1994b. "Ruptures et Continuit s dans la Pens e et les Politiques de Développement et de Reconstruction au Liban depuis l'Indépendance," *Proche-Orient Etudes Economiques*, 43, Université Saint Joseph, Beirut.

CRD (Council for Reconstruction and Development), 1995. *A Progress Report*, Beirut.

Eken, Sena, S. Nuri Erbas, Jose Martelino, and Adnan Mazarei, 1995. "Economic Dislocation and Recovery in Lebanon," *Occasional Paper*, 120, International Monetary Fund, Washington, D.C.

Gannagé, Elias, 1994. "Du Plan Lebret au Plan 2000: Etude Comparative," *Proche-Orient Etudes Economiques*, 43, Université Saint Joseph, Beirut.

Hamdane, K., 1995. "Le Malaise Social: Quelle guaranti?", *Commerce du Levant*, 18 (January).

IMF (International Monetary Fund), 1994. *International Financial Statistics, Annual Year Book*, Washington, D.C.: International Monetary Fund.

Iskandar, M., and E. Baroudi, 1994. *The Lebanese Economy in 1982–83*, Beirut: Middle East Economic Consultants.

Kabbani, O., 1982. *The Reconstruction of Beirut*, Oxford: Centre for Lebanese Studies.

Kasparian, R., 1995. *La Population Déplacée au Liban*, Paris: L'Harmattan.

Khalaf, N., 1985. "Policy Measures for the Control of Inflation in Lebanon," *Bulletin trimestriel*, 24–27 (Fourth quarter), Banque du Liban.

Khalaf, N., and N. Munla, 1984. "Some Propositions on the Understanding and Control of Inflation in the Lebanese Economy," *Bulletin trimestriel*, 20 (First quarter), Banque du Liban.

Khalaf, S., and Ph. Khoury (eds.), 1993. *Recovering Beirut: Urban design and Post-War Reconstruction*, Leiden: E.J. Brill.

Labaki, B., 1993. *Bilan des Guerres du Liban*, Paris: L'Harmattan.

Lebanese Banks' Association, 1992. *Annual Report 1991/92*, Beirut.

————— 1995. *Monthly Bulletin*, 1, Beirut.

Menassa, G., 1946. *Plan de Reconstruction de l'Economie Libanaise et Réforme de l'Etat*, Beirut: The Société Libanaise d'Economie Politique.

Ministry of Finance, 1995. "Fazlaket Mashrou' Kawanin al Bournamej al Inmaï," Beirut.

Ministry of Planning and Institute de Recherches et de Formation en vue du Développement, 1961. *Besoins et Possibilités de Développement du Liban*, Beirut.

RDCL (Rassemblement des Dirigeants et Chefs d'entreprises Libanais), 1993. *Le Livre Blanc de L'Economie Libanaire*, vol. 2, Beirut.

Sbaiti, A., 1994. "Reflections on Lebanon Reconstruction," in D. Collings (ed.), *Peace for Lebanon? From War to Reconstruction*, Boulder, Col.: Canadian Institute for International Peace and Security.

8 Syria: Strategic Economic Issues

Nabil Sukkar

The Syrian economy has been growing rapidly over the past few years because of recent oil finds, but it faces serious internal and external challenges as the twenty-first century approaches. The response to these challenges has been slow, with the government giving priority to short-term stability rather than new economic thought. Economic progress will require considerable effort: long-term development to increase productivity as well as structural reform aimed at openness, liberalization, and improved efficiency. Science, technology, and human resource development are of particular importance if Syria is to compete in the global economy. Structural adjustment and long-term development should also be accompanied by a social program that compensates for rapid population growth, the negative consequences of reform, and failures of the market system.

During the 1970s and early 1980s Syria received a substantial amount of official aid, mainly from countries in the Gulf region and the former Soviet Union, that helped fuel relatively high annual growth of about 10 percent. Capital inflows dried up when a drop in oil prices strained the resources of the Gulf countries and when the Soviet Union went into domestic crisis. The drop in oil prices not only cut off aid to Syria but also precipitated a foreign exchange crisis. Economic activity slowed, and the 1980s saw negative growth in per capita gross national product (GNP). In response to the crisis, the government introduced various reforms: exchange rate adjustments, moderate relaxation of trade and price controls, reduction of subsidies, an increased role for the private sector, and a new emphasis on exports (Sukkar, 1994).

Economic growth resumed during the first half of the 1990s, partly because of these reforms but mainly because of the export of high-quality crude oil, which was discovered in 1984. Production of oil, until then mostly heavy crude, doubled over an eight-year period and transformed Syria from a net importer into a net exporter of oil.

Foreign exchange proceeds from oil exports reignited the engines of public enterprises, many of which had come to a virtual standstill during the crisis. Meanwhile, the larger role given to the private sector helped unplug supply bottlenecks. Higher prices paid to farmers encouraged agricultural production, as did the removal of a government monopoly on the importation and distribution of agricultural inputs. Industrial investment and production were given a boost by the removal in 1988 of restrictions on private entry into once exclusively public industries. Thus new oil and improved efficiency are responsible for recent growth. Investment remains low, at 16 percent during 1991–3 compared with 27 percent during 1974–80, but the private sector's share in investment exceeds that of the public sector, and private enterprises account for about two-thirds of non-oil trade.

PROSPECTS FOR GROWTH

In next few years Syria should experience growth on account of the oil sector, which generates about 65 percent of foreign exchange proceeds and 17 percent of gross domestic product (GDP). From 390,000 barrels a day in 1990 crude oil production reached 600,000 barrels a day in 1994. Of this, 360,000 barrels a day were exported, yielding $2.0 billion ($1.2 billion after deducting foreign partners' share). This level of production is expected to continue through the end of the century. Production will fall gradually thereafter unless new discoveries are made.

Syria's proven recoverable oil reserves are estimated at more than 3 billion barrels, but only a third of the country's area has been drilled (*Middle East Economic Survey*, March 1 1993). Shell and Elf Equitaine are signing contracts for further exploration, while other companies are hoping for contract terms that allow more flexible investment and better cost recovery (*Petroleum Intelligence Weekly*, August 29 1994; *Energy Business Review*, July–September 1992). The leveling off of oil production and its subsequent decline will likely be offset by an increase in oil prices by 2005.

Estimates for gas reserves vary between 4 trillion and 8 trillion cubic feet. Gas, consumed mainly in the home, by industry, and for power generation, is becoming increasingly useful. The government is converting cement, fertilizer, steel, and electricity generation plants from oil to gas for two reasons: to free up more oil for export at a time when domestic consumption of oil is growing rapidly, and to make up for the decline in hydroelectric power capacity resulting from a decline in the flow of the Euphrates River. The country's hopes for a balanced energy supply and a steady level of foreign exchange earnings depend on the development of gas reserves and the conversion of power stations and heavy industry to using gas as fuel (*Middle East Economic Survey*, March 1 1995).

Economic reforms and the new role given to the private sector will continue to have a positive but limited impact on sectors other than oil and gas. Agriculture, industry, and services, while constrained by macroeconomic imbalances and other factors, will continue to grow. The economy's ability to generate foreign exchange outside the oil sector will not expand significantly beyond current levels – $1,178 million for non-oil merchandise exports and $800 million for tourism – though tourism will increase somewhat. Policies to increase merchandise exports other than oil will take time to materialize. Remittances from Syrians working in Gulf nations and in Libya are likely to diminish as employment opportunities in these countries continue to shrink.

CHALLENGES TO GROWTH

As it pursues its prospects for growth, Syria faces five main challenges: rapid population growth, unsustainable economic growth, insufficient economic reform, heavy defense spending, and changing international and regional economic structures.

Syria's population of 13.8 million people faces a demographic problem of major proportions. Because of a high fertility rate (5.9 percent) and a sharp drop in the mortality rate over the past three decades – from 15.6 per 1,000 in 1970 to 6.0 per 1,000 in 1994 – the population is growing at about 3.4 percent a year. Complicating matters is the fact that more than half the population is less than nineteen years old. The fertility rate started to drop during the 1980s, so the rate of population growth is not expected to rise further (Ali, 1995). Still, at the current rate Syria's population will double by 2012. With growth high and weighted toward youth there will be an increasing demand for education and other social services, straining budgetary resources. Meanwhile, the continuing flood of entrants to the labor force, about 200,000 a year, will aggravate unemployment. Continued high population growth will constrain Syria's economic development.

Syria is in the unenviable position of having to depend on foreign aid, a depletable mineral reserve, and scarce rainfall for its economic well-being. During the first half of the 1980s economic growth fell for two reasons – drought and the drop- off in official aid. Only when newly discovered oil reached full- capacity production in the 1990s did high growth resume.

It was during this period of setback, in the mid-1980s, that the foreign exchange crisis occurred, prompting economic reform. The government invited the private sector to help reduce emerging supply bottlenecks by expanding its role in imports (particularly of inputs and basic foods), exports, and industry. Reform measures, introduced piecemeal and without the involvement of international aid agencies, expanded gradually and included devaluations, fewer exchange rates, streamlined import regulations, fewer bans on imports, and relaxed price controls. Reform culminated in the 1991s Investment Law 10, which offered tax and duty incentives to private domestic and foreign investors alike.

While the response to these reforms has been positive – commodity shortages have been eased and agricultural and industrial production have increased – they have not gone far enough in restoring balance to the economy. For example, although inflation has fallen from its 1986– 8 levels of 36 percent and more, it is still high, at 10–15 percent. The actual fiscal deficit also continues to be high, in the range of 35–45 percent of expenditures after allowing for extrabudgetary allocations.

Reform has been insufficient in several respects. Devaluations were not accompanied by fiscal and monetary policies adequate to contain aggregate demand, or by liberalization in factor markets that would enable production units to adjust to market forces. Despite private sector incentives (in the form of tax and duty exemptions), the old regulatory framework remained in place, and the banking system, created in the mid-1960s, did not cater to the needs of a market-oriented economy. Although the increase in prices paid to farmers for major crops boosted agricultural production, it also increased pressure on the resources of the state-owned banking system. The public enterprise sector, exposed to devaluations, relaxation of price controls, and increased competition from the private sector, was not given the tools to adjust to such pressures. Finally, measures such as less emphasis on price stabilization, a freeze on public sector employment, and a reduction in direct consumer subsidies were not accompanied by social safety nets to compensate those affected.

What makes reform all the more urgent is Syria's heavy defense spending because of the conflict with Israel. Military spending amounted to 16.6 percent of GDP in 1992. Although a settlement agreement is being brokered between Syria and Israel, it is not expected to result in a significant drop in defense spending for several reasons. Current negotiations do not cover arms supplies to the region or local arms production, nor do they cover demilitarization and denuclearization. Syria is not likely to reduce its military spending unilaterally as long as military unbalance prevails in the region, with the United States still officially committed to the maintenance of Israel's technological and military superiority, and as long as the region's political environment remains unstable. Furthermore, with the demise of the Soviet Union and the disappearance of the budgetary support Syria used to receive from Gulf countries, Syria will finance a large part of its future defense spending from taxes and foreign exchange revenues – adding to pressures on budgetary resources.

The demise of the Soviet Union, Syria's former ally and most powerful political and economic supporter, is just one sign of the changing international environment that is challenging Syria's regional role and model of development. The country will also have to adapt to the approaching settlement of the Arab–Israeli conflict, new political and economic alliances in the region, the globalization and liberalization of world trade and capital movement, and the move to market and expanded role for the private sector in domestic economies around the world.

STRATEGIC ECONOMIC ISSUES

In response to these internal and external challenges, Syria will have to accelerate economic reform and deal with development issues, particularly in the areas of international and regional integration, local science and technology, human resources, and equity and poverty.

Accelerating economic reform

What Syria needs first is a program that creates both a stable macroeconomic framework and an incentive system for a sustainable supply response. Such reform would go far toward improving efficiency and increasing investment, in particular enabling the country to sustain growth after the decline in oil revenues. Interrupted production and rising prices and unemployment are short-to medium-term costs that will have to be borne to make possible a move to sustainable development. Having social and economic programs prepared in advance would help ease the consequences of reform.

The second stage of reform would involve major structural adjustments in banking, fiscal policies, public enterprises, and other areas. Since these adjustments are interlinked, they require a comprehensive, not a piecemeal, approach. Syrians tend to be skeptical about the value and consequences of stabilization and structural adjustment, especially when supervised from abroad. But now that the country is less dependent on external assistance it has an opportunity to prepare its own program at a pace and with a social component that suits its circumstances.

A basic strategy of Syria's domestic reform has been to encourage the private sector first, leaving more difficult public sector reform for later. Privatization in the sense of selling fixed public assets to the private sector is not favored, and the government has made it clear that it intends to reserve a role for all three sectors – public, private, and mixed – in productive activities. The term 'economic pluralism' was coined in 1990 to reflect this strategy.

This strategy is a prudent one in principle. It has expanded employment opportunities in preparation for eventual public sector reform, which will disrupt production and labor. But while the strategy may have achieved its initial objective, it is now hindering further private sector development and stabilization measures for fear of the impact on public enterprises. The public enterprise sector's claims on the treasury and the state-owned banking system have risen, while the markedly different set of rules for the public and private sectors is preventing the free flow of resources. A point will be reached where the economic costs of restraining the private sector and postponing stabilization measures will far exceed the costs of public sector reform – modernization, compensation, and training.

Although the government insists that it intends only to reform and not privatize public enterprises, privatization, at least in part, may prove unavoidable. Restructuring and rehabilitating the equipment of public enterprises, recapitalizing these enterprises, and setting up training programs and social safety nets would require borrowing on a scale that Syria would not accept and could not afford. The public enterprise sector consists of some 200 companies, predominantly manufacturing, construction, and foreign trade firms. In the financial sector there is one commercial bank, five specialized banking institutions, and one insurance company. The only alternative to borrowing is to privatize these enterprises, at least in part. A politically acceptable formula would be to transfer many public enterprises into the mixed sector.

In encouraging the private sector, Syria has resorted to generous exemptions from taxes, duties, and foreign exchange and import regulations instead of making hard decisions about stabilizing the macroeconomic framework and streamlining regulations. Incentives like these, sporadically scheduled and covering different sectors, accentuate distortions in the economy. Currently, for example, there are exemptions for investment in hotel accommodations that were issued in 1985, exemptions for mixed-sector investment in agriculture that were issued in 1986, and the exemptions of Investment Law 10 (1991). Carrying out structural reform and maintaining a stable macroeconomic environment would obviate the need for such incentives and give the treasury the revenues it badly needs.

While encouraging the private sector, Syria should also streamline business laws and regulations, ensuring equal opportunity and maintaining transparency. This would prevent the emergence of private monopolies, the abuse of power, and the legislative gaps and ambiguities that plague today's transition economies.

Promoting international integration and export growth

The Syrian economy has not been integrated with the world economy. Imports represent 16 percent of GDP and non-oil exports, 9 percent. The economy has grown behind protective walls, with quantitative restrictions (QRs) widely used, tariff rates high, and public sector monopolies dominant.

Quantitative restrictions include outright import prohibitions, notably on imports that compete with domestic products for which local supply is sufficient. Duties ranging between 5 percent and 235 percent (including surcharges) tend to increase gradually with the degree of manufacturing, with imports that compete with domestic products charged higher rates. Tariffs on raw materials, inputs for agriculture, and industry and manufacturing equipment are kept low to reduce production costs (IMF, 1990). Protection is not withdrawn when it is no longer necessary.

International integration will require structural adjustments in the trade regime, with an emphasis on tariffication and reducing nominal and effective protection. Reform should be carried out within the framework of the Uruguay Round agreements and the recently established World Trade Organization (WTO), which Syria will likely join in the next few years. Even if it does not join the WTO, Syria will be affected by the new regulations. Integration will also require rationalization and unification of exchange rates. With Syria's trade regime so protective and the Uruguay Round agreements so far-reaching, adjustments in trade and production will be deep. They should be carried out gradually to minimize painful dislocation, including job losses. Adjustments should be accompanied or preceded by measures that help the public and private sectors adjust to external changes.

Syria has preferential trade agreements with industrial countries – EU countries, the United States, Canada, and Japan – that will be eliminated by the Uruguay Round agreements. But elimination of these preferences will be significant only in the case of trade with the EU countries. In 1993 Syria's exports to the United States represented less than 2 percent of total exports, to Canada and Japan less than 1 percent each, and to the European Union 61 percent (Table 8.1). Of exports to the European Union, 19 percent were non-oil commodities.

Textiles and clothing, which account for 15 percent of Syria's non-oil exports to the European Union, will be most affected by the removal of preferences. Syria will face a more competitive environment when, in accordance with the Uruguay Round agreements, the international quota system is lifted along with restrictions on low-cost Asian textiles entering world markets. Outside of agriculture, however, textiles and clothing hold the most hope for export expansion. This sector should be targeted for a major upgrading, including the acquisition of new technologies, enlarged production units, and strengthened links among spinning, weaving, and garment-making entities.

The Uruguay Round agreements also open up opportunities for Syria's agricultural production. The intended reduction of agricultural subsidies in industrial countries is likely to raise prices, encouraging Syria to increase its agricultural production and exports. Over the past three years Syria has already increased such production considerably, particularly in grains. As a result the country's dependence on food imports, estimated at about 32 percent of total consumption in 1988–90 (UNDP, 1994), has dropped sharply. By the end of 1994 wheat production had increased dramatically, quadrupling since 1989 (from 1.0 to 4.2 million tons), and strategic reserves of wheat had reached 2.8 million tons and of barley, 2.0 million tons. Both cereals will soon be exported.

Table 8.1 Destination of Syrian exports, 1991–3
(thousands of Syrian pounds)

Region	1991	1992	1993
Arab countries	8,838,420	8,615,826	8,352,935
	(23)	(25)	(24)
Egypt	152,531	189,777	144,345
Jordan	768,436	581,712	820,597
Lebanon	3,695,195	4,516,345	3,717,797
Saudi Arabia	2,238,448	1,498,098	1,729,161
European Union	18,432,263	21,814,688	21,449,182
	(48)	(63)	(61)
Other Western Europe	281,477	223,712	211,223
	(0)	(0)	(0)
Transition economies	9,252,191	2,166,006	1,888,809
	(24)	(6)	(5)
China	8,420	8,795	2,134
Russia	7,259,629	533,973	984,001
North America	232,053	298,601	1,080,574
	(0)	(0)	(3)
Canada	4,979	6,634	328,275
United States	208,459	273,563	674,640
Other	1,467,534	1,600,954	2,335,292
	(4)	(5)	(7)
Japan	28,479	102,699	106,404
Turkey	1,036,385	481,968	761,839
Total	38,503,938	34,719,787	35,318,015

Note: Numbers in parentheses are percentages.
Source: Syrian Arab Republic, Central Bureau of Statistics, *Statistical Abstract*, various years.

The export market for Syria's cotton also looks promising. Cotton production rose by 45 percent between 1990 and 1995, from 440,000 to 640,000 tons. About 60 percent of this is exported as raw cotton, representing about 6 percent of Syria's exports including oil. With an expected strengthening of cotton prices and markets abroad this export should continue to grow in importance (Golden and Kherallah, 1995).

Recent liberalization in world trade, improvements in transport and communications technology, and the formation of regional trading blocs around the world are making international trade increasingly competitive. Still, Syria should be able to find a niche for itself. Given its agricultural potential and low wage costs, it should attempt to meet a substantial portion of the Middle East's demand for food and agroindustries while strengthening its position as an exporter of raw cotton-based and textiles and clothing.

Building science and technology capability

Science and technology are critical to growth and development. But there are only 3.6 scientists and technicians per 1,000 people in Syria, and less than 0.2 percent of GNP is spent on research and development (Mullin, 1991). The few scientific research institutions are linked either to the government or to one of the four universities. These institutions suffer from a scarcity of funds and faculty, outdated equipment, and limited information flow (both regionally and internationally). Research links with industry are weak, and industry itself spends practically no money or effort on research and development. The number of scientific publications from Syria in international journals is telling: in 1989 there were only 42 articles, compared with 1,955 from Egypt and 348 from Iraq (Zahlan, 1992).

This state of affairs has emerged because the development of science and technology has not been an objective of Syria's development efforts. There is no national science and technology strategy, and no higher authority is responsible for the application of science and technology to national objectives or needs. The cultural and religious environment, as in the larger Arab world, does not encourage scientific inquiry. The education system puts more emphasis on learning facts and storing information than on developing observation and analysis skills (Daghestani, 1993). Researchers and professors are relatively isolated, without easy access to international scientific publications or travel. Finally, the technology that is imported is rarely adapted to local needs.

If Syria hopes to increase productivity and compete internationally, it must make science and technology a major part of its development strategy. An important first step would be to set up a specialized ministry to replace the existing Supreme Council of Science, which is attached to the Ministry of Higher Education, or to place the Supreme Council of Science in the prime minister's office. Building the capacity to acquire and adapt existing information technology, if not to produce it, should also be part of the strategy. To this end, policies should be introduced that enhance the flow of information and ideas to the country and that help develop skills for applying available information technology.

Focusing on human resource development

Over the past two decades Syria's human resource development has advanced in quantitative but not qualitative terms. Life expectancy is up and infant mortality is down. Adult literacy went from 40 percent in 1970 to 68 percent in 1992. Primary school enrollment increased from 78 percent in 1970 to 109 percent in 1990, achieving a universal level for both males and females. Secondary school enrollment rose from 38 percent to 50 percent between 1970 and 1991, which is above average for Arab countries (UNDP, 1994, 1995).

Syria's spending on education (4.1 percent of GNP, 17.3 percent of total public spending) is not low by international standards, but the demand for education is being accommodated at the expense of quality. The education system is politicized and suffers from an inadequate curriculum and teaching that focuses on memorization, not reasoning. Furthermore, there is a prevailing bias against rural education, and education is not tailored to labor market needs.

Syria's rapid population growth and young population continue to put pressure on the education system, which will deteriorate unless action is taken. If Syria hopes to raise its current level of labor productivity and realize its aspirations for integrating with the world economy, it must spend more on education as well as improve teaching methods and curriculums. Allowing private participation at the university level would reduce the pressure on public resources for education.

Increasing equity and reducing poverty

Equity, a major objective of the ruling party, was until recently pursued by increasing the public sector's role in the economy through direct consumer subsidies, price stabilization, job security, free education, and other social services. Although some of these measures likely reduced inequity in certain areas, there is no evidence that these measures, or the overall development plan in place since the mid-1960s, have reduced economic inequity. While most people now have access to health services, safe water, and sanitation in rural and urban areas (Table 8.2), a sizable percentage of the population lives in absolute poverty. According to the World Bank, 54 percent of the rural population lived in absolute poverty during the 1980s (World Bank, 1995b).

Unemployment in Syria, for which figures vary – official data put it at 6.7 percent, while other estimates put it at 10.0 percent and others

Table 8.2 Access to health services, safe water, and sanitation, Syria, 1988–93
(percentage of population)

Sector	Health services	Safe water	Sanitation
Rural	84	58	82
Urban	96	90	84
Total	90	74	83

Source: UNDP, 1995.

still claim it is as high as 20.0 percent – is threatening to rise (Layous, 1993; Arab Labor Organization, 1994; Diwan and Squire, 1992). Rapid population growth is producing more entrants to the labor force than the economy can absorb. The labor supply is expected to grow by 4.5 percent a year over the next thirty years, compared with 3.7 percent a year in the previous thirty years (World Bank, 1995b). Compounding the problem, once the public sector (which represents 31 percent of the workforce) is restructured and job security laws are relaxed, labor will be shed. This trend will be further reinforced by the expected reduction in the armed forces (408,000 people in 1992) following the signing of a peace treaty with Israel.

Economic growth is the most effective way of promoting equity, but it may not be enough. Growth should be broadly based, addressing labor-absorbing sectors such as agriculture and small- and medium-scale industry, and it should be accompanied by social safety nets and increased investment in human capital.

Participating in regional integration

Integration and preferential trade arrangements would, in principle, help Syria mitigate losses from globalization and international trade liberalization. An economic integration agreement signed by Syria and Lebanon in 1993 aims to establish a customs union. Syria would benefit from Lebanon's skilled labor, more advanced banking and education facilities, and international trade connections, while Lebanon would benefit from Syria's market depth and unskilled and semiskilled labor. The changing orientation of the Syrian economy generated the proposed scheme, though the vast difference in the two countries' trade and exchange rate regimes and the slow pace of economic reform in Syria remain major obstacles. No target date has been set for the completion of the customs union, though agreements for closer cooperation in various sectors have been concluded.

The Syrian–Lebanese integration scheme will gain strength if it is extended to include neighboring Iraq (once that country introduces some fundamental reforms). Iraq and Syria are 'natural' trade and economic partners: each has a diversified resource base for agricultural, industrial, and hydrocarbon development. Iraq is a capital-surplus, labor-shortage economy, while Syria is a capital-shortage, labor-surplus economy. Syria provides a cost-effective outlet for Iraqi products through the Mediterranean, and Iraq provides an outlet for Syria's rapidly rising labor supply. The Euphrates River, which passes through both Syria and Iraq, is critical for irrigation and power generation in both. In the extended integration plan, which might be called the Arab Mashreq scheme, Lebanon would benefit from further expansion of the market and act as the banking and service center.

Syria and Israel are not likely to become members of the same regional economic integration scheme. Even if the two countries sign a peace agreement, they will be competing intensely for influence in the region. Syria suspects Israel, with its superior military and economic power, of aspiring toward hegemony in the Middle East (Peres, 1993). Many Syrian observers believe that the regional transportation network of roads, railways, ports, airports, and oil pipelines proposed by Israel at the 1994 Casablanca conference would favor Israel and is a clear indication of Israel's desire for regional hegemony. If implemented, these projects, together with trade and other projects proposed by Israel in Casablanca, will only aggravate regional economic disparities.

Pursuing the Euro-Mediterranean partnership scheme

Syria has an opportunity to join the new European initiative for the establishment of a partnership and free trade area with the southern and eastern shores of the Mediterranean, targeted for completion by 2010. The European Union will allocate $7 billion over the next five years for structural adjustment and economic reform to help countries in the region integrate with the countries of the north. By joining the scheme Syria would benefit from European investment and technology and preferential access to EU markets. These gains would give it an advantage in the EU market over products from low-wage countries in Asia.

The potential impact of the initiative on Syrian industry should not be underestimated. It will not be easy for Syria to remove its custom duties on European industrial imports by 2010 without completely restructuring its industry, both public and private. Nor will negotiations be easy: Europe may want to impose limitations on imports of agricultural products and agroindustries from Syria, and Syria will have to request a slow opening of its industries to unrestricted European competition. Syria should request that European official assistance include support for its long-term development efforts, particularly in strengthening human resource development and local science and technology capability. It should also examine ways in which European private investment can be directed toward development priority sectors.

While the scheme would give EU countries preferential access to markets relative to other industrial blocs and to low- cost labor for setting up manufacturing activities, in a wider context it aims to foster stability in the Mediterranean basin (European Commission, 1993). A potential threat to this goal is the scheme's failure to recognize the vast wealth gap between Israel and the rest of the countries on the eastern and southern shores of the Mediterranean. EU partners should examine the potential consequences of this gap and direct official assistance to national development efforts and projects that help reduce economic disparities in the region.

FINANCING GROWTH

Substantial funds are needed to support Syria's domestic economic reform and long-term development. Over the past few years domestic savings and foreign exchange have permitted rates of investment in the range of 15–17 percent. These levels are inadequate. Syria is in critical need of higher and more efficient investment, especially given the expected drops in oil production and export. To raise investment, domestic savings will have to be mobilized and external capital brought in. With international aid diminishing, Syria will have to rely increasingly on private external capital. But substantial capital from abroad, be it official or private, will not materialize unless Syria goes further with economic reform and improves its creditworthiness.

Private capital inflows

Until recently it was not Syrian policy to encourage foreign investment. An exception was made in the late 1970s when the government decided to invite foreign investment in the oil sector (Table 8.3). Western companies responded, and two of them were successful in discovering oil in commercial quantities.

Table 8.3 External financing, Syria, 1977–89
(billions of U.S. dollars)

Source	1977–81	1982–5	1986–9
Arab assistance	6.2	2.8	1.4
Other official transfers	0.3	0.2	0.4
Net multilateral loans	0.4	0.3	0.2
Private net flows	0.1	0.2	0.1
Total net financing	7.0	3.5	2.1
Total net financing/GNP (percent)	12.7	5.4	2.4

Source: Diwan and Papandreou, 1993.

Investment Law 10 represented a major departure in the government's attitude toward foreign investment. It offered foreign investors tax and duty exemptions, permission to retain foreign exchange earned from exports, and assurances about the transfer of annual profits and the repatriation of capital. Although domestic response to the law was promising, foreign response was mute. Little data are available on foreign participation in licensed projects, but most has been limited to investment from Syrians abroad and from Gulf nationals. A more active foreign investment policy is needed. More than tax and duty exemptions, external investors should have the encouragement of a freer foreign exchange regime, a developed banking system, improved creditworthiness, and the rule of law.

Private Syrian savings abroad, estimated at $26 billion in 1991 (Diwan and Squire, 1992), are the most likely source of private external capital inflow and should be a target of Syrian policy. The government should introduce measures that attract these savings for the development and technological benefits they offer.

External debt

The 1986 foreign exchange crisis forced Syria to suspend servicing on some of its external debt, including debt owed to the World Bank and to commercial creditors. In 1991 it also stopped servicing its debt to the dissolving Soviet Union. The government started to repay some of its arrears when the external foreign exchange position improved, but clearance has been slow. The delays have not developed because Syria cannot service its debt, but because it wants to maintain adequate reserves in the face of external pressures while the Middle East is changing. Arrears on long-term debt at the end of 1993 stood at $4.7 billion in principal and interest, owed mostly to the former Soviet Union, the World Bank, and Western European export guarantee agencies. Syria's total external debt stood at about $20.0 billion at the end of 1993, of which $16.2 billion was in the form of long-term debt; $11.0 billion of this debt is owed to the former Soviet Union. The Soviet debt is inflated by the fact that it is calculated at the official exchange rate of the ruble, which bears no resemblance to the ruble's current market rate. The debt service exports ratio was reasonable, standing at 18.2 percent in 1992, but external debt as a share of exports of goods and services and of GNP stood well above the critical levels (or standard ratios) established for international creditworthiness (Table 8.4).

Table 8.4 External debt ratios, Syria, 1989–93
(percent)

Ratio	1989	1990	1991	1992	1993
Total debt stock/exports of goods and services	399.1	312.6	385.3	380.4	374.7
Total debt stock/GNP	169.5	125.5	116.9	—	—
Total debt service/exports of goods and services	—	—	14.6	18.2	—
Short-term debt/total debt stock	9.8	12.6	13.7	16.3	18.7
Concessional debt/total debt stock	60.1	76.9	77.2	75.4	73.8
Multilateral debt/total debt stock	4.7	5.1	4.5	4.5	4.2

Source: World Bank, 1994, 1995a.

Despite the fact that 74 percent of Syria's external debt was lent on concessional terms, debt stock and arrears hinder its ability to attract external capital, both official and private, for investment and growth. Clearance of arrears and major debt relief would be extremely helpful. Such relief could come first from a rescheduling of former Soviet debt. Over the past two years discussions with the Russian Federation have tried to reach agreement on, first, the exchange rate that will be used to assess the size of the debt and, second, whether a major part of this debt can be written off and the balance rescheduled. Outstanding debt is payable by 2005. Syria is asking for a writeoff of 80 percent of that, with the balance to be rescheduled until 2014 and paid partly in convertible currencies, partly in commodities. An agreement close to these terms would raise Syria's debt position and creditworthiness to acceptable levels.

Peace in the region will create the momentum for increasing aid flows, but new aid is not likely to reach pre-1986 levels, and its sources will probably be more diversified, with major donors expected to be Arab development institutions, the European Union, Japan, and multilateral assistance organizations. Resumption of bilateral assistance from Western countries and multilateral assistance from international organizations will be linked to progress in debt clearance and economic reform. Western countries and international aid institutions prefer settlement of arrears in the context of Paris Club arrangements for aid coordination and debt relief. Syria does not favor this arrangement, which it feels carries too many conditions and would interfere with internal economic policy. It is more likely to secure its requirements for official development and debt clearance on a bilateral, case-by-case basis. In all cases it will seek new aid on concessional terms, both to carry a smaller debt burden and to expand the scope for independent political action.

CONCLUSION

The Syrian economy is currently enjoying rapid growth on the strength of its oil sector, but as it approaches the twenty-first century the economy faces serious challenges that, if not addressed, could exacerbate unemployment and cause Syria to slip down the international development ladder. If proper measures are taken, growth will be sustained and development will improve, carrying the economy into the post-oil era.

Aside from the need to prolong the life of the oil sector through exploration, Syria must first adopt a development strategy that looks both outward – reducing protection, promoting exports, and inviting private capital from abroad – and inward – developing human resources, building science and technology capacity, and improving productivity and the supply response. Second, Syria should raise the rate of investment from the current level of 15–17 percent to about 30 percent through incentives to private investment (public investment will be constrained by budgetary pressures and the scarcity of official aid). Third, Syria should prepare a social and economic assistance program to cope with the threat of increasing unemployment, the temporary setbacks of adjustment, and failures in the market system.

To meet these challenges, it is important that Syria adopt a strategy combining comprehensive economic reform and long-term development. Trade liberalization without simultaneous efforts to increase productivity will damage the economy. Priority should be given at an early stage to rationalizing and unifying exchange rates, streamlining business regulations, and reforming the financial and banking system to help raise private investment and attract Syrian savings abroad. Immediate efforts are also needed to prepare a human resource development plan and a science and technology development strategy.

Many factors could interfere with reform and development, such as the bureaucracy, the difficulty of penetrating world export markets, and Syria's external debt – but there are reasons for hope. The availability of oil funds will make it easier for the government to take austerity measures and improve its negotiating position with donors, warding off conditionalities and minimizing interference in economic policies. A debt relief agreement with the Russian Federation would provide an opportunity for Syria to grow out of debt with moderate austerity. Drawing on their substantial savings abroad, Syrians could make a major contribution to the development effort. In addition to the external capital benefit, such capital would bring with it a return of Syrian enterpreneurship and skill. Finally, peace in the Middle East should encourage private and official capital inflows. However, a substantial diversion of resources from defense to development in Syria is unlikely unless a better military and technological balance is achieved in the region.

The challenges ahead will require resolute action on the part of the Syrian government. The prevailing political style is one of caution, along with complacency generated by the availability of oil funds and concern over economic and social dislocations. Above all, economic reform is being delayed because Syria has not yet reconciled its outdated ideology with current global economic thought. Some efforts have been made. Syria's leadership and press have worked slowly over the past few years to shift mainstream Baath Party thinking toward a better appreciation of the new international economic precepts. There is increasing agreement on the shortcomings of the old system, accompanied by doubt about the virtues of the free market and deep bewilderment over how to reconcile marketization and globalization with the cherished concept of economic self-reliance.

Before Syria prepares its economic reform and long-term development programs, it must conceptualize its new economic thinking, officially recognizing the significance of internal and external reform in the context of a rapidly changing international and regional political and economic environment. Conceptualization will open the way for transparent plans and programs, and while Syria will still have to cope with the issue of reform versus stability, at least the choices will be clearer.

References

Ali, Ibrahim, 1995. *Trends of Population Growth in Syria in Light of the 1994 Census*, Damascus: Economic Science Association (in Arabic).

Arab Labor Organization, 1994. *Confronting Unemployment While Raising Economic Efficiency in the Context of Economic Reform* Cairo (in Arabic)

Daghestani, Fakhruddin A., 1993. 'Status of World Science: The Arab States,' in UNESCO, *World Science Report*, Paris: United Nations Educational, Scientific, and Cultural Organization.

Diwan, Ishac, and Nick Papandreou, 1993. 'The Peace Process and Economic Reform in The Middle East,' in Stanley Fischer, Dani Rodrik, and Elias Tuma (eds.) *The Economics of Middle East Peace*, Cambridge, Mass: MIT Press.

Diwan, Ishac, and Lyn Squire, 1992. 'Economic and Social Development in the Middle East and North Africa,' *Middle East and North Africa Discussion Paper*, 3, World Bank, Washington, D.C.: World Bank.

Energy Business Review, various issues. Nicosia.

European Commission, 1993. 'Strengthening the Mediterranean Policy of the European Union: Establishing a Euro–Mediterranean Partnership,' A Communication from the Commission to the Council and the Parliament, Brussels.

Golden, Ian, and Mylene Kherallah, 1995. 'The Uruguay Round and International Trade in Agricultural Products: Implications for Arab Countries,' prepared presented at a conference on the effects of the GATT agreements on Arab countries, sponsored by the Arab Fund for Economic and Social Development, the Arab Monetary Fund, the International Monetary Fund, and the World Bank (June 17–18), Kuwait.

IMF (International Monetary Fund), 1990. 'Syrian Arab Republic: Taxation and Possibilities for Reform,' Middle East Department, Washington D.C.

Layous, Michael, 1993. 'Employment and Unemployment in the Syrian Arab Republic,' paper presented at a conference on unemployment sponsored by the Economic and Social Commission of West Asia (July 26–29), Amman (in Arabic).

Middle East Economic Survey, various issues. Cyprus.

Mullin, James, 1991. 'Toward a Science and Technology Strategy for Syria,' United Nations Development Programme report submitted to the Scientific Studies and Research Center of the Syrian Arab Republic, Damascus.

Peres, Shimon, 1993. *The New Middle East*, London: Element Books.
Petroleum Intelligence Weekly, various issues. New York.
Sukkar, Nabil, 1994. 'Banking Reform in Syria', Economic Science Association, Damascus (in Arabic).
UNDP (United Nations Development Programme), various years. *Human Development Report*, New York: Oxford University Press.
World Bank, 1994. *World Development Report 1994: Infrastructure for Development*, New York: Oxford University Press.
———— 1995a. *World Debt Tables*, Washington, D.C.: World Bank.
———— 1995b. *World Development Report 1995: Workers in an Integrating World*, New York: Oxford University Press.
Zahlan, A. B., 1992. 'Advances in Materials Sciences: Challenges and Implications to the Arab Countries,' paper presented at a workshop on the implications of new and advanced materials technologies sponsored by the Economic and Social Commission of West Asia (September 21–24), Damascus.

Part III

Perspectives from Turkey, Sudan, Iran, and the Gulf

9 Determinants of Economic Growth in Turkey[1]

Sübidey Togan

Rapid, sustained economic growth is one of the main objectives of Turkish policymakers. Because total factor productivity plays a big role in growth, policies that increase education levels, achieve more equitable distribution of income, and secure high rates of investment are essential. In addition, prudent macroeconomic policies are needed to avoid balance of payments crises, eliminate industrial incentives that inhibit competition, and further lower nominal and effective rates of protection.

To better allocate resources and create a more enabling climate for innovation and technical progress, in 1994 Turkey adopted a new competition policy modeled on European Union practice. Further liberalization of trade should also help achieve growth. In addition, public enterprise performance must improve, barriers to entry and exit of firms should be removed, and privatization should be encouraged. The success of these reforms will depend, to some degree, on regional political developments and international economic developments. Membership in a customs union with the European Union and participation in the General Agreement on Tariffs and Trade (GATT) will also contribute to competition and growth.

During the past forty-five years per capita gross national product (GNP) in Turkey has increased threefold. Although the country remains poor by industrial country standards, it has placed itself among the world's rapidly growing middle-income countries. Still, policymakers are eager to bolster growth, and so are pursuing efforts to foster competition and trade.

SOURCES OF GROWTH ANALYSIS

The average annual growth of gross domestic product (GDP) during 1950-94 averaged 5.1 percent, but it has fluctuated considerably,

Figure 9.1 GDP growth, Turkey, 1950–94

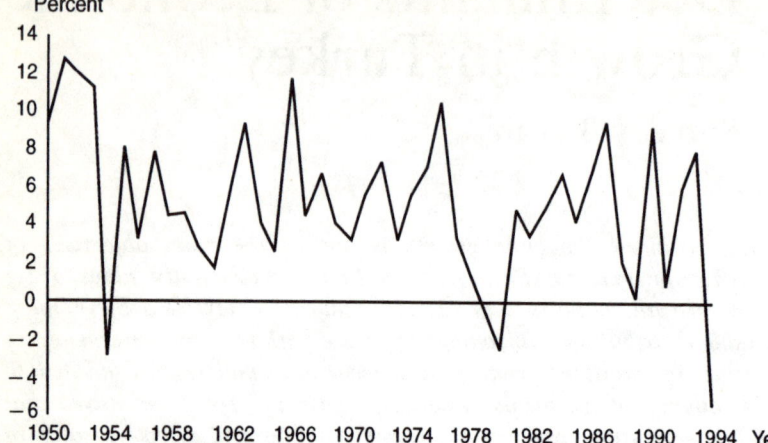

Source: World Bank data.

moving between -5.4 and 12.8 percent (Figure 9.1). The variability of GDP measured by the standard deviation was 4.0. The main objective of economic policy in Turkey has been to increase average growth as well as narrow its variability.

Economists analyzing the behavior of growth generally consider one of two approaches: growth theories and models and sources of growth analysis. This chapter employs the sources of growth method developed by Jorgenson and Griliches (1967), which is an accounting identity. As such the analysis is grounded in national accounts and aggregate production function theory. The basic formula of the sources of growth method states that the rate of output (GDP) is equal to the rate of growth of capital times the capital income share, *plus* the rate of growth of labor times the labor share, *plus* total factor productivity change. The various factors affecting economic growth in Turkey are also examined qualitatively.

From State Planning Organization data on capital stock, labor, and gross output (Maraslioglu and Tiktik, 1991, as revised by Maraslioglu) and shares of capital and labor in value added as weights (Celasun, 1986; De Santis and Özhan, 1994), total value added in the economy was calculated for 1978–92. Total value added increased by an average of 4.022 percent a year, with capital contributing 1.619 percentage points, labor 0.712 percentage point, and total factor productivity (TFP) growth 1.691 percentage points. Thus 40.25 percent of the average growth rate is explained by capital, 17.70 percent by labor, and 42.05 percent by total factor productivity growth.

These figures refer to aggregate data. Sectoral figures reveal that total factor productivity growth explains more than 60 percent of the growth of value added in agriculture, 59 percent in mining, and 63 percent in manufacturing. The contribution of total factor productivity growth is higher than 80 percent in energy but only 11 percent in services. While the data suggest the importance of total factor productivity growth, other important contributors to Turkish economic growth include labor force characteristics, the expansion in capacity achieved through investment, technological change, international developments, and the country's economic policies.

Labor force characteristics

About 60 percent of Turkey's 62.5 million people are 15–64 years old. Annual population growth slowed from 2.5 percent during the late 1950s to 2.2 percent during 1985–90. The population is quite young, with a median age of 21. The labor force participation rate (the share of civilian labor force in the population aged 15–64) fell from 75 percent in 1970 to 54 percent in 1993, with the civilian labor force totaling 20.2 million. Unemployment is about 7.6 percent.

Education levels and income distribution are the main factors determining labor productivity in Turkey. Enrollments in primary and secondary schools have increased since the 1970s, when secondary enrollments were substantially lower than the average for middle-income countries. By the 1990s enrollments were still lower than those of the average middle-income country, but the gap had narrowed substantially (World Bank, various years). A major shortcoming of the education system is its emphasis on general curriculum schools and neglect of technical and vocational schools (OECD, 1993). Total spending for education was just 1.9 percent of GDP in 1988, compared with 2.8 percent in Greece, 3.9 percent in Spain, and 5.0 percent in United States. However, the government recently boosted the share substantially, declaring its commitment to educational attainment.

Education contributes to economic growth through several channels. The most obvious is that educated workers are more productive than uneducated workers. But other factors are important as well, as emphasized by Barro (1991) and Hamilton (1995). Regression of the productivity of labor, measured by GDP per unit of labor (*GDP/L*), on the aggregate capital-labor ratio (K/L) and secondary enrollment rates (SER) over 1978–92 yields the following result:

$$\ln(GDP/L) = -0.9495 + 0.4350\ln(K/L) + 0.6246\ln(SER)$$
$$(-8.2855) \quad (2.0911) \qquad\qquad (5.1182) \qquad\qquad (9.1)$$
$$n = 15; \ R^2 = 0.9536; \ DW = 1.9736$$

where the terms in parentheses are t-statistics. Thus besides the capital–labor ratio a main determinant of labor productivity is human capital proxied by the number of students enrolled in secondary schools relative to the total population of the corresponding age group. (8.1) shows that raising the fraction of children going to secondary school by 10 percentage points can be expected to boost subsequent annual output per unit of labor employed by about 6.2 percent. Empirical studies have shown that the quality of education is also a significant determinant of economic growth. Thus if Turkey to attain rapid, sustainable economic growth it must place a higher value on education. Enrollment in junior high schools could be increased from 50 percent to 60–70 percent by channeling additional funds into the sector and by improving the quality of education in these schools.

Restrictive wage policies kept labor unrest and union activity low during the 1980s. But the continuation of peaceful labor relations will depend on achieving relative equality in income distribution. As with most developing countries, distributional data in Turkey are less reliable than national accounts data, but much of the country's inequality can be explained by the economy's dual structure. In 1970 Turkey was an overwhelmingly rural, agricultural economy, with 37 percent of GDP and 64 percent of total employment generated by agriculture (Dervis and Robinson, 1980; Celasun, 1989). Since then extremely rapid urbanization has led to a structural transformation of the economy. By 1994 agriculture accounted for just 15 percent of GDP, although it still generated 47 percent of employment. The productivity ratio of nonagriculture to agriculture (calculated using the employment and value added data of Maraslioglu) has fluctuated around 4, which suggests that the large income differential between agricultural and nonagricultural sectors is the main reason for rapid urbanization.

Distributional statistics reveal estimated Gini coefficients of 0.509 for 1978, 0.522 for 1983, and 0.44 for 1987. The share of households under the poverty line was 25 percent in 1978 and 30 percent in 1983, while the ratio of highest to lowest income groups was 42.01 for 1978 and 47.27 for 1983. Income distribution analysis, following the work of Celasun (1989), shows that the main source of income inequality is the wide gap between the average incomes of agricultural and non-agricultural households. The income disparities within agriculture also constitute a significant source of overall inequality. Such disparities can be attributed to variations in regional conditions and uneven patterns of land ownership.

Capacity expansion

Various economists, including Maddison (1982) and Levine and Renelt (1992), have shown that rapid, long-term economic growth requires large investments in fixed capital. Turkey is no exception, as evidenced by (8.1). Large investments in fixed capital over long periods require large and sustainable domestic or foreign savings.

Calculations using the national income data series for 1987–94 developed by the State Institute of Statistics indicate an average investment to GNP ratio of 24 percent. The domestic savings rate averaged 22.5 of GNP; the foreign savings rate averaged 1.5 percent. Domestic savings peaked at 27.2 percent in 1988, dropped to 22 percent in 1989, and remained there until 1994, when they fell to 20.8 percent. Foreign savings reached 3.1 percent of GNP in 1990 and 5.0 percent in 1993; during the rest of the period it fluctuated between –1.1 percent and 2.1 percent.

The State Planning Organization defines public disposable income as the difference between public sector gross revenue, including state enterprise profits and depreciation, and income transfers to the private sector and the rest of the world, including interest payments. Private disposable income is the difference between GNP and public disposable income.

Consideration of the relevant accounts over 1987–94 reveals that:

- The ratio of public consumption to GNP averaged 9.9 percent and that of public savings to GNP averaged 2.1 percent. The ratio of public consumption to GNP climbed from 7.0 percent in 1987 to 12.7 percent in 1993. The ratio of public disposable income to GNP declined from 13.6 percent in 1987 to 9.9 percent in 1993. As a result the ratio of public savings to GNP declined from 6.6 percent in 1987 to –2.8 percent in 1993. In 1994 the ratio of public consumption to GNP fell to 10.6 percent and the ratio of public savings to GNP increased to –1.8 percent.
- The ratio of public investment to GNP averaged 7.5 percent, fluctuating between 3.7 percent and 10.3 percent. In 1993 it amounted to 7.2 percent and in 1994 to 3.7 percent.

- These developments in the public sector savings–investment gap reflect a deterioration in public finances. The gap increased from 1.6 percentage points in 1988 to 10.1 percentage points in 1993. In 1994 the gap was reduced to 5.5 percentage points.
- The ratio of private consumption to GNP averaged 67.6 percent and varied little over 1987–94. The ratio of private savings to GNP, on the other hand, fluctuated between 17.3 and 24.8 percent of GNP, averaging 20.5 percent.
- The ratio of private investment to GNP averaged 16.6 percent, ranging from 14.9 percent to 19.7 percent. After reaching 19.7 percent in 1993, the ratio fell to 16.2 percent in 1994.

The national accounts data reveal that the ratio of public savings to public disposable income fell from 48.5 percent in 1987 to −28.8 percent in 1993. Since domestic savings is the sum of private and public savings, the deterioration in public finances during 1987–92 and the accompanying decline in public savings led to the drop in total domestic savings. For capital accumulation the country can undoubtedly rely on foreign savings. But excess reliance on foreign savings may lead to unsustainable debt finance and hence to a loss of creditworthiness. The country will have to follow prudent macroeconomic policies in order to avoid issuing debt at a rate higher than the growth rate of the resources available for eventual debt service. Thus Turkey must apply effective macroeconomic policies to increase domestic savings as well. The domestic savings rate of 22.5 percent and investment rate of 24.0 percent during 1970–93 compare unfavorably with the average domestic savings rates of 33.0 percent in Indonesia, 32.4 percent in Korea, 33.5 percent in Malaysia, and 28.7 percent in Thailand. The average investment rate was 30.7 percent in Indonesia, 31.9 percent in the Republic of Korea, 31.5 in Malaysia, and 32.6 percent in Thailand.

Sectoral data on the distribution of fixed investment during 1980–93 show the emphasis the government has placed on capital formation in basic infrastructure systems (communication, transportation, and energy). It is because of these large investments that Turkey now has adequate communication and transportation networks. Furthermore, several projects now under way will bring major improvements. For example, the Southern Anatolian Project will construct twenty-one dams and seventeen hydroelectric power plants on the Euphrates and Tigris rivers and their tributaries. About 1.6 million hectares will be irrigated and 26 billion kilowatts of electrical energy generated each year with the installed capacity of 7,500 megawatts. Furthermore, investments in the tourism sector raised tourism revenues from $326 million in 1980 to $4.32 billion in 1994. Finally, additional investment in education should substantially increase the quality of the labor force during the second half of the 1990s.

Technical progress

Because total factor productivity growth accounted for 42 percent of GDP growth over 1978–92, it is likely that even with no changes in the supply of factors of production (such as capital and labor), production will expand through improvements in technology and increasing returns to scale.

A number of economists have shown that two factors are key to total factor productivity growth: competitive pressure (as measured by market concentration ratios, import penetration ratios, and effective rates of protection) and research and development expenditures as a share of GDP (Grossman and Helpman, 1992; Urata, 1994; Goel and Ram, 1994). A consistent set of data on market concentration ratios – the share of total domestic sales accounted for by the largest producer – is not available. However, concentration ratios for selected goods during 1989–90 are quite high – 100 percent for plate glass and automotive tier cords, 95 percent for pencils and buses, 90 percent for minibuses, and 80–90 percent for acrylic fiber, electrical porcelain goods, and washing machines (Dutz, 1996). Such markets are clearly oligopolistic, and competitive pressure must be weak. As such there was not much pressure to improve production efficiency until the 1980s.

During the 1980s Turkey opened its economy to foreign competition by substantially lowering nominal and effective rates of protection. The average value of the economywide nominal protection rate fell from 66 percent in 1983 to 28 percent in 1991. Similarly, the effective protection rate dropped from 71 percent in 1983 to 38 percent in 1991 (Togan, 1994). As a result competitive pressure from abroad has increased. Thus the concentration ratios reported by Dutz (1996) are expected to fall over time. Turkey will further lower nominal and effective protection rates during the second half of the 1990s as part of its customs union with the European Union. As competitive pressures develop, production efficiency and hence total factor productivity growth should increase.

Data on enterprises' spending on research and development are available only for 1990–92. Such spending amounted to just 0.11

percent of GNP during 1991 and 0.12 percent during 1992. Similar figures for industrial countries are in the range of 2 percent. Since it appears that the effect of research and development on total factor productivity is negligible, total factor productivity growth must be the result of increased competitive pressure from abroad and Turkish firms imitating foreign products.

Developments on the international scene

Turkey has been a signatory to the General Agreement on Tariffs and Trade (GATT) since 1951. In the GATT context Turkey is defined as a developing country. This classification allows it to maintain quantitative restrictions when confronting scarce foreign exchange reserves, which it did until the late 1980s.

The two most important trade agreements Turkey has concluded are the agreements with the European Union (EU) and the Economic Cooperation Organization. Under the EU agreement Turkey joined a customs union on January 1 1996. The Economic Cooperation Organization, which consists of Iran, Pakistan, and Turkey, established preferential tariffs for its members in 1992. The agreement liberalizes trade among the member states for four years, after which it can automatically be renewed for another two years. Thus competitive pressures are increasing, and with the new agreements it will keep increasing, leading to increases in total factor productivity growth.

Macroeconomic policies

Sustainable economic growth rests on effective macroeconomic policies. By the late 1970s it had become apparent that Turkey's strategy of economic growth based on import substitution, fixed exchange rates, regulation of imports through quotas, and high nominal and effective protection rates was no longer sustainable. In 1980 the government introduced reforms to reduce inflation and control the balance of payments deficit. Policymakers also tried to make the economy more dynamic by fostering competition through trade.

During the 1980s various economic reforms improved export performance, eased the balance of payments deficit, and boosted real income. Exports grew from $2.9 billion in 1980 to $11.6 billion in 1989. The current account deficit moved from a deficit of $3.4 billion in 1980 to a surplus of $0.96 billion in 1989. Real income increased by an average of 4.8 percent a year during 1981–9. Inflation went from

116 percent in 1980 to 39 percent in 1987. During the late 1980s, however, the government started to move away from market-oriented policies and switched over to populist policies. The ratio of public sector borrowing to GNP rose from 4.8 percent in 1988 to 11.7 percent in 1993. Because this borrowing was increasingly financed by the central bank, the money supply increased rapidly, leading to higher inflation. In 1989 the capital account was liberalized and the government allowed the real exchange rate to appreciate. As a result the trade deficit increased from $1.78 billion in 1988 to $14.1 billion in 1993, while the current account deficit went from a surplus of $1.6 billion in 1988 to a deficit of $6.4 billion in 1993. External debt reached $67.4 billion by the end of 1993, and domestic debt exploded. In April 1994 the government entered into negotiations with the International Monetary Fund to address the balance of payments crisis. The resulting stabilization package caused real GDP to drop by 5.4 percent in 1994, but the current account deficit was completely eliminated. Still, inflation during 1994 accelerated to 106 percent. Against this background the government introduced measures – such as the EU customs union agreement – to further open up the economy.

The 1994 crisis was caused by deteriorating public finances. As the inflation rate exploded, the real exchange rate appreciated. Consideration of the relation between the real exchange rate (*RER*) and the values of the share of exports in GNP (*X/GNP*) reveals that:

$$\ln(X/GNP) = -4.5289 + 1.5252\ln RER$$
$$(-9.8967) \qquad (15.1084) \qquad\qquad (9.2a)$$
$$n = 31; \ \rho = 0.1114; \ R^2 = 0.9094; \ DW = 1.9966$$
$$(0.6292)$$

The estimation of the import demand function yields:

$$\ln(m) = 12.4847 + 0.2063\ln GDP - 0.8929\ln pm$$
$$(5.8666) \qquad (1.8544) \qquad\quad (-2.7086) \qquad (9.2b)$$
$$n = 31; \ \rho = 0.5581; \ R^2 = 0.5425; \ DW = 2.3626$$
$$(3.0915)$$

where *m* is real imports and *pm* is the relative price of imports, defined as $pm = [pm * E(1 + t)]/p$. In this formulation *pm** is the foreign price of imports, *E* is the exchange rate, *t* is the average tariff rate, and *p* is the price of domestic goods.

(9.2a) and (9.2b) reveal that the balance of payments crisis in 1994 could have been avoided if policymakers had allowed the real exchange rate to depreciate sufficiently. In that case exports would have increased, imports would have decreased, and the large trade deficit would have been avoided. Furthermore, policymakers should not have used the liberalization of the capital account to finance the balance of payments deficit by borrowing from abroad.

Investment incentives

Since 1967 the government has granted a number of incentives to promote investment in production activities. These incentives have been directed to reducing the cost of investment, reducing the need for external financing, and increasing profitability. The incentive scheme contains a number of peculiarities. First, incentives are differentiated by region: developed regions (consisting of cities of the Istanbul and Kocaeli and the municipal districts of Ankara, Izmir, and Bursa), priority normal regions (provinces like Afyon, Kirikkale, and Trabzon), regions enjoying first degree priority in development (provinces like Van, Agri, and Kars), and regions enjoying second-degree priority in development (provinces like Çankiri, Yozgat, and Malatya). Second, the government imposes certain conditions on lower limits, investment totals, minimum level of own sources, and export levels that investments have to satisfy in order to benefit from the incentives. Third, all incentives originate from the central government's Undersecretariat for Treasury. Only the investments that are granted incentive certificates by this agency are eligible for incentives.

In 1995 the investment incentives consisted of (in decreasing order of importance) an investment incentive allowance, customs exemptions, exemptions from the value-added tax, a premium on domestically produced capital goods, state aid to certain activities, investment credits, energy incentives, postponement of the value-added tax, and land allocations. By using these measures to reduce the effective cost of borrowing to investors, the government reduces the cost of investments, increasing their profitability. In addition, public investments in infrastructure lower the cost of private production and distribution.

Although the investment incentives are intended to overcome the barriers to entry into industry imposed by capital market imperfections – and thus increase competition – they have become a barrier to competition and structural change. Established firms obtain unit cost advantages through the incentive system that help them consolidate their market position. New entrants with scarce fiscal resources are at a disadvantage relative to well informed incumbents. Thus credit incentives often reinforce the position of large incumbents. Furthermore, because the government directly controls the allocation of credit, credit from public banks is often not extended on a commercial basis. To a large extent the high concentration values discussed earlier can be attributed to these investment incentives. With the phasing out of this system barriers to industrial entry will be reduced, leading to increases in competitive pressures and thus in total factor productivity growth.

Foreign trade policies

Besides the investment incentives, government aid to industry is concentrated in trade-related measures. Until the 1980s all imports entering Turkey were regulated by annual import programs. These programs itemized commodities under a liberalization list, a quota list, and a list enumerating the commodities to be imported under bilateral trade arrangements. Goods not included on the lists were prohibited. In 1981 the quota list was partly phased out, and a large number of commodities was transferred from the restricted list to the free import list. In 1984 imports were reclassified as prohibited, subject to permission, or liberalized, and tariffs were reduced substantially. However, a number of levies and surcharges were introduced to constrain import demand, including a municipality tax, a transportation infrastructure tax, a minerals surcharge, a stamp duty, a value added tax, a housing fund tax (which finances low-cost housing for poor and middle-income families), a resource utilization and support fund tax, and a support and price stabilization fund tax. At the beginning of the 1990s the import permit system was eliminated, import formalities were eased, and quantitative restrictions were abolished. Furthermore, as of 1993 all charges except for customs duties, the housing fund tax, and the minerals surcharge were abolished. Imports exempt from duties under GATT represented about 38 percent of total imports in 1992. In addition, holders of investment incentive certificates are allowed to import machinery and equipment duty-free and exporters are allowed to import intermediate inputs and other capital goods duty-free.

In 1989 Turkey adopted a Law on the Prevention of Unfair Competition in Importation that contained antidumping and antisubsidy provisions. A Law on the Protection of Competition, modeled largely on EU practice, was adopted in December 1994. This statute contains rules on forbidden practices, provisions against the abuse of a dominant market position, and regulations on acquisitions and mergers. Further liberalization of foreign trade and effective application of this law would cause levels of domestic industrial concentration to fall over time. As a result competitive pressures will rise, leading to increases in total factor productivity growth and hence in GDP per capita.

Public enterprise policies

Turkey's public enterprise sector is very large. During the 1930s the government formulated an ideological position called *étatism*, defined as state intervention to direct industrial activity in the interest of national development. These policies were implemented within the frameworks of five-year plans that assigned a leading role to the public sector in saving generation and in carrying out key entrepreneurial functions in industrial development. As a result of the étatist and import substitution policies followed until the end of the 1970s the share of state-owned enterprises in total value added amounted to 11.5 percent in 1985 and 10.6 percent in 1990 (OECD, 1992). Until March 1996 the state held monopolies in tobacco, weapons, air transportation, sugar prodution, and telecommunications. In the manufacturing sector state-owned enterprises were concentrated in basic metals, chemicals, petrochemicals, fertilizers, newsprint, paper, oil refineries, cement, and textile production. (In March 1996 state-owned enterprises gave up their monopolies in production of fertilizers, paper, cement, and textiles.) These enterprises generally exhibit poor economic performance, mainly because of the soft budget constraints they face. Politicians force them to pursue such objectives as agricultural income support and employment creation. Public firms are not subjected to commercial code, and so avoid bankruptcy laws. Pricing, employment, and investment decisions require the approval of the Treasury, the State Planning Organization, and sometimes ministers. Although privatization has been a prominent part of the structural adjustment program since 1983, the difficulties it has encountered have limited its momentum.

It should be emphasized that, besides the barriers to entry imposed by the investment incentives, Turkey also limits exit. Public firms are often not allowed to go bankrupt. The government protects workers from unemployment by subsidizing unprofitable firms. Such policies make firms more risk averse in undertaking new activities and block a more decisive approach to resource allocation. Because proper functioning of the price system requires both free entry and free exit of firms from markets, the privatization of public enterprises should be considered. Privatization would increase efficiency and hence total factor productivity growth, leading to increases in the rate of GDP growth.

PROSPECTS FOR THE FUTURE

In addition to the factors just discussed, Turkish economic growth over the next several decades will be determined by regional political developments and international economic developments.

Regional political developments

Turkey has been directly affected by the downfall of communism in Eastern Europe and the disintegration of the Soviet Union. As a result of these changes the centuries-old Turkish–Russian borders have ceased to exist; Moscow's power around the Black Sea coast has been fragmented; in the Southern Caucasus Soviet sovereignty has been replaced by Georgia, Armenia, and Azerbaijan; in Central Asia the Turk-speaking republics have been freed from Russian rule; and in the Balkans an entirely new political landscape has emerged. The changes have also aroused sentiments, perceptions, and aspirations about group identities, preferred lifestyles, and cross-national and cross-cultural experiences. To the east Turkey enjoyed a long period of harmonious relations with Iran. But Irans efforts to export the Islamic revolution, competition for influence in Central Asia, and Iran's backing of the Kurds have strained relations between the two countries. The Iraqi quest for advanced weaponry, friction over Turkish control of the sources of the Tigris and Euphrates rivers, and the Gulf war have generated tensions between Ankara and Baghdad. Turkish–Syrian relations have long been corroded by disputes over Hatay province, and Syrian accumulation of advanced weaponry, water issues, and Syrian backing of Kurd separatists all present conflict areas. Besides the conflicts over Cyprus and control over the Aegean Sea Turkeys most challenging problem is the growth of Kurdish nationalism. Developments on these fronts will determine the extent of the resources Turkey will have to devote to security and national defense in the future. The volume of resources diverted from such areas as education and infrastructure investments to security and national defense will determine the reduction in resources for productive investments and hence in rates of economic growth.

International economic developments

Integration with the European Union

On March 6, 1995, it was agreed at the Association Council meeting in Brussels that Turkey would join the European customs union starting January 1, 1996. Under the timetable specified in the agreement, Turkey:

- Eliminated all customs duties, quantitative restrictions, charges equivalent to customs duties, and measures equivalent to quantitative restrictions in trade with EU countries on January 1, 1996.
- Adopted the Common Customs Tariff against third-country imports on January 1, 1996, and will adopt the preferential agreements the Union has concluded with third countries by 2001 (for certain products Turkey will impose higher tariffs than those in the Common Customs Tariff for another five years).
- Will adopt within five years EU instruments relating to the removal of technical barriers to trade. The list of these instruments will be laid down within a year. Effective cooperation will be achieved in the fields of standardization, quality, and certification.
- Will implement EU commercial policy regulations, including procedures for administering quantitative quotas, antidumping rules, and procedures for officially supported export credits. Turkey will also adopt the EU's textile and garments agreement with third countries.
- Will adjust policies in order to adopt the common agricultural policy required to establish freedom of movement of agricultural products.
- Adopted EU customs provisions on origin of goods, customs declarations, release for free circulation, customs debt, and right of appeal.
- Will ensure adequate and effective protection and enforcement of intellectual, industrial, and commercial property rights.
- Will adopt EU competition rules, including measures regarding public aid, within two years. However, aid for structural adjustment purposes will be considered compatible with the functioning of the customs union for another five years.

- Will adopt until 1998 legislation to secure the patentability of pharmaceutical products and processes.

The European Union, on the other hand, will abolish the system of quotas in textile and clothing products as soon as Turkey has implemented EU garments and textile agreements with third countries; measures regarding intellectual, industrial, and commercial property; and competition (including the measures regarding public aid). The Framework Agreement is silent on three issues: supply of services, movement of capital, and movement of labor.

The customs union between Turkey and the European Union will allow goods to circulate freely between the two parties. In addition, Turkey will implement the EU's Common External Tariff (CET) on goods from third parties and adopt all of the EU's preferential trade agreements. To calculate the effect of these changes on the Turkish economy it is necessary to obtain figures on nominal protection rates for trade with the Union and third countries for periods before and after the formation of the customs union. The Framework Agreement distinguishes between two sets of commodities: products in which it was thought that Turkey could achieve international competitiveness relatively soon were placed on a twelve-year list; other industrial products were placed on a twenty-two-year list. In January 1996 the nominal protection rate for both sets of commodities was lowered to zero.[2]

The average weighted tariff rates prevailing in 1994 and that will prevail in 2001 when Turkey adopts the Common External Tariff and all the preferential EU trade agreements were estimated by Togan (1995). These agreements include free trade agreements with Central and Eastern European countries, Baltic countries, and Israel; preferential trade agreements between the European Union and African, Caribbean, and Pacific countries; and the Generalized System of Trade Preferences that the EU has granted to developing countries. The weighted average nominal protection rate during 1994, weighted by the share of the respective country groups in Turkish imports, was 13.16 percent. The weighted average nominal protection rate that will prevail in 2001 is 3.16 percent. The input–output table prepared by the State Institute of Statistics for 1990 was used to calculate effective protection rates. The economywide effective protection rate will fall from 18.44 percent in 1994 to 1.12 percent in 2001 (Togan, 1995). The effects of the customs union on sectoral value-added is calculated by subtracting the value of the effective protection rate for 1994 from the value of the effective protection rate for 2001. Thus membership in the customs union will increase value-added in such sectors as grain mill products, sugar refining, and clothing and lower value-added for processed tobacco, petroleum refining, and nonalcoholic beverages.

Membership in the customs union will lower annual tariff revenue by about $2.4 billion. Turkey will have to compensate for this loss by increasing other taxes or reducing public spending. In either case output will decrease and unemployment will increase in the short run – at the same time that adjustment takes place under the standby agreement concluded with the International Monetary Fund in 1994. Furthermore, adjustment will raise employment in sectors where the country has comparative advantage and lower it in sectors where it does not. The country will also have to adjust to the changing conditions regarding competition policy and new rules on intellectual, industrial, and commercial property rights. These adjustment costs will be rather costly in the short run.

Turkey considers membership in the customs union as an intermediate step toward the achievement of full membership in the European Union. The country recognizes that the increased competition achieved through the customs union will lead, in the long run, to improved resource allocation and thus to welfare gains. Policymakers are willing to bear the short-run costs of establishing the customs union, even in the absence of the kind of assistance Greece, Portugal, and Spain received when they joined the Union. Membership in the Union is desirable for a number of reasons. The Union will be Turkey's main trading partner and primary source of technology and investment over the next few decades. Membership will lock in political and economic reforms, providing credibility to these reforms. Membership will increase competition for Turkey within the Union, leading to improved allocation of resources and hence to increases in long-run per capita income. As a result of these changes the customs union will cause – once short-run adjustments in the economy are complete – total factor productivity to grow and per capita incomes to rise over time.

Multilateral agreements

The Uruguay Round is the most comprehensive round launched by the GATT. Besides tariff reductions, this round addressed complex issues like agriculture, trade in services, intellectual property rights, and trade-related investment measures (TRIMs).

For Turkey the implications of the Uruguay Round are similar to those of the customs union agreement. According to the Uruguay

Round the average tariffs on industrial goods will fall by more than a third until January 1 1999 (the customs union requirements are more demanding). In the case of agriculture the Uruguay Round requires that member countries convert all nontariff barriers to trade to tariffs and reduce the tariffs by about 24 percent. Export subsidies will be reduced by 36 percent in value terms and 21 percent in volume terms from their 1986–90 base. The reductions in tariffs and subsidies will take place over six years for industrial countries and ten years for developing countries. These requirements are more demanding than those of the customs union agreement, which did not clearly specify requirements on the adoption of the common agricultural policy. For textiles and clothing the Uruguay Round requires that bilateral quotas negotiated under the Multifiber Arrangement be completely phased out over a ten-year period. Under the customs union agreement the Union will eliminate quotas on Turkish textile and clothing exports once Turkey has effectively implemented the measures regarding intellectual, industrial, and commercial property; competition (including the measures on public aid); and EU garments and textile agreements with third countries.

In the case of intellectual property the requirements of the customs union agreement are similar to those of the Uruguay Round. According to the Uruguay Round Turkey will have to adopt the Trade-Related Aspects of Intellectual Property Rights agreement until 2000; the customs union agreement requires that Turkey implement this agreement until 1999. Furthermore, the customs union requires that Turkey adopt until 1998 legislation to secure the patentability of pharmaceutical products and processes.

For subsidies the Uruguay Round defines three categories of subsidies: prohibited subsidies (those contingent on export performance or the use of domestic rather than imported goods), actionable subsidies (those that have demonstrably adverse effects on other member countries), and nonactionable subsidies. The agreement also restricts the use of countervailing measures introduced in response to competitors' subsidies. The customs union agreement, on the other hand, requires that Turkey adopt EU competition policies. As such the customs union agreement is much more restrictive than the Uruguay Round agreement.

CONCLUSION

Turkey's economic policies during the early and mid-1980s were extremely successful at liberalizing the economy. The formation of a customs union with the European Union will further open the economy. By allowing greater competition in domestic markets by reducing barriers to imports, eliminating export and production subsidies, introducing competition policies and laws regarding intellectual property rights, privatizing state-owned enterprises and subjecting them to market rules, and allowing foreign direct investment Turkey will be able to achieve sustainable real growth. Turkey recognizes the importance of the customs union agreement and the Uruguay Round agreements. The government's long-run objective – increasing the welfare of its citizens by achieving steady growth in GNP per capita – will be achieved by the EU customs union. But it certainly was not the only approach. If the customs union agreement had not been ratified by the European Parliament in October 1995, Turkey could have increased competition and elevated national welfare by opening the economy to foreign trade, taking the necessary measures to increase competitive pressures, following the rules of the Uruguay Round, and establishing free trade agreements with the European Union, the United States, and other countries.

Notes

1. The author is grateful to Professor Hanaa Kheir-El-Din for helpful comments and suggestions.
2. Three other types of commodities were also considered under the agreements: agricultural products, products within the province of the European Coal and Steel Community (ELSC), and products within the province of the European Atomic Energy Community. In order to establish freedom of movement of agricultural products, Turkey will have to adopt the EU's common agricultural policy, which provides the main framework for agricultural support. The policy is based on three principles: free movement of agricultural commodities through the common market order system, protection of agricultural markets from foreign competition through market interventions, and financing of agricultural support program from the EU budget, mainly through the European Agricultural Guidance and Guarantee Fund (EAGGF). Thus Turkish agricultural commodity prices should rise to EU levels, and Turkey should finance its agricultural support program from a fund similar to the European Agricultural Guidance and Guarantee Fund. The State Planning Organization estimates the amount of required annual support at $3.1 billion. Since Turkey cannot devote this amount to agricultural support, free movement of agricultural products will not be achieved in the near future.

References

Barro, Robert J., 1991. "Economic Growth in a Cross Section of Countries," *Quarterly Journal of Economics*, 106: 407–3.

Celasun, Merih, 1986. "A General Equilibrium Model of the Turkish Economy, Simlog-1," *Middle East Technical University Studies in Development*, 13: 29–94.

———— 1989. "Income Distribution and Employment Aspects of Turkey's Post-1980 Adjustment," *Middle East Technical University Studies in Development*, 16: 1–30.

Dervis, Kemal, and Sherman Robinson, 1980. "The Structure of Income Inequality in Turkey," in E. Özbudun, and A. Ulusan, (eds.), *The Political Economy of Income Distribution in Turkey*, London: Holmes & Meier.

De Santis, Roberto, and H. Gazi Özhan, 1994. "A Social Accounting Matrix for Turkey 1990," University of Warwick, Development Economics Research Centre.

Dutz, Mark, 1996. "Competition Law and Its Relevance for Turkey," in Refik Erzan (ed.), *Policies for Competition and Competitiveness: The Case of Industry in Turkey*, Vienna: United Nations Industrial Development Organization.

Goel, Rajeev K., and Rati Ram, 1994. "Research and Development Expenditures and Economic Growth: A Cross-Country Study," *Economic Development and Cultural Change*, 42: 403–11.

Grossman, Gene M., and Elhanan Helpman, 1992. *Innovation and Growth in the Global Economy*, Cambridge, Mass.: MIT Press.

Hamilton, Bruce W., 1995. "Education and Development," report prepared by Bilkent University faculty members for Prime Ministry of the Republic of Turkey, Bilkent University, Ankara.

Jorgenson, Dale W., and Zvi Griliches, 1967. "The Explanation of Productivity Change," *Review of Economic Studies*, 34: 249–83.

Levine, Ross, and David Renelt, 1992. "A Sensitivity Analysis of Cross-Country Growth Regressions," *American Economic Review*, 82: 942–63.

Maddison, Angus, 1982. *Phases of Capitalist Development*, Oxford: Oxford University Press.

Maraslioglu, Haryi, and Ahmet Tiktik, 1991. "Turkiye Ekonomisinde Sektorel Gelismeler: Uretim, Sermaye Birikimi ve Istihdam 1968–1988," State Planning Organization, Ankara.

OECD (Organization for Economic Cooperation and Development), 1992. "OECD Economic Surveys: Turkey 1991–1992," Paris: OECD.

———— 1993, "OECD Economic Surveys: Turkey 1993," Paris: OECD.

Togan, Sübidey, 1994. *Foreign Trade Regime and Trade Liberalization in Turkey during the 1980s*, Aldershot: Avebury.

———— 1995. "Turkey and the European Union," in H. Ersel, (ed.), *Towards A New Medium-Term Stabilization Program for Turkey*, Istanbul: Turkish Industrialists' and Businessmen's Association.

Urata, Shujiro, 1994. "Trade Liberalization and Productivity Growth in Asia: Introduction and Major Findings," *The Developing Economies*, 32: 363–72.

World Bank, various years. *World Development Report*, New York: Oxford University Press.

10 Sudan: Toward a Strategic Vision for Peace and Development[1]

Ibrahim A. Elbadawi

This chapter proposes a development vision for Sudan. Given the current extreme conditions of raging civil war and declining economic fortunes, political and economic reforms that bring internal peace, minimize risks, and achieve basic macroeconomic stability and structural reforms are proposed as essential components of the strategy. Complementary components of the strategy include measures for moving from stabilization to sustained growth, with an emphasis on the key role of external support in consolidating internal reforms; measures for strengthening the institutions and policies required to achieve agricultural transformation, economic diversification, and flexibility against external and natural shocks; initiatives to foster regional cooperation and complementarities; and efforts to redefine the role of the state under the new development paradigm given the economic and social conditions prevailing in Sudan.

Sudan, situated at the southern threshold of the Arab world, is divided into north and south along ethnic, cultural, and to some extent religious lines.[2] This diversity, which could be a source of enrichment and strength, has instead led to civil wars and protracted episodes of political instability since the country's independence in 1956. It is thus not surprising that, despite its enormous economic potential, Sudan is one of the poorest countries in the Arab world. Not only has civil unrest inhibited the country's economic development, it has also precipitated an atmosphere of "crisis management" that has blurred a broader vision of nation building.

Given its difficult political and social climate, Sudan's economic development is predicated on a lasting internal peace built upon a participatory and transparent political process. As a fundamental precondition for generating a self-enforcing reform process, the strategy for economic development should seek immediately to restore macroeconomic stability as the basis for economic growth, structural diversity and flexibility as the basis for medium- to long-term sustainability, and an equitable, broadly-based social agenda as the basis for meaningful reductions in poverty. These are the essential components of a strategy for effecting the political and economic reforms that bring internal peace. The complementary components of the strategy include measures for moving from stabilization to sustained growth, with an emphasis on external support to consolidate internal reforms with responsive, coordinated investment; stronger, more focused institutions and policies for enhancing agricultural productivity; and initiatives to foster regional cooperation and complementarities.

RECENT ECONOMIC DEVELOPMENTS

Sudan's economic fortunes have declined sharply since the mid-1970s. Despite its enormous size and economic potential, the country has been unable to achieve sufficiently high rates of growth on a sustained basis.[3] Only in the second half of the 1970s did it experience strong growth, averaging a more than 10 percent annual increase in GDP (Table 10.1). But this period was the by-product of two unique circumstances: the cessation of hostilities in southern Sudan on the heels

Table 10.1 Economic indicators and gross domestic product, Sudan, fiscal 1971–91
(percentage of GDP except GDP growth)

Indicator	1971–74	1975–78	1979–87	1988–89	1990–91
GDP growth	−3.94	10.78	−2.89	−3.70	2.10[a]
Gross domestic investment	11.6	19.2	14.4	15.1	13.3
Public investment	—	37.2	35.9	34.2	—
Consumption	88.2	84.3	95.1	88.7	91.8
Gross domestic savings	11.1	11.1	4.1	9.5	1.8
Gross national savings	10.6	11.9	4.7	8.3	−0.2
Agriculture	38.4	36.6	33.0	32.2	28.9
Industry	12.2	12.1	13.4	15.7	15.7
Services	36.8	40.1	45.6	48.4	51.4

— Not available.
a 1990–94.
Source: World Bank, 1994.

of the 1972 Addis Ababa agreement (forged between the Numeiri regime and the rebel Anya Nya movement) and the influx of substantial investment funds, primarily from the oil-surplus countries of the Arab world, to finance an ambitious development plan. Yet the government was unable to sustain this high rate of economic growth. To maintain the pace of its development plan, the government relied on monetary expansion and external financing, as a series of adverse external shocks, including the 1973 oil price shock and its aftermath, threatened macroeconomic stability (Elbadawi, 1988, 1992). Gross implementation and planning deficiencies not only brought growth to a halt, they also led the country to the brink of a major economic crisis by 1978.

In 1979 Sudan became one of the first countries to adopt International Monetary Fund (IMF) and World Bank macroeconomic stabilization and structural adjustment programs. The reforms emphasized two central policies: successive devaluations and trade liberalization measures that shifted imports (and to some extent exports) from the official market to the free market (Elbadawi, 1992).[4] Sudan was also able to seize upon the oil boom that followed the 1973 Arab–Israeli war, emerging into a major labor-exporting country to the oil-surplus economies of the Middle East. Remittances from Sudanese nationals working abroad averaged more than three times the dollar value of official exports during 1983–84 (Elbadawi, 1992).[5] These huge foreign exchange resources prompted the government to adopt reforms to unify the exchange rate. So far, however, its efforts have been unsuccessful, and Sudanese nationals have continued to send the bulk of their remittances through the parallel foreign exchange market, attracted by its more depreciated exchange rate.

Sudan's quest for economic reform has been a dismal failure for three broad reasons. First, the early IMF and World Bank macroeconomic stabilization and structural adjustment programs were fraught with sequencing and design problems. Although methodological advances and practical experience have since significantly improved these reform packages, the learning curve was costly, especially for poor countries in Africa (Ndulu, 1995). Second, the Sudanese government lacked the political will to implement the reforms and the broad development vision to guide them. The third and most critical factor was the resurgence of civil war in 1983, which precluded the emergence of credible political and social institutions for fostering national consensus as part of a participatory political process. For example, when the democratically elected Prime Minister Sadig Al-

Mahdi attempted to initiate dialogue on a "social contract" for the Sudan after the 1985 popular uprising, the lack of political consensus prevented the democratic regime from undoing the economic legacy inherited from the previous sixteen years of the Numeiri regime.

In June 1989 a military takeover put an end to the short-lived third democracy in the Sudan.[6] After a brief reversal of economic reform and a failed attempt to restore economic controls, the new regime quickly embarked on a massive deregulation and privatization program. The government also introduced a long-term strategic plan for development. But macroeconomic instability prevailed as the sweeping structural and microeconomic reforms were executed. For example, between fiscal 1990 and 1994 the deficit as a share of GDP averaged more than 16 percent, domestic credit grew by an average of 60 percent (more than double the annual rate for the 1978–87 period), and annual inflation reached almost 100 percent, compared with 6.6 percent a year during 1978–87 (Table 10.2).

Despite some recovery in aggregate output, particularly in agriculture, the extreme macroeconomic instability in and weak export performance by Sudan, coupled with one of the largest external debts of all Sub-Saharan African countries, indicate that the country is experiencing a major economic crisis. The fact that per capita income has grown by an average of 2.1 percent a year since fiscal 1990 reflects primarily a cyclical phenomenon – poverty also has increased sharply since 1991, suggesting that the data on growth are inaccurate or that the patterns of growth have been very skewed. The prospects for the future are also dim, particularly if two necessary development are absent – a peaceful settlement of the civil war and the emergence of a participatory and accountable political system that provides a foundation for development.

Table 10.2 Macroeconomic indicators, Sudan, 1970–94 (percent)

Indicator	1971–73	1974–77	1978–87	1990–94
Domestic inflation	3.3	3.8	6.6	99.3
Change in domestic credit rate/M2	17.9	37.1	28.2	59.2
Public sector share of domestic credit	58.2	64.8	64.4	—
Overall deficit/GDP	3.4	4.5	8.7	16.1
Deficit/GDP	4.3	5.8	13.0	—

— Not available.
Source: Estimates based on information provided by Sudanese authorities.

THE ECONOMIC IMPACTS OF CIVIL WAR

Sudan's disappointing economic performance, especially since the second half of the 1970s, suggests that the protracted civil strife has been one of the main causes of its declining economic fortunes. The country's population is estimated at 27 million people, about 80 percent of whom live in the north. The population in the north consists primarily of Muslims who speak Arabic as their native language. Most of the population in the south consists of animists or the adherents of traditional African religions, but almost all speak Arabic as a second language. These cultural, ethnic, and religious differences divide the country and drive the legacy of civil war – a war that has consumed twenty-eight of the thirty-nine years of modern, independent Sudan.[7] But the more fundamental reason for the north–south disunity is a tale of divisive colonial policies, adverse external political interventions, and the absence of political vision by national political leaders (both northerners and southerners).

In the early days of the Anglo–Egyptian Condominium (during the first half of the twentieth century) the north–south divide was fostered to position the south as the exclusive region for the activities of Christian missionaries. In 1922 the colonial authorities decreed the "Closed Districts Area," which for the next twenty years effectively closed the south to the northern Sudanese in order to promote the spread of Islam and the Arabic language throughout the southern region (First, 1970). But when the British administration decided to oppose the creation of a Nile valley state between Egypt and northern Sudan, it abandoned its plans for annexing the south to East Africa, and allowed the two halves of the country to integrate. On the eve of independence in 1956 national leaders from both sides agreed to a unified, independent Sudan, with southern leaders maintaining the option of a federal form of government. In the same year, however, the southern Sudanese military broke from its national leaders, and Prime Minister Azhari subsequently declared the Sudan's independence without regard to the federation of the south. Then, after more than eleven years of peace following the Addis Ababa accord, the unconstitutional and unilateral 1983 decision by Numeiri to subdivide the south into three units sparked the second, current cycle of the civil war. Since the fall of the Numeiri regime in 1985, the northern political leaders have put the federation for the South back on the political agenda, but not enough to appease southern political and military opposition.

Costs

Civil war in the Sudan – like all wars – has collapsed output and, because it has lasted for so long, has destroyed most of the physical, human, and social capital in southern Sudan. The loss of human and social capital is particularly critical because their recovery will take a long time. As such, to the extent that their loss dominates the direct loss of output attributable to war-induced disruptions of economic activity, the economic payoffs of a peace accord may be scant in the short run.

Both the direct loss of output and the destruction of productive capacity in the Sudan have been substantial. In particular, the war delayed and has subsequently disabled two major projects – the oil production in Baht Al Gazal and the Jonglei Canal projects – that have inflicted heavy damage on the Sudanese economy. The termination of the Jonglei Canal has also hurt Egypt's economy. The loss of petroleum production since 1985 has cost $2.04 million a day, reaching a total of $2,938 million by September 1989 (Mohammed, 1993; Kok, 1992). By the time work on the Jonglei Canal project was halted by the war in 1983, it had cost $150 million over six years, and by 1986 the drilling equipment was damaged. In addition to enhancing agricultural development throughout the south, the project would have secured 4.7 billion cubic meters of White Nile water, to have been shared equally by Sudan and Egypt.

Civil war also had a devastating effect on agriculture (Mohammed, 1993). It is estimated that 7.0 million head of cattle, 2.0 million sheep, and 1.5 million goats were lost in the South, and at least six major agricultural schemes were destroyed. Due to the mass displacement of people, most of the traditional agriculture in the South has ceased to exist. The war has had similarly devastating impacts on the educational and health infrastructure of the South. Of 1,415 primary, intermediate, secondary, and technical schools in 1983, only 244 were open in 1989; of 32 hospitals, only six were operational in 1989.

Except for the loss of oil revenue and the immense water supply that the Jonglei Canal could have made possible, the core productive capacity of the northern Sudanese economy remains unaffected by civil war – the destruction of physical and human capital has been confined largely to the south. But a relatively localized war can still have a devastating impact on a country's development in the form of lost opportunities, distorted spending patterns, political instability, and social relations marked by hatred and distrust. These developments erode regional and global legitimacy, compromising a country's external economic relationships and jeopardizing much-needed support for economic reform and long-term development.

The costs of the war to Sudan's per capita GDP growth and its rate of investment relative to GDP can be simulated by proxying the effects of two war-related developments: political instability (between 1956 and 1989 power changed hands fourteen times), along with the erosion of state and civil institutions and the consequent loss of property rights and enforceable contracts; and the diversion of human, financial, and physical resources to the military. The impact of political instability can be proxied using an index of civil liberties or the number of war casualties per 1,000 (both soldiers and civilians) in endogenous growth cross-country models; both measures have consistently been found to have a significant and deleterious impact on growth. Empirical evidence about the second effect (proxied by the ratio of military expenditures to GDP) has been less conclusive, in that military spending generates two opposing influences. In the short run military spending can stimulate aggregate demand and boost employment. In the long run heavy military spending can depress productive fixed and human capital formation and aggravate distortions in resource allocation, thereby lowering capacity output (Knight, Loayza, and Villanueva, 1995). But an econometric methodology that accounts sufficiently for these long-run influences is likely to generate a net negative effect of military spending on growth.

The simulation results suggest that, compared with the average military spending–GDP ratios that prevailed in Sub-Saharan Africa during 1986–90 (about 2.52 percent), military spending ratios in the Sudan were quite high during fiscal 1990–94 (at about 7.92 percent), reducing investment–GDP by 16.16 percentage points and lowering per capita GDP growth by 1.55 percentage points. The direct costs of war are even more devastating: when the war intensified from 956 noncivilian casualties in 1984 to more than 4,000 in 1989, the investment–GDP ratio fell by 196 percent, and per capita GDP growth slowed by 6 percent (Table 10.3). Overall, the current civil war has reduced the country's investment to just one-third of its potential ratios and lowered GDP paperper capita by a cumulative 7.37 percent.

Potential peace dividends

If Sudan ultimately achieve peace, should it expect a huge peace dividend in the form of a stable economy and strong productive and

Table 10.3 Costs of civil war in Sudan
(percent unless otherwise specified)

Indicator	Cost
GDP (billion Sudanese pounds)	639.43
Total spending (billion Sudanese pounds)	161.08
Military spending (billion Sudanese pounds)	50.65
Military spending/GDP	7.92
Military spending/total spending	31.44
The direct impact of war	
On investment/GDP	−196.93
On *per capita* GDP growth	−5.83
The impact of military spending	
On investment/GDP	−16.16
On *per capita* GDP growth	−1.55
The overall impact	
On investment/GDP	−212.05
On *per capita* GDP growth	−7.37

Source: Mohammed, 1993; Knight, Loayza, and Villanueva, 1995.

social sectors?[8] In the long run, yes. But the initial phases of any development strategy must first address some major economic and social constraints.

First, the current fiscal situation does not leave much hope for redeploying public expenditures toward peace dividends. Given the comparatively ineffective fiscal performance during fiscal 1990–94, when total annual revenue averaged just 8.4 percent of GDP against total average expenditures of 24.5 percent, the Sudan faces staggering fiscal deficits. Even cash-basis deficits (mainly excluding interest payments) soared during the period, at an annual average of more than 9 percent. The financing of such huge deficits has led to distortionary financing methods, such as inflation and a seigniorage tax. The seigniorage tax ratio, for example, averaged more than 5.30 percent – almost double the 3.0 percent level that indicates major macroeconomic imbalances (Fischer, and Easterly, 1990). As the war continues, this fragile and distorted budgetary environment will only deteriorate, leaving little room for major new spending if peace restores fiscal discipline.

A second constraint encompasses the costs and time required to rebuild the lost physical and human capital, particularly social capital, in the south. Prolonged social disturbance undermines defenses against opportunism by increasing insecurity – both microeconomic insecurity, which is violence against individual and property, and macroeconomic insecurity, which is the dissolution of many of the organizations of civil society and the state (Collier, 1995). These insecurities shorten time horizons, thereby reducing incentives to build and maintain credible policies and institutions and substantially undermining (if not totally eliminating) the crucial role of the state as an impartial guardian of the law and enforcer of contracts. Under such circumstances the most profitable form of behavior can flip from honesty to opportunism, increasing the risks involved in transactions and jeopardizing assets. This mistrust can be seen in the eleven-year period of peace following the 1972 Addis Ababa peace agreement. Although the Numeiri regime was far from a participatory, account-able, or transparent political system, it did attempt to restore political and economic gains to the south. But the inherent difficulties of the transition, the lingering scars of the war between the north and south, and the tribal conflicts within the south conspired to halt the devel-opment of genuine social and political norms and systems in southern Sudan.

Collier (1994) argues that, although the time required to realize the peace dividend after the cessation of hostilities is influenced by factors beyond the control of governments, it is not completely exogenous. Government policy can play a role in accelerating dividends in Sudan, and the government should make several measures part and parcel of the peace process itself. First, it should create a fully accountable, transparent, and participatory political system that protects the legit-imate rights of ethnic, religious, and cultural minorities (such as the southern Sudanese). In doing so, it will begin to resolve the problem of macroeconomic insecurity. Second, it should shift financial and human resources toward legislative and judicial institutions, as well as form a smaller, unified, more capable army. These moves would begin to address microeconomic insecurity and help consolidate the broader political process. Third, the government should create the regulatory and incentive environment needed to restore professional ethics, and promote the effectiveness and vitality of both formal and informal institutions of civil society. These broader measures for achieving peace dividends by improving institutional, social, and economic prospects are fundamental to more specific measures that would constitute a socioeconomic development strategy for Sudan. These measures are delineated in the remainder of the charter.

A DEVELOPMENT VISION FOR SUDAN

As stated earlier, the overall development strategy consists of two broad components. One component includes measures that are necessary to the strategy – the basic political and economic reforms that minimize risks and promote macroeconomic stability and structural reform. The other component consists of complementary measures – a host of initiatives to foster the credibility of policies and accelerate economic development. These include steps to enhance regional cooperation and external economic relationships, and to support the structural transformation of the Sudanese economy. Still another aspect of the strategy pertains to the respective roles of the state and the private sector in the development process.

Essential political and economic reforms: The new development paradigm

Political instability, including protracted civil war, is arguably the most severe type of shock affecting many African countries, including Sudan. Investments in peace-keeping policies could offer the best social rate of return among African investment opportunities (Azam, 1994a). Avoiding political instability, particularly civil war, not only eliminates the direct negative externalities associated with lost productivity and human capital, it also enhances the prospects for regional and global support for a national reform program. The surge of regional and international goodwill with the peaceful resolution of a major civil war could yield immediate economic gains as a more credible political system and welldesigned economic policies make foreign investment more attractive. Regional and international support could yield immediate, substantial peace dividends.

Fundamental to a lasting, genuine peace in a unified Sudan is a sociopolitical order that fully but judiciously respects the country's ethnic, cultural, and religious diversity. Political settlement must also be genuinely participatory and transparent, and apply equally to the north and the south. In short, a peaceful and unified Sudan is predicated on a more democratic governance process, which in turn is a basic prerequisite for economic reform and development.

Macroeconomic imbalances are a comparatively new target of the development paradigm in developing countries. The drive toward macroeconomic stability comes after the failed development strategies of the early 1980s, which emphasized development financing and a dominant government role in economic transformation at the expense of transparent state intervention, private sector development, and market discipline. This new paradigm has come at great cost, however. As Ndulu (1995: 6) observes, the new strategy has sought "macroeconomic stabilization at any cost and the restructuring of incentives and other supply-side factors to encourage output growth. Concerns for other development fundamentals, including national capacities to initiate and sustain change, have been pushed to the background."

But lessons from practical experience with and more advanced research on economic development suggest that a new paradigm is emerging – one that combines market discipline and private sector involvement with a redefined role for the state. The economic development strategy should consist of two broad measures:

- Structural adjustment to correct macroeconomic imbalances (encompassing fiscal and monetary restraint and exchange rate reform) and to change incentive structures and eliminate microeconomic distortions (encompassing trade liberalization, financial sector reform, and public sector reform). These efforts must be accompanied by capacity building in institutions to provide an enabling environment for restoring and accumulating physical and human capital.
- Sustained growth per capita income to support a sustainable reduction in poverty.

Structural adjustment

A comparison of Sudan's fiscal indicators with those across southeast Asia suggests the depth of the Sudan's adjustment needs.[9] During 1980–90 the average fiscal deficits of Indonesia was 1.8 percent and of Thailand, 2.3 percent. Sudan's deficit ratio during 1990–94 was about 16 percent – more than eight times the average for Indonesia and Thailand. Although a simple comparison of budget ratios can be misleading, Sudan's weak GDP growth rates, consistently negative national savings, and enormous stock of external debt ($17.8 billion in fiscal 1994) and debt servicing burden (more than 200 percent of current receipts) support the view that its macroeconomy is in turmoil.

Efforts to stabilize Sudan's fiscal performance must be accompanied by deeper structural reforms in policy institutions and production incentives. In particular, the reform agenda in the Sudan should seek to liberalize further the domestic goods markets and external trade, restructure the financial sector, privatize state enterprises, and deregulate private sector production and investment.[10] These measures are the most difficult part of the economic reform agenda, but they are also the most rewarding (Easterly and Schmidt-Hebbel, 1994).

Poverty alleviation

A meaningful and lasting reduction in poverty is predicated on sustained growth. Evidence indicates that the incidence of poverty – the proportion of population below the poverty line – declines rapidly as consumption grows, with an elasticity of -2.0 (Ravallion, forthcoming). Experience from East Asia and Latin America also shows that poverty reduction is strongly correlated with growth. Although sustained structural adjustment (particularly fiscal reform) is fundamental to restoring growth, sufficient investment in human capital formation is also integral to a long-term poverty alleviation program. Sudan will not be able to achieve sustainable growth without substantially increasing its spending on public education and health.[11] In turn, enhancing the efficiency of greater social investment is predicated on modifying the underlying incentive structure and institutional aspects of delivery systems, as well as on tapping private contributions to these sectors (Shafik, 1994).

The evidence from East Asia falls short of claiming that growth is sufficient for alleviating poverty or that short-term policy measures to alleviate poverty are ineffective (Bruno, 1995). Indeed, given the alarming spread of poverty in Sudan in the 1990s such measures not only make sound economic sense, they are also necessary for the survival and stability of any political regime in the country, especially if the regime happens to be a product of the peace process.[11] Despite the depth of poverty in the Sudan, a frontal attack is both feasible and not necessarily distortionary. Eradicating rural poverty would require transferring only 7 percent of available resources to the sector; eliminating urban poverty would require transferring only 4 percent of resources (Ali, 1994). Still, targeted programs of this type require considerable institutional capacity to ensure efficient delivery systems.

Complements to the development strategy

The strategy for economic development must include a framework that provides sufficient guidance for making the switch from adjustment to growth – that is, for bridging the gap between necessity and sufficiency (Dornbusch, 1991). Sudan must develop the capacity to manage its affairs in an uncertain internal, regional, and global environment and to guide the implementation of reforms and the efficacy of state intervention. In short, it must establish its credibility as an economic player. What enabling measures does Sudan require to put it on the path toward economic development?

From stabilization to growth: A case for debt relief

The most immediate challenge facing Sudan is restoring growth in the short run following a structural adjustment program. One of the main impediments to short-run growth is that the extent to which firms are willing to invest in export expansion or import substitution depends on how they perceive the depth of policy reform under the program. Even if they are offered substantial incentives up front – which may be difficult politically, since doing so would affect the distribution of income – they may prefer to delay investment (Dornbusch, 1991).

The experience with macroeconomic stabilization efforts in Latin America and Sub-Saharan Africa indicated that capital (new or flight) normally does not return to a region. Even if it does, it is usually placed in liquid form rather than in irreversible productive assets. In essence, investors choose to wait "until the front-loading of investment returns is sufficient to compensate them for the risk of relinquishing the liquidity option of the wait and see position" (Dornbusch, 1991: 43). Where the domestic rate of returns is not sufficient to warrant the risk of repatriation, no capital comes in. Where sufficient capital returns, the risk is low, making the required excess returns fall off to nothing.

This review suggests that stabilization alone may not be enough to trigger the "optimum equilibrium" that is needed to move from stabilization to growth. Sudan thus requires an external mechanism that resolves this coordination failure and breaks the tendency of the market to wait. This external mechanism should be in the form of substantial debt relief. A reduction in or complete suspension of debt service would relieve Sudan of its substantial external debt and debt service burden. This, in turn, would dramatically enhance the policy credibility of the governing regime, attracting the enormous savings of Sudanese nationals abroad (conservatively estimated at 6 percent of GDP: Elbadawi, 1992). If one also considers the potential for repatriating the savings that went out as capital flight during the 1980s – estimated at more than 9 percent of GDP (Elbadawi, 1992) – it becomes clear that remittances could play a key role in financing economic growth.[13] Realizing these gains, however, would require not only deep economic reform but also an effective strategy for developing external economic relationships at both the regional and global levels. Peace would provide a window of opportunity for seizing on regional and international goodwill as substantial, immediate dividends.

Agricultural development and environmental sustainability

The agricultural sector is the mainstay of the Sudanese economy. It accounts for more than 35 percent of GDP, more than 90 percent of export earnings, 75 percent of the productive sector's value added, 90 percent of national food requirements, and 70 percent of total employment. The rest of the economy depends on agriculture as a source of raw material, foreign exchange, and wage goods, and as a market for goods and services produced by other sectors (Hag Elamin and El Mak, 1995). Any successful development strategy in Sudan must start with agriculture.

Yet, despite successive development plans that focused on agriculture as an engine for economic growth, the sector and the economy remain relatively undeveloped. As with many African economies, Sudan's economy is structurally weak and disarticulated, and is arguably more vulnerable to external shocks. In addition to the direct cost of these shocks, economies that are perceived to react with inflexibility to adverse external and natural shocks may not be able to reap the benefits of enhanced investment under structural adjustment, since investors are wary of the same types of risk that are caused by political uncertainty. Diversifying the agriculture sector, especially its export base, in an effort to stabilize earnings and enhance the links between domestic production and domestic supply and demand, should thus be at the top of the poststabilization policy agenda for the Sudan.

One key challenge in the sector will be to enhance the structure of incentives. Although recent evidence suggests that the bias against agriculture through sector-specific policies (such as high taxes and fixed prices) was reduced substantially during the 1990s,[14] the dramatic macroeconomic policy failures of recent years have completely eroded the incentives in agriculture. The real exchange rate-induced effect on agricultural incentives, reflecting the macroeconomic policy-induced effect, was a staggering −43 percent during 1990–93, compared with −13 percent during 1979–85 (Hag Elamin and El Mak, 1995). The evidence clearly suggests that Sudan's agricultural policies – and, more important, its macroeconomic policies – should be reformed substantively before the playing field is level enough to support rapid agricultural growth and export expansion commensurate with the country's agricultural potential. Also lacking is a broader development strategy for agriculture that goes beyond macroeconomic and price reform – encompassing reform in, for example, marketing and financial mechanisms, the regulatory framework, cooperative and private sector participation, human capital development, rural infrastructure, technological support, and environmental sustainability (for a detailed discussion of these reforms in Sub-Saharan Africa, see Elbadawi, 1994).

The supply response of agriculture, which will ultimately determine the success of reforms and whether the sector can be the engine of growth in the Sudan, will not happen immediately, and its extent will vary according to the different components of the strategy. Macroeconomic and price reform, for example, can generate a supply response in the short run, but only a limited one. This response can be enhanced, however, if other agricultural policy reforms, such as extension services and improved input supply, are added. As observed by Cleaver (1993), the really huge payoffs may come only in the medium to long run. Such activities as credit, privatization, road construction, soil conversation, and land tenure reforms would yield effects in the medium term. Other components of the strategy, such as education, population policy, biodiversity conservation, and sound urban policy, will have an impact in the long run. These steps coincide with the four stages of agricultural transformation, each of which requires a specific set of policies (Table 10.4). As with many African countries, Sudan's agricultural sector is still at stage 1.

Table 10.4 Four stages of agricultural transformation

Phase	Defining characteristic	Key policies	Degree of government intervention
1	Factor productivity increases	Infrastructure development, research and extension efforts	High
2	Agricultural surplus develops	Taxation (through prices)	High
3	Private markets develop	Aggressive promotion of private markets	Indirect
4	Agriculture-like manufacturing	Income distribution, environmental protection	Outside agriculture sector

Source: Delgado, 1995.

The objective of Sudan's agricultural transformation should be to develop an environmentally sustainable, diversified agricultural base as a spearhead for another phase of diversification in which agro-industrialization and mining would be expanded. With the ratification of the Uruguay Round, developing countries should now find it easier to penetrate the markets of industrial countries, especially those in the European Union, with their processed agricultural exports (Chabrier, El-Erian, and Moalla-Fetini, 1995). Countries like Sudan, which produce both substantial and comparatively diversified primary agricultural products for export, can substantially enhance their terms of trade by expanding their processed agricultural export base. Aside from determining the most appropriate approach for effecting diversification, a breakthrough in the political impasse will be required in order to tap the vast and diversified agricultural potential and mineral resources of the south. In addition to achieving peace, Sudan will have to secure strategic regional cooperation arrangements before it can develop its irrigation and hydroelectric potential.

Industrialization and structural transformation

According to recent analyses of longitudinal data on international terms of trade for primary commodity exports relative to manufactured goods, the recent slowdown in terms of trade is part of a long-run secular decline, hence corroborating the famous Prebisch–Singer hypothesis (see Cuddington and Feyzioglu, 1993; Reinhart and Wickham, 1994). These findings suggest that the deteriorating terms of trade facing an agricultural export-based economy like Sudan is decidedly secular and that even temporary shocks tend to persist over several years. This prospect indicates that the importance of export diversification beyond agriculture as a paramount development objective cannot be overstated. The key question is, what is the best strategy for diversification?

One of the key implications of the Prebisch–Singer hypothesis is that the government should play a proactive role in determining the pattern of specialization. The deteriorating terms of trade for primary goods increases the relative prices of capital goods and thus provides an incentive for starting up a capital goods sector. But relative productivities matter, and for each price path one can imagine a path of relative labor productivities whereby capital goods production does not become profitable because productivity in that sector is growing at a low rate (Ziesemer, 1994). Governments can influence the pattern of specialization, particularly when there are significant effects for externalities and public goods. The example of human capital is a case in point. When the scarcity of progress-enhancing human capital makes the production of capital goods too expensive to be internationally competitive, investment in education can reduce the cost of producing capital goods and thus influence the pattern of specialization.

This view appears to be corroborated by the successful experience in East Asian countries. The initial industrialization in these countries exploited primarily their comparative advantage in unskilled labor. But as their industrial experience grew, real wages rose and the educational attainment and skills composition of their labor force increased, leading to the emergence of new industries with a comparative advantage (Krueger, 1981). Skills formation and an increase in technological capabilities were thus part of the experience of successful industrialization, and not merely a precondition for industrialization. As such, industrialization provided important feedback for building these capabilities, ultimately supporting shifts in comparative advantage.

The implication of this analysis for Sudan is that, given its baseline economic and social conditions, the government should help effect the transformation to a more diversified economy by investing in education and human capital, thus enhancing the international competitiveness of domestically produced capital goods. To effect this transformation, Sudan's economy would have to reduce its debt overhang substantially in order to free resources for investment and growth. Given the dominance of public debt in servicing requirements, reducing the debt overhang will help boost public investment and, through it, private investment and the absorptive capacity of the economy for growth.

Regional cooperation and integration

One of the basic arguments for economic cooperation is its potential impact on the credibility of national policy, providing a mechanism for collective commitment to economic reform in the context of a reciprocal threat-making arrangement (Collier, 1991). Furthermore, deeper economic integration in a given region can support the expansion of the regional economy, in that it generates the threshold scales needed to trigger strategic complementarity and to attract adequate levels of investment for developing modern manufacturing cores and the transfer of technology within the region (Krugman, 1991). The empirical literature also supports the growth-enhancing effects of economic integration. The most significant findings come from Sub-Saharan Africa: when, in addition to the standard growth fundamentals, spillover effects (such as those due to public investment or political instability) are accounted for, the process of economic growth in the region can be fully explained by variations in the growth fundamentals (Chua, 1993a,1993b). Furthermore, regional cooperation and coordination has been one of the primary determinants of the stellar performance of Southeast Asian countries (Elbadawi, 1995).

A new paradigm for regional integration in Africa and the Middle East, inspired by the experiences of postwar Europe and the recent "miracle" in East Asia, could be designed not only to foster the credibility of national policy but also to accumulate physical and human capital, triggered initially by enhanced foreign direct investment and later by regional savings and investment surges. Developing this strategy in the region could lead to the development of a participatory, supranational agency of restraint (like the European Union), and some of the stronger economies in the region could anchor this arrangement (see Collier, 1991; Collier and Gunning, 1993). As such, an otherwise poor and fragile economy such as the Sudan could gain policy credibility by committing to these arrangements, thus enhancing its ability to lure back flight capital and attract foreign direct investment.

Thus regional cooperation could have tangible benefits for Sudan. In fact, during its twelve years of peace (1972–83), when the (aborted) settlement of the southern problem was achieved, the country was able to use its geopolitical advantage and agricultural potential to attract petrodollar investment funds from the Arab world, and to serve as a base for an important pan-Arab development institution. Another important regional link comes from the significant number of migrant Sudanese working in the oil-surplus economies of the Arab world. Again, peace is a prerequisite if Sudan is to exploit its unique position in the Arab world – as a gateway to Africa – and develop a regional strategy conducive to its national development aspirations.

The state's role in development

Given the evidence on the importance of macroeconomic stability, microeconomic efficiency, and property rights to economic growth, the endogenous growth model identifies three broad roles for the state:

- To create an enabling environment for the private sector by delivering a stable macroeconomic environment and efficient microeconomic and institutional structures.

- To provide the necessary incentives for promoting adequate production and the transfer of technology through training, education, and research and development.
- To provide a level of public services and public goods (such as infrastructure, legal and regulatory frameworks, and so on) that is sufficient to generate maximum spillovers and serve as complementary inputs to the development process.

Given the unequal income distribution and vast poverty that prevails in Sudan, the endogenous growth-specified role for the state may not be enough to sustain growth and make a lasting impact on poverty. It is known that certain types of public spending on health and nutrition (and to some extent education) contribute simultaneously to consumption (and thus current utility) and human capital investment (and thus growth). The policy implications of this focus on a more comprehensive concept of human capital could be far-reaching. Unlike the contention in the endogenous growth literature that investment in physical capital and education can be achieved only through foregone consumption, this formulation posits that sustained growth requires a minimum level of consumption *above* the subsistence level. Indeed, a skewed income distribution and mass poverty may substantially inhibit the widespread accumulation of human capital and thus growth. Furthermore, to the extent that these undesirable social and economic conditions can cause social and political unrest that induces capital flight and reduces national savings, economic growth will be retarded even further.

A "basic needs" strategy (poverty alleviation, equitable income distribution, and so on) to support sustainable growth based on the accumulation of human capital could profoundly enhance the role of the state in the development process (Pio, 1994). According to this expanded paradigm of development, the state may also have to engage in a deliberate program of wealth and human capital redistribution (encompassing, for example, land reform, intensive scholarization, and targeted social assistance) if massive poverty or extreme income inequalities are baseline economic conditions. But two requirements must be met before the government can execute this added role successfully. First, it must implement growth-enhancing policies, since experience suggests that virtually no poverty reduction programs have succeeded with a "shrinking pie." Second, as with industrial policy programs, the government must enhance its implementation capacity to ensure that the targeted poverty reduction measures are efficient and effective. Experience also suggests that the extent of the government's intervention in these areas must be tailored to existing state capacity, as well as to its ability to mobilize political consensus behind the programs. Again, for Sudan, the governing regime must secure at least this last requirement as part of the national reconciliation process, while putting its implementation capacity at the top of the agenda in the economic reform program.

CONCLUSION

One of the main purposes of this paper has been to illustrate the potentially devastating implications of protracted political uncertainty for Sudan's capacity to conceive and implement a coherent development strategy. Civil war has destroyed both actual and potential productive capacity, particularly human, physical, and social capital. Rebuilding this capital, especially social capital, will take time. When and if peace is achieved, the Sudan should not expect substantial peace dividends in the short run. But with the flows of regional and international goodwill that normally follows the peaceful resolution of a major civil war, the country could reap immediate economic gains both directly from financial assistance and indirectly from the enhanced credibility of its political system and national economic policies.

Notes

1. The author is grateful to Dr. Mohamed El-Erian for helpful comments on an earlier draft. The author also acknowledges the research assistance of Sheila Nyanjui.
2. Although religious division has been the factor most often attributed to the separation of Sudan into the north and south, particularly by the Western media, a careful analysis of the crisis suggests that its origin is much more complicated. For example, although the majority of the educated elites in the south are Christians, fewer Christians than Muslims live in the south. Both cycles of civil war (1955–72 and 1983–present) also started when religious considerations were not among the major factors in the national political debate.
3. Sudan is the largest country in Africa and is endowed with a wealth of agricultural resources. It has a total cultivable area of 207 million acres, less than 10 percent of which is currently being cropped. It also has substantial water resources; all three Niles flow through the country, and an enormous amount of ground and surface water is available. Water resources are vastly underexploited, however, with about half of the

water potential being realized. Sudan's agricultural potential also lies in its sectoral diversity, with more than 4 million acres of irrigated land, more than 7 million acres of mechanized rainfed land, and about 10 million acres of rainfed land.

4. See Ali, 1985, and Brown, 1992, for a comprehensive assessment of the IMF-inspired reforms.

5. By 1984 an estimated 300,000–350,000 Sudanese nationals were working abroad, primarily in the Gulf states, earning a total annual income of $5.5 billion and accounting for 77 percent of recorded GDP (Brown, 1992). During 1983-84 remittances from Sudanese nationals ranged from $1.5 to 3.1 billion (Choucri, 1986).

6. Two other democratic regimes held power during 1956–58 and 1964–69.

7. The first period of civil war between Anya Nya (the military wing of the Southern Sudan Nationalist Liberation movement) and the government of Sudan began in 1955 and continued until 1972. The second period of civil war involving the Sudan's People Liberation Army – which is the military wing of the Sudan's People Liberation Movement – and splinter military and political groups began in 1983.

8. This section abstracts from a detailed discussion of the requirements for a peaceful settlement in Sudan. The literature on this area is vast (see, for example, Mohammed, 1993; Khalil, 1991, 1994). A small but growing literature on the political economy of civil wars and the conditions for peace is also emerging (Azam, 1994a, 1994b, 1995; Bates and Collier, 1995; Alesina and Spolare, 1994; Buchanan and Faith, 1987; Findlay, 1994; Wittman, 1991).

9. World Bank, 1993, provides a more comprehensive analysis of development experiences in East Asia. Lindauer and Roemer, 1994, provide a comparative analysis of economic development in Asia and Sub-Saharan Africa.

10. The government has recently undertaken drastic restructuring and privatization measures, but under an explosive macroeconomic environment. In addition, the policy reforms have been neither transparent nor free from political interests.

11. Spending on public health and education relative to GDP is much lower now than it was during the 1980s. At 4.0 percent in 1986, education expenditures in the Sudan were already lower than the average for the Middle East and North Africa (5.8 percent). Health spending that year was a meager 0.2 percent, less than a quarter of the average for Sub-Saharan Africa.

12. Ali, 1994, using the headcount method, estimates that the overall incidence of poverty in Sudan in 1993 was 91 percent (93 percent in rural areas and 84 percent in urban areas), compared with a rate of 78 percent in 1986. The current estimates suggest that poverty rose by 2.3 percent a year during 1986–93.

13. Sudanese nationals who acquired Egyptian real estate between 1982 and 1984 may alone have accumulated at least $1.25 billion (Harris, 1986). Harris estimates that foreign assets accumulated by Sudanese nationals are between $7 billion and $15 billion in recent years, while Ali, 1987, using a different methodology, arrives at $14 billion between

1977/78 and 1983/84. Elbadawi 1992, using yet another methodology, arrives at $12 billion for the 1973–88 period. These estimates suggest that Sudan accounts for about a quarter of the total flight capital from Sub-Saharan Africa (Brown, 1992).

14. The net protection coefficient, reflecting the effect of sector-specific policies on overall incentives for agriculture, increased from -16 percent during 1979–85 to 1 percent during 1990–93.

References

Alesina, A., and E. Spolare, 1994. "On the Number and Size of Nations," Harvard University, Department of Government, Cambridge, Mass.

Ali, A., (ed.), 1985. *The Sudan Economy in Disarray: Essays on the IMF Model*. London: Ithaca Press.

————— 1987. "How Wrong Can the World Bank Be? A Note on Capital Flight," University of Gezira, Sudan.

————— 1994. *Structural Adjustment Programs and Poverty in the Sudan*, Cairo: Arab Research Center for Studies, Documentation, and Publication (in Arabic).

Azam, J.P., 1994a. "Democracy and Development: A Theoretical Framework," *Public Choice* 80: 293–305.

————— 1994b. "Development Policy for Africa: A Research Agenda," Paper presented at the Organization for Economic Cooperation and Development's Development Centre Export's meeting on the future of Africa, (October), Paris.

————— 1995. "How to Pay for the Peace? A Theoretical Framework with References to African Countries," *Public Choice* 83: 173–84.

Bates, R., and P. Collier, 1995. "Wars of Secession," Harvard University, Department of Government, Cambridge, Mass.

Brown, R., 1992. *Public Debt and Private Wealth: Debt Capital Flight and the IMF in Sudan*, London: Macmillan.

Bruno, Michael, 1995. "Development Issues in a Changing World: New Lessons, Old Debates, Open Questions," in Michael Bruno and Boris Pleskovic, (eds.), *Proceedings of the World Bank Annual Conference on Development Economies 1994*, Washington, D.C.: World Bank.

Buchanan, J.M., and R.L. Faith, 1987. "Secession and the Limits of Taxation: Toward a Theory of Internal Exit," *American Economic Review*, 77(5):1023–31.

Chabrier, P., M. El-Erian, and R. Moalla-Fetini, 1995. "Implications of the Uruguay Round for the Arab Countries: A General Analysis," Presented at the seventh annual joint seminar on the Uruguay Round and the Arab Countries, (January 17–18), Kuwait.

Choucri, N., 1986. "The Hidden Economy: A New View of Remittances in the Arab World," *World Development*, 14(6): 697–712.

Chua, H., 1993a. "Regional Public Capital and Economic Growth," New Haven, Conn. Yale University, Economic Growth Center.

————— 1993b. "Regional Spillovers and Economic Growth," *Discussion Paper*, 700, New Haven, Conn. Yale University, Economic Growth Center.

Cleaver, K., 1993. *A Strategy to Develop Agriculture in Sub-Saharan Africa and a Focus for the World Bank*, World Bank Technical Paper, 203, Washington, D.C.: World Bank.

Collier, P., 1991. "Africa's External Economic Relations: 1960–90," *African Affairs*, 360 (July):339–56.

————— 1994. "Demobilization and Insecurity: A Study in the Economics of the Transition from War to Peace," *Journal of International Development*, 3.

————— 1995. "Civil Wars and Economics of the Peace Dividend," Oxford: University of Oxford, Centre for the Study of African Economies.

Collier, P., and J. Gunning, 1993. "Linkages Between Trade Policy and Regional Integration," paper presented at an African Economic Research Consortium conference on trade liberalization and regional integration in Sub-Saharan Africa (December), Nairobi.

Cuddington, J., and T. Feyzioglu, 1993. "Long-Run Trends in Primary Commodity Prices: Resolving Our Differences using the ARFIMA Model," Washington, D.C.: Georgetown University, Department of Economics.

Delgado, C., 1995. "Agricultural Transformation: The Key To Broad-Based Growth and Poverty Alleviation," presented at the Overseas Development Council conference on Africa's economic future (April 24–25), Washington, D.C.

Dornbusch, Rudiger, 1991. "Policies to Move from Stabilization to Growth," in Stanley Fischer, Dennis de Tray, and Shekhar Shah (eds.), *Proceedings of the World Bank Annual Conference on Development Economics 1990*, Washington D.C.: World Bank.

Easterly, William, and Klaus Schmidt-Hebbel, 1994. "The Macroeconomics of Public Sector Deficit: A Synthesis," in William Easterly, Carlos Rodriguez, and Klaus Schmidt-Hebbel (eds.), *Public Sector Deficit and Macroeconomic Performance*, Oxford: Oxford University Press.

Elbadawi, Ibrahim, 1988. "The Extent and Consequences of Direct and Indirect Taxation of Sudanese Agriculture," University of Gezira, Sudan.

————— 1992. "Macroeconomic Management and the Black Market for Foreign Exchange in Sudan," *Policy Research Working Paper*, 859, Washington, D.C.: World Bank.

————— 1994. "The Structure of Incentives, the External Environment, and Agricultural Supply Response in Sub-Saharan Africa," paper presented at the second international conference on African economic issues, (October 10–1), Arusha.

————— 1995. "The Impact of Regional Trade/Monetary Schemes on Intra-Sub-Saharan Africa Trade," paper presented at an African Economic Research Consortium research workshop on regional integration and trade liberalization in Sub-Saharan Africa, (March 5–8), Harare.

Findlay, R., 1994. "Towards a Model of Territorial Expansion and the Limits of Empire," New York: Columbia University, Department of Economics.

First, R., 1970. *The Barrel of a Gun: Political Power in Africa and the Coup d'Etat*, London: Allen Lane.

Fischer, Stanley, and William Easterly, 1990. "The Economics of the Government Budget Constraint," *World Bank Research Observer*, 5(2):127–42.

Hag Elamin, N., and S. El Mak, 1995. "Adjustment Programs and Agricultural Incentives in Sudan: A Comparative Study." final report presented at the African Economic Research Consortium research workshop, May 27–June 1, Nairobi, Kenya.

Harris, L., 1986. "Conceptions of the IMF's Role in Africa," in P. Lawrence, (ed.), *World Recession and Food Crisis in Africa*, London: James Curry.

Khalil, M., 1991. "The Crisis of Democracy and National Reconciliation in Sudan." paper presented at the Sudan Studies Association annual conference, (April 3), Lexington.

———— 1994. "Sudan's Democratic Experiment: Present Crisis and Future Prospects," *Northeast African Studies*, 1(2–3).

Knight, M., N. Loayza, and D. Villanueva, 1995. "The Peace Dividend: Military Spending Cuts and Economic Growth," International Monetary Fund, Middle Eastern Department, Washington, D.C.

Kok, P., 1992. "Adding Fuel to the Conflict: Oil, War, and Peace in Sudan," in M. Doornbos *et al.*, (eds.), *Beyond Conflict in the Horn: Prospects for Peace, Recovery, and Development in Ethiopia, Somali, and Sudan*, The Hague, *Netherlands*: Institute of Social Studies, in association with London: James Curry.

Krueger, Anne, 1981. "Export-Led Industrial Growth Reconsidered," in Wontack Hons and Lawrence Krause, (eds.), *Trade and Growth in the Advanced Developing Countries in the Pacific Basin.*, Seoul: Korean Development Institute.

Krugman, Paul, 1991. *Geography and Trade*, Cambridge, Mass.: MIT Press.

Lindauer, D., and M. Roemer, (eds.), 1994. *Asia and Africa: Legacies and Opportunities in Development*, San Francisco: ICS Press.

Mohammed, N., 1993. "Conflict in Southern Sudan," *Occasional Paper* 2. Cambridge: University of Cambridge, Global Security Programme.

Ndulu, B., 1995. "Economic Reforms and Development in Sub-Saharan Africa: What Have We Learned and What Are the Challenges Ahead?," paper presented at the Global Coalition for Africa meeting, (April), Washington, D.C.

Pio, A., 1994. "New Growth Theory and Old Development Problems: How Recent Developments in Endogenous Growth Theory Apply to Developing Countries," *Development Policy Review*, 12:277–300.

Ravallion, Martin, 1995. "Growth and Poverty: Evidence from the Developing Countries," *Economic Letters*, June.

Reinhart, C., and P. Wickham, 1994. "Commodity Prices: Cyclical Weakness or Secular Decline," *IMF Staff Papers*, 41(2):175-213.

Shafik, Nemat, 1994. "Big Spending, Small Returns: The Paradox of Human Resource Development in the Middle East," World Bank, Middle East and North Africa Regional Office, Washington, D.C.: World Bank.

Wittman, D., 1991. "Nations and States: Mergers and Acquisitions, Dissolutions and Divorce," *American Economic Review*, 81(2):126–9.

World Bank, 1993. *The East Asian Miracle: Economic Growth and Public Policy*, A World Bank Policy Research Report, New York: Oxford University Press.

———— 1994. *World Tables*, Washington, D.C.: World Bank.

Ziesemer, T., 1994. "Economic Development and Endogenous Terms-of-Trade Determination: Review and Reinterpretation of the Prebisch – Singer Thesis," *Discussion Paper*, 87, New York: United Nations Conference on Trade and Development.

11 Structural Adjustment and the Iranian Economy

Massoud Karshenas

Over the past twenty years Iran's relative ranking in the world economy has declined considerably. Comprehensive institutional reform is essential if this process of economic retrogression is to be reversed and sustainable growth achieved. This chapter identifies the needed reforms by studying the ill-fated reforms of the First Five-Year Plan. Contrary to the claim frequently made by critics of economic reform, Iran's current economic problems are not due to the excesses of economic liberalization and price adjustments under the plan, but rather to the reforms not being sufficiently far-reaching. A number of complementary institutional reforms are suggested as necessary prerequisites for the success of any future price reform and liberalization program.

After the Iran–Iraq war ended in 1988, the Iranian government embarked on a substantial economic reform and adjustment program within the framework of its First and Second Five-Year Plans. Foreign exchange reform, the relaxation of price and quantity controls, the removal of quantitative trade restrictions and a move toward trade liberalization, and the gradual removal of direct price subsidies were important elements of the program. A March 1993 attempt to unify the exchange rate was the high point of the reforms, followed by a phased reduction of government subsidies and increased trade liberalization. Inflationary pressures in winter 1993, however, led the government to once again delink the official exchange rate from the market rate. As a result the gap between the two rates has widened considerably. In addition, the system of government-controlled foreign exchange allocation has been partially reinstated, along with quantitative import restrictions. The slowdown in economic growth (particularly in industry and services), coupled with an acceleration in the inflation rate, has jeopardized the reform program.

Although the economic reforms were well-conceived and forcefully implemented, they failed to address the fundamental distortions in the real economy that developed during the second half of the 1970s. The remarkable regression of the Iranian economy during the 1980s, in addition to highlighting the adverse implications of poorly conceived policies and the need for economic reform, exacerbated these distortions. It is against this background that this chapter analyzes the economic reform program and its shortcomings, and offers suggestions for more comprehensive reform.

REGIONAL AND INTERNATIONAL PERSPECTIVES

The performance of the Iranian economy, whether considered in absolute terms or relative to other countries or regions, has deteriorated remarkably since the mid-1970s. Although the past two decades have seen a deterioration in growth for all the countries in the Middle East and North Africa, among the region's economies Iran's phenomenal decline in per capita income stands out (Figure 11.1).

During 1955–76 Iran exhibited growth rates achieved by only a few other major economies in the Middle East and North Africa or Asia.

Figure 11.1 Per capita income, Iran and various regions, 1955–92

1985 U.S. dollars

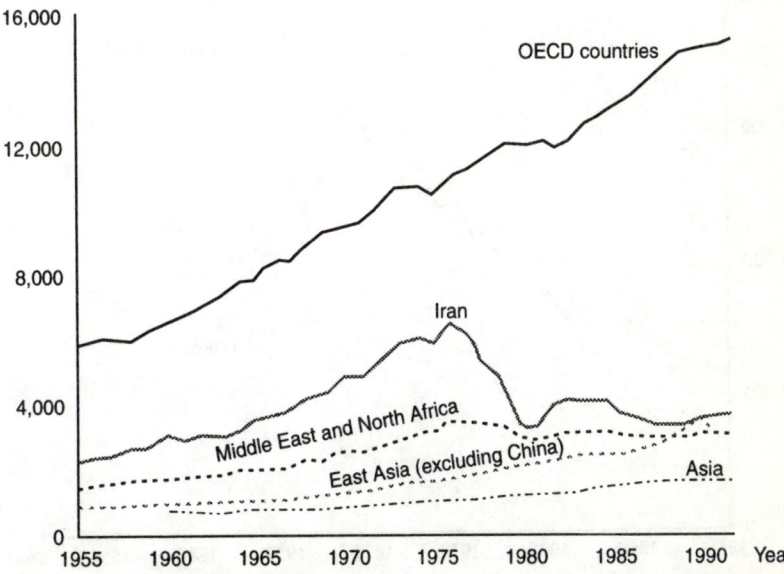

Source: PENN World Table (Mark 5).

Starting from already-high per capita income levels, by the mid-1970s
per capita income in Iran was nearly twice the regional average.
During this period the growth of gross domestic product (GDP) in
Iran was also higher than in the advanced industrial countries, making
Iran one of the few developing countries to reduce its income gap
relative to the industrial countries during this period. In 1975 Iran's
GDP per capita was far above any of the newly industrializing economies in East Asia. Since then, however, the Middle East and North
Africa in general and Iran in particular have seen growth slacken. By
the end of the 1980s East Asia had surpassed both Iran and the region
in this respect.

A comparison of the per capita incomes of Iran, the Republic of
Korea, and Turkey highlights the dramatic reversal of fortunes in the
Iranian economy since the mid-1970s (Figure 11.2). Until 1976 the
Iranian economy outperformed Turkey and kept pace with Korea in
terms of per capita growth. In 1976 per capita GDP in Iran was more
than twice the levels attained in the other two countries. During 1976-
90, however, per capita income in Iran collapsed, while the growth of

Figure 11.2 Per capita income, Iran, Republic of Korea, and Turkey
1985 U.S. dollars

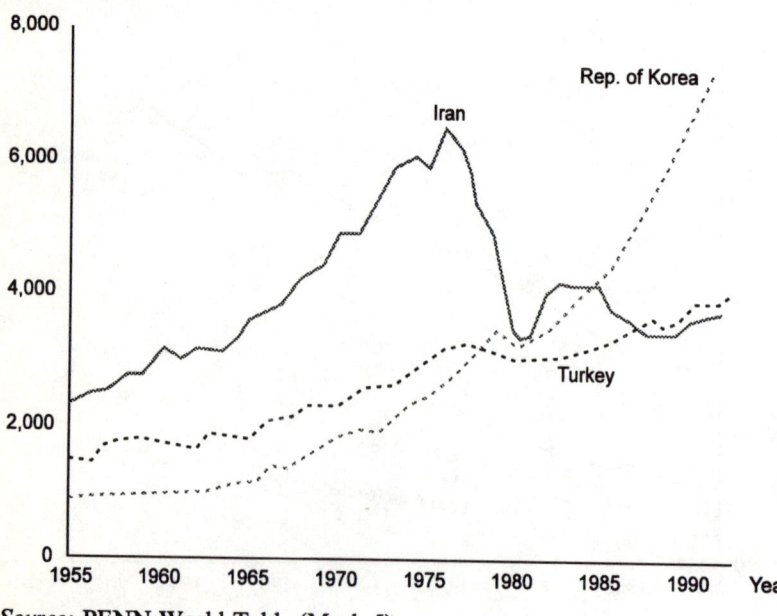

Source: PENN World Table (Mark 5).

the Korean economy continued and that of Turkey slowed. By 1990 GDP per capita in Iran had dropped by half – to levels prevailing in the early 1960s – while Korea had achieved per capita income levels twice those in Iran. Turkey also overtook Iran. By 1990 per capita income levels in Iran were closer to the Middle East and North Africa average, at a level close to those in Korea and other newly industrialized countries during the mid-1970s.

CAUSES AND CONSEQUENCES OF ECONOMIC DECLINE

The fundamental factors hindering economic reform and growth in Iran stem from the internal conditions that developed during the past two decades of economic stagnation. In addition, since the 1979 revolution the Iranian economy has been subjected to a number of external shocks. The revolution itself, the protracted war with Iraq, the freezing of Iranian assets, economic isolation, and the oil price shocks of the 1980s have taken their toll on the economy. The developments in the Iranian economy over the past fifteen years have been shaped by the government's policy response – within the preexisting structures of the economy and the newly emerging postrevolutionary institutions – to these debilitating circumstances.

The rapid economic growth in the two decades preceding the revolution occurred in the context of a strict import-substitution industrialization strategy in a highly protected domestic economy. Paradoxically, this strategy made the economy increasingly dependent on oil export revenues in order to finance the needs of the industrial sector for imported raw materials and capital goods. The problems associated with the distorted and inflexible industrial structure that developed during the prerevolutionary period were felt most acutely during the 1980s, when three decades of rapid growth in oil export revenues came to an end.

The postrevolutionary response

Early signs of stress, indicating the need for industrial restructuring, began to manifest themselves in the Iranian economy in 1976. The postrevolutionary regime, free from the political constraints that normally hinder the introduction of fundamental economic reforms, was in a unique position to introduce the needed economic restructuring. But policy interventions by the postrevolutionary government during the 1980s only increased the inefficiency and rigidity of the industrial structure that it had inherited from the old regime.

Immediately following the revolution, a considerable portion of the large-scale modern industry and the entire banking and insurance system were nationalized. To some extent these nationalizations were forced on the government, because in many cases the owners and managers of factories had fled the country and enterprises were on the verge of collapse. During the 1980s the regime continuously debated the role of the private sector and markets – as direct government controls over the economy increased. This process was spurred on by the demands of running a war economy. During the war the government introduced a complex system of rationing and direct subsidies for a large number of commodities. Government controls over other economic spheres also increased significantly during this period. Foreign exchange shortages led to import compression and foreign exchange controls and rationing. Shortfalls in oil revenue, at a time of increasing demand for government resources, led to substantial budget deficits that heightened inflationary pressures. Inflation also intensified the growing shortages resulting from import restrictions, economic sanctions, and war damage, encouraging further commodity rationing and government controls in the product markets.

Thus the government's expanded role during the postrevolutionary period was not solely or even primarily the result of a shift from private to public ownership. It was manifested in direct interventions in the operation of markets – foreign exchange controls, maintenance of a system of multiple exchange rates, control over interest rates and bank credits – as well as in direct price controls in a large number of product markets. Substantial price distortions gradually developed, with serious consequences for all economic activity, from investment to production, trade, distribution, and consumption (Karshenas and Pesaran, 1995).

The overvalued official exchange rate maintained by the government during the 1980s has received much attention (see Lautenschlager, 1986; Behdad, 1988; Pesaran, 1992; Karshenas and Pesaran, 1995). The premium on the black market rate increased rapidly from the time of the revolution, reaching 200–300 percent by the early 1980s, 500–600 percent by the mid-1980s, and more than 2,000 percent by the end of the 1980s. This twentyfold premium in the parallel exchange markets reflected the enormous subsidies the government was providing to the institutions and individuals that benefited from the government's foreign exchange rationing system. Similar subsidies were granted, directly or indirectly, to various consumer goods and key producer goods, such as energy. The government's consumer pricing policy during the war years combined subsidies, direct price controls, and a two-tier pricing mechanism for certain products. By the end of the war there was an extensive network of official markets for some 300 price-controlled products, with the prices of some key products (such as energy and bread) set at less than 10 percent of their international price.

Once the war ended, the disequilibrium and inefficiencies associated with the exchange rate and other controls forced the government to pursue a comprehensive liberalization and restructuring program. But the disequilibrium and distortions reflected deep-seated and fundamental maladjustments in the real economy, which made the task of reform particularly challenging. Because resource allocation and use during the war were based on administrative directives and quantity controls, these processes must be examined in order to assess the problems facing the government as it attempted reform. The developments in the manufacturing sector epitomize the problems arising from the distorted development of the Iranian economy during the 1980s.

Productive efficiency and the real exchange rate

Despite its criticism of the industrialization policies of the previous regime, the postrevolutionary government also pursued import-substitution industrialization policies. In fact, the import compression and various subsidies introduced in response to foreign exchange shortages increased the protection given to the domestic manufacturing sector. During the postrevolutionary period the public sector became more involved in industrial production, mainly through semipublic charities with strong political ties to the regime (for example, the Foundation of the Oppressed and Disabled). The public sector's enhanced role ensured continued subsidization of the manufacturing sector and the allocation of foreign exchange to enterprises at highly undervalued official rates during periods of severe foreign exchange shortages. Such policies exacerbated the distortions and inefficiencies that already existed in the sector.

Output, employment, and productivity in the manufacturing sector during 1963–90 are shown in Figure 11.3. During the postrevolutionary period the slowdown in the growth of foreign exchange revenues from the oil sector led to a considerable decline in the growth of

Figure 11.3 Manufacturing output, employment and productivity, Iran, 1963–90
Log (1980 = 100)

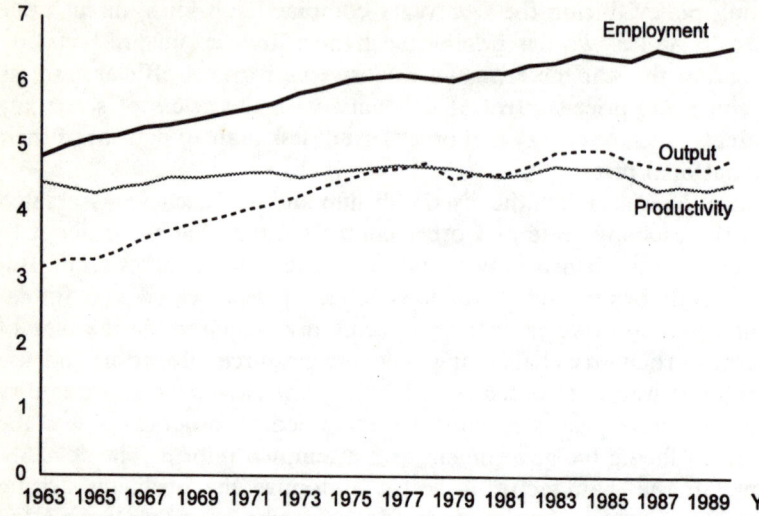

Source: UNIDO, 1994.

manufacturing output. The average annual rate of growth of output fell from about 11.6 percent a year during 1963–75 to 1.5 percent during 1975–90 (Table 11.1). Despite this decline, manufacturing employment continued to grow during the 1980s, leading to a phenomenal drop in labor productivity. Labor productivity in the manufacturing sector during 1977–90 fell by 2.3 percent a year, so that by the end of the 1980s productivity had fallen to levels prevailing in the mid-1960s – commensurate with the decline in overall GDP per capita discussed earlier.

Part of this decline in labor productivity can be explained by low investment and a lack of industrial renovation, as well as by the underutilization of capacity due to foreign exchange shortages and a lack of raw materials. But the main source of productivity decline was the continued growth of employment in the face of stagnant industrial output. Such inefficient labor policies could only take place in public enterprises, or in enterprises run by charities receiving sizable state subsidies. Such developments would be extremely unlikely in private enterprises subject to commercial norms, even if they were supported by large-scale state subsidies. The extreme inefficiency and low productivity in the manufacturing sector were major destabilizing factors for the reforms attempted in the 1990s.

Table 11.1 Structure and growth of the manufacturing sector in Iran, Turkey, and Republic of Korea
(percent)

Indicator	Iran	Turkey	Rep. of Korea
Output growth[a]			
1963–75	11.6	8.2	19.2
1975–90	1.5	6.4	10.5
Employment growth[a]			
1963–75	9.0	6.8	10.9
1975–90	3.7	2.0	4.5
Productivity growth[a]			
1963–75	2.6	1.4	8.3
1975–90	−2.0	4.4	6.0
Growth of real product wages[a]			
1963–75	4.3	1.3	7.2
1975–90	1.5	−1.1	7.1
Share of wages in value-added[b]			
1967–75	23.3	27.1	24.1
1980–5	53.9	24.8	27.2
1987–90	44.8	18.3	28.5
Raw material costs/wage bill[b]			
1967–75	6.9	5.4	6.8
1980–5	2.0	7.6	7.2
1987–90	2.4	9.4	6.0
Industrial markups[b]			
1967–75	41.9	42.6	41.0
1980–5	29.3	36.1	32.7
1987–90	36.1	44.0	36.2

a Annual average growth rates.
b Period averages.
Source: UNIDO, 1994.

The manufacturing sector also maintained distorted movement of wages and an inefficient cost-price structure. The trends in real product wages, the share of wages in value added, and the ratio of raw material costs to the wage bill in the manufacturing sector are shown in Figure 11.4. Despite the phenomenal decline in labor productivity during the 1980s, real product wages were higher in 1990 than in 1977 – when labor productivity in the manufacturing sector was at its

fffffdd*Figure* 11.4 Real wages and the cost and price structure in manufacturing, Iran, 1963–90

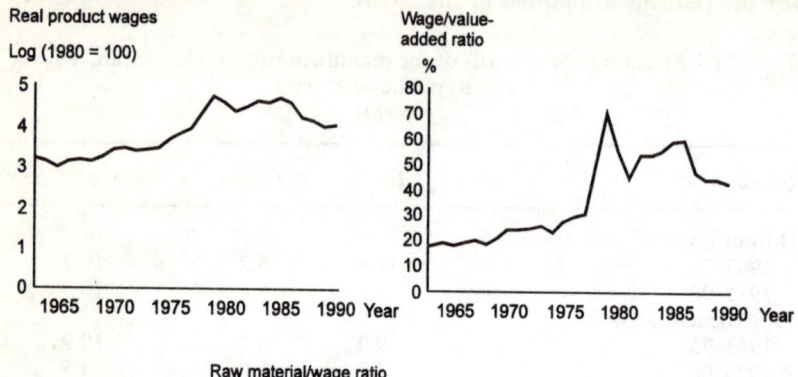

Source: UNIDO, 1994.

peak. Real wages increased substantially just before the revolution, when the old regime granted substantial wage hikes to appease striking workers. During the postrevolutionary period workers in the manufacturing sector were able to prevent this wage grant from eroding, despite their declining productivity. Considering that between 1977 and 1990 labor productivity in the manufacturing sector and real per capita incomes fell by more than half, this maintenance of real wages came at the expense of workers outside the manufacturing sector.[1]

The maintenance of real wages has resulted in a substantial increase in the share of wages in value added in the manufacturing sector. This share increased from an average of about 23 percent during 1967–75 to about 54 percent during 1980–85, falling to 45 percent during 1987–90 (see Table 11.1). A comparison with the share of wages in value-added in Korea and Turkey reveals Iran's abnormally high levels. In Korea wage shares ranged from 24–28 percent during 1965–90 despite the rapid growth of real product wages, mainly because of an equally rapid growth in labor productivity. In Turkey wage shares fell from a 27 percent average during 1967–75 to about 18 percent during the late 1980s, partly because of a relative improvement in labor productivity but to a larger extent because of real wage compression. Wage shares in Iran, which were similar during the prerevolutionary period to those in Korea and Turkey, increased in the 1980s to almost twice the levels in those two countries.

Even more significant, however, is that despite the phenomenal increase in the share of wages in value-added during the 1980s, industrial markups did not exhibit a commensurate decline. Industrial markups fell from a 42 percent average during 1967–75 to about 30 percent during the first half of the 1980s, and climbed to 36 percent during the second half of the decade. This approximates the movement of markups in the Korean manufacturing sector. The dramatic decline in the cost of raw materials in Iran made this apparently paradoxical outcome possible. The ratio of raw material costs to the wage bill in the Iranian manufacturing sector fell from about 7 during the prerevolutionary period to just over 2 in the 1980s.

To some extent the decline in the cost of raw materials was the result of excessive growth in the wage bill, as already discussed. But to a larger extent it resulted from huge government subsidies to the manufacturing sector in the form of substantially overvalued foreign exchange at the official rate and other price subsidies on raw materials (for example, cheap energy). In fact, without such subsidies – other things, including nominal and product wages and labor productivity, being the same – markups would have plummeted to 10–12 percent during the 1980s. It was only through these enormous subsidies that the manufacturing sector was able to finance the prevailing levels of real wages despite the rapid decline in labor productivity.

Using the ratio of the cost of raw materials to the wage bill as a proxy for the real exchange rate (the relative price of traded to non-traded goods), the drop in this ratio between the pre- and postrevolutionary periods reflects the substantial overvaluation of the exchange rate during the prerevolutionary period.[2] This index also helps identify the sources of the overvaluation: wage and price distortions and the low degree of production efficiency. The first source of overvaluation, wage and price distortions, can be corrected with price and exchange rate reforms, such as a unification and devaluation of the exchange rate with fixed money wages. The second source, however, requires that industrial production be restructured and production efficiency be improved. When this source of overvaluation is predominant, there may be no exchange rate at which the domestic industry is competitive, because domestic output prices will always be excessive compared with international prices, even at international input prices.

As noted above, the overvaluation of the Iranian rial in the postrevolutionary period was related to both these factors, but predominantly the second. On the one hand, given the drop in labor productivity, product wages were high, as were money wages relative to the highly subsidized prices of other inputs. But the overstaffing of the manufacturing sector and other production inefficiencies in the sector rendered the industry noncompetitive at international input prices. A successful reform and restructuring program requires that both these problems be addressed. If the problem of production inefficiency is neglected, the adjustment program may lead to excessive real wage compression, which in the long run may exacerbate production inefficiencies. Such a lopsided adjustment program, where an excessive burden is imposed on real wage compression, is likely to fail even in the short run, either because of political concern over declining real wages or financial instability and inflationary pressures resulting from real wage resistance on the part of workers.

EXCHANGE RATE REFORM AND ECONOMIC RESTRUCTURING

After the Iran–Iraq war the Iranian government embarked on an economic reform program within the framework of the First Five-Year Plan (1989–93). This program dismantled the network of price and quantity controls, planned for the gradual reduction of price subsidies on basic consumer goods and energy, reformed the foreign exchange system, removed quantitative trade restrictions, and gradually liberalized foreign trade. The exchange rate was unified in March 1993, followed by moves toward greater trade liberalization.

The reform program, however, has been impeded by the buildup of inflationary pressures and the rapid depreciation of the market exchange rate, with the reemergence of a widening gap between the official exchange rate and the market rate. As a consequence the government has reinstated the administered foreign exchange budgeting procedures and reintroduced some quantitative import restrictions. Though the setback to the price reforms and the foreign exchange unification program is intended as a temporary response to the foreign exchange crisis, delays in the urgently needed economic reforms will make future economic restructuring increasingly difficult. The continuation and smooth implementation of the reform program require an understanding of the factors that led to macroeconomic instability and the failure of the exchange rate unification program.

Booms and busts

Economic performance during the First Five-Year Plan, as gauged by overall growth indicators, was favorable. During 1989–93 the average annual growth rate of GDP was about 7 percent, with private consumption growing at 7.4 percent a year and gross fixed investment growing at 12.5 a year. Private fixed capital formation increased by more than 12 percent a year during the same period. But economic growth during this period had a haphazard quality and was clearly unsustainable. The economy was plagued by the boom and bust policies that had followed sudden jumps in oil prices in the past (Karshenas, 1990).

After the foreign exchange revenues from oil doubled between 1988 and 1990, the government embarked on a massive reconstruction and investment program.[3] Public sector investment during the 1989–91 period grew by more than 30 percent a year. The liberalization of foreign trade and the dismantling of the system of rationing and quantitative controls also led to extremely rapid growth of private consumption during this period. Private consumption increased by 19.5 percent in 1990 and 9.5 percent in 1991, as pent-up consumer demand was unleashed following partial liberalization of the economy (Table 11.2). Propelled by the rapid expansion of domestic demand, and eased by access to cheap credit and the easy availability of foreign exchange, private investment increased by more than 20 percent a year during 1989–91.

An economic boom of this scale was bound to be short–lived. Merchandise imports increased from about $13 billion in 1989 to well over $25 billion in 1991, giving rise to a current account deficit of $9.4 billion in 1991. Weaknesses in the oil market led to a considerable deterioration in the terms of trade, which further exacerbated foreign exchange shortages in 1992 and 1993.[4] The rapid buildup of foreign debt meant that growth eventually would have to come to an end. The plunge came sooner rather than later, due to the fact that a large part of the foreign debt incurred during 1991–92 was in the form of short-term suppliers' credits. By 1993 the stock of foreign debt was

Table 11.2 Macroeconomic indicators, Iran, 1988–93

Indicator	1988	1989	1990	1991	1992	1993
GDP (percentage change)	−7.8	3.5	11.6	11.5	5.9	1.6
Private consumption (percentage change)	0.5	2.5	19.5	9.5	5.4	2.3
Fixed investment (percentage change)	−15.9	6.4	13.3	40.9	6.9	2.7
Public	−18.5	1.0	30.8	31.6	3.3	n.a.
Private	−14.1	10.1	2.4	48.4	9.8	n.a.
Oil export revenues (million U.S. dollars)	9,673	12,037	17,993	16,012	16,880	14,333
Non-oil exports (million U.S. dollars)	1,036	1,044	1,312	2,649	2,988	3,747
Current account balance (million U.S. dollars)	−1,869	−191	327	−9,448	−6,504	−3,765
Government revenue (percentage of GDP)	12.2	14.2	18.5	17.2	18.1	21.6
Oil revenue	3.7	5.6	9.4	7.3	8.0	15.7
Exchange differential	0.7	2.8	6.3	5.2	6.3	8.2[a]
Tax revenue	4.5	4.4	4.7	5.7	5.9	4.3
Government spending (percentage of GDP)	21.6	18.2	20.5	19.5	20.0	21.7
Budget deficit (percentage of GDP)	−9.4	−4.1	−2.0	−2.3	−1.9	−0.6
Non-oil budget deficit	−13.1	−9.7	−11.5	−9.6	−9.8	−16.3
Domestic credit (percentage change)	17.8	21.5	18.5	23.2	21.0	25.2
Net credit to central government	22.3	16.6	2.4	9.4	0.7	−11.9
Credit to official entities	10.4	18.6	44.8	36.0	36.7	104.0
Private sector credit	11.7	32.4	41.2	38.2	38.2	32.8
Money supply (M2) (percentage change)	23.8	19.5	22.7	24.3	25.3	34.2
Wholesale prices (percentage change)	22.2	20.4	20.6	25.8	33.0	25.6
Interest rate[b]	8.5	8.5	9.0	9.0	10.0	11.5
Exchange rate						
Official rate (rials/dollar)	68.6	70.2	65.3	64.6	67.0	1,758.6
Weighted average (rials/dollar)[c]	236.6	302.8	415.6	511.2	579.0	1,224.2

a Measured as the domestic currency value of oil revenues converted at the unified rate minus the the value at the weighted average rate prevailing before the unification.
b Banking system's one-year deposit rate.
c Trade-weighted index of different exchange rates.
Source: Central Bank of Iran; IMF, 1995.

$19 billion, 70 percent of it short term. As a consequence, debt service obligations, equivalent to 3 percent of exports in 1990–91, reached more than 65 percent of exports in 1993, posing severe cash flow problems. Debt payment arrears reached $10 billion that year. The collapse of growth in 1993 was as abrupt as the short–lived boom of 1990–91. GDP growth in 1993 fell to 1.6 percent (IMF, 1995), with investment and private consumption growth falling to just over 2 percent (see Table 11.2). Because of the large current account deficit and substantial debt payment arrears in 1993, however, even these low rates of growth were unsustainable.

Exchange rate adjustments

Until the exchange rate unification of March 1993 a system of multiple exchange rates prevailed, with a wide spread between the official exchange rate and the free market rate. In January 1991, along with the partial liberalization of foreign trade, the multiple exchange rate system was simplified and the foreign exchange revenues from nonoil exports were allowed to be converted at the free market rate.[5] During 1988–92, however, the effective exchange rate was continuously devalued as various imports were shifted from the official to the competitive exchange category and others were shifted from the competitive rate to the free market rate category. (Of course, the devaluation of the free market rate resulting from inflationary pressures was another factor underlying the devaluation of the effective exchange rate.)

The effective nominal exchange rate – weighted by the share of trade conducted at various exchange rates – was devalued by about 100 percent during the 1988–92 period. This amounted to a substantial devaluation of the real exchange rate, considering that during this period the government also continued to subsidize basic food items and energy, and that a large share of industrial raw materials were imported at the low – and mostly fixed – competitive exchange rate. The value of nonoil exports increased from about $1 billion in 1988 to about $3 billion in 1992 in response to this devaluation (see Table 11.2).

The 1993 exchange rate unification at the prevailing free market rate implied a substantial further devaluation of the effective exchange rate. The impact of this devaluation, however, was very different from those implemented under the multiple exchange rate system. Under the unified exchange rate regime industries that had previously been able to acquire their imported raw material imports at the "competitive" exchange rate found themselves at a disadvantage. At the time such a move was essential in order to redirect scarce foreign exchange away from the old, inefficient industries with strong ties to the state toward new, export-oriented industries.

In November 1993, however, the free market rate begun to depreciate rapidly, and since December 1993 the government has effectively abandoned its exchange rate unification policy by severing the link between the official and the free market exchange rates. By December 1994 the free market rate was 50 percent higher than the official rate, and by May 1995 the premium on the free market rate was 260 percent of the official rate (which had remained fixed at 1,750 rials to the U.S. dollar since December 1994). At the end of May 1995 the government devalued the official exchange rate to 3,000 rials to the U.S. dollar and declared foreign exchange transactions in the free market illegal. Exporters were required to surrender their foreign exchange earnings to the banking system at the new official rate.

The instability of the exchange rate and the failure of the exchange rate unification scheme has received much attention both within and outside Iran. The timing of the exchange rate unification attempt, at a time of severe foreign exchange shortages, has been criticized. Some critics argue that it would have been more appropriate to unify the exchange rate all at once, at the beginning of the First Five-Year Plan. To minimize the inflationary impact of such a move and to allow sufficient time for the production structure of the economy to adjust to the new exchange rate, at the outset the indirect subsidies that accrued to the producers benefiting from the old preferential rate would have been replaced by direct subsidies. These direct subsidies, which could have been financed through revaluation of oil export revenues at the new unified exchange rate, would then be phased out according to a predetermined timetable. Considering that a large share of the industrial sector belongs either to the public sector or to semi-public charities, such a program could also have provided information on the extent of the indirect subsidies provided through the multiple exchange rate system, which would have been useful in planning a realistic restructuring program. The government's gradualist approach to exchange rate reform has also been criticized for its excessive encouragement of imports during the 1991–92 import boom, just prior to the planned 1993 unification of the exchange rate (Mazarei, 1995).

Having missed earlier opportunities to unify the exchange rate, however, does not necessarily imply that the government's attempt to unify the exchange rate in 1993 was unwise. Nor does it explain the instability of the exchange rate in the subsequent period. Some observers have blamed the instability of the exchange rate after the 1993 unification on the level at which the new unified exchange rate was established (Farzin, 1995). But even if there was a lower real equilibrium exchange rate that could reinstate external and internal equilibrium under the economic conditions prevailing in 1993, this does not address the stability of the nominal exchange rate, which is the main issue here.[6]

The stability of the nominal exchange rate following unification depends, first of all, on inflationary pressures in the economy, which in turn result from the fiscal and monetary stance of the government and the manner of resolution of the distributional conflicts that unification inevitably gives rise to.[7] In particular, in an oil-exporting economy like Iran, where exchange rate devaluation has important fiscal and monetary implications, the manner in which the government handles the financial consequences of the devaluation would significantly affect the stability of the exchange rate.

The devaluation of the exchange rate during 1988–93 substantially increased the government oil revenues denominated in domestic currency (see table 11.2). Until the 1993 exchange rate unification such increases were shown in the general budget as profits from the sale of foreign exchange at higher than the official rate. As a result of the devaluation of the exchange rate – despite the decline in the dollar value of oil exports from $17 billion in 1992 to just over $14 billion in 1993 – the domestic currency value of government oil revenues increased from 8 percent of GDP in 1992 to nearly 16 percent in 1993. Between 1988 and 1993 government revenue increased from about 12 percent of GDP to nearly 22 percent, a significant portion of which was accounted for by the revaluation of oil revenues at the depreciated exchange rate. Clearly, the government's approach to disposing of the increased revenues would have crucial implications for macroeconomic stability, particularly in the post–unification period. If the government had used these funds to subsidize imports – in order to neutralize the impact of the exchange rate depreciation on import prices – there would have been no major economic consequences and the move would have remained purely an accounting one.

Instead, the Iranian government opted to use the new funds to reduce its budget deficit. Government spending remained at about 20 percent of GDP during the First Five-Year Plan period, while the general budget deficit fell from 9.4 percent of GDP in 1988 to 0.6 percent in 1993. This may give the impression that the government followed a restrictive financial policy during the plan period, and hence that inflationary pressures and exchange rate instability, particularly after the 1993 exchange rate unification, remain paradoxical. But the general budget does not include the accounts of public enterprises and the semipublic charities. The general budget's revenue increases resulting from the devaluation of the rial, particularly after the exchange rate unification, were predominantly an income transfer to the central government from the public enterprises and semipublic charities that were the main beneficiaries of the multiple exchange rate system.[8]

The consolidated accounts of the public sector (including public enterprises and the semipublic charities) may therefore show a very different picture from that conveyed by the government's general budget. To the extent that such income transfers are not compensated for by either efficiency improvements in the public and semipublic enterprises or by the curtailment of their activities, the resulting deficits are likely to lead to credit expansion beyond the normal requirements to finance investment in the economy. The phenomenal increases in credit expansion to public enterprises and to the private sector, particularly after the unification of the exchange rate in 1993, attest to the highly inflationary fiscal stance of the state (see Table 11.2). The rate of private credit expansion, which stood at 12 percent in 1988, increased to 32 percent in 1989 and remained between 30 and 40 percent through 1993. Until 1992 these rates were commensurate with the high growth rates of real private consumption and investment. After the 1993 exchange rate unification, however, private credit expansion remained at 33 percent while private investment had come to a standstill.

This phenomenon is even more alarming in terms of credit extended to public enterprises. After the exchange rate unification the credits extended by the banking sector to public enterprises increased by 104 percent. At a time when public investment had come to a halt, this phenomenal increase signified the need for public enterprises to cover the losses resulting from the exchange rate unification.

This strategy was particularly profitable for the public and semipublic charities because they were able to access cheap credit at negative real interest rates. The inflationary pressures and exchange rate instability that resulted from the overexpansion of bank credit allowed these enterprises to exploit the government's policy of centrally administered credit rationing at low nominal interest rates. Exchange rate instability and inflationary pressures thus seem to have been the outcome of distributional conflicts that resulted from the exchange rate unification attempt and the government's inability to resolve these conflicts in accordance with the needs of its structural adjustment policies.

In particular, the move from a command economy to a market-based system required the restructuring or closure of the old, inefficient industrial establishments as resources shifted toward new, more efficient establishments. Instead, newly emerging private enterprises, encouraged by price incentives and relaxation of official controls, had to compete with the old establishments for scarce resources, predominantly foreign exchange. The ability of the old public enterprises and semipublic charities to rely on cheap bank credits put the private sector at a disadvantage in this competition. Yet the government and the central bank did not have the political clout to restrict credit to these establishments. The reintroduction of foreign exchange rationing and the substantial divergence between the official exchange rate and the market rate is a political victory for the interest groups connected to the old establishments, and for those who would benefit from access to rationed foreign exchange at the official rate due to their political influence. If this kind of rent-seeking behavior continues, it will thwart future reform programs, with serious consequences for economic growth.

SUGGESTED INSTITUTIONAL REFORMS

Iran's current economic crisis is rooted in instability – of industry, exchange rates, public sector management, and so on. Efforts to address these weaknesses have failed to achieve their goals because they have failed to go far enough. Iranian institutions and systems of governance must change if they are to cope with reform and its attendant challenges.

Fiscal reform

A major prerequisite for economic reform in Iran is the restructuring of inefficient industrial enterprises, which will involve major expenses for the government. In addition, successful adjustment will require additional government spending on education, health, economic infrastructure, and other core economic activities. The substantial reductions in the government budget deficit and the achievement of apparent fiscal balance during the adjustment program, noted above, were made possible by a general neglect of these essential items. The balanced budget was achieved largely through the use of the funds made available by the revaluation of oil revenues at an increasingly depreciated exchange rate. These funds should have been used to finance the renovation and restructuring of old industrial enterprises.

Evidence suggests that the balanced budget was also achieved through the neglect of other core government activities, particularly infrastructure investment. In order to finance the required spending of the adjustment program without incurring unsustainable budget deficits, the government will have to increase domestic resource mobilization by reforming the taxation system.

Central government tax revenue in Iran has fluctuated at about 5.0 percent of GDP for the past five years, with 2.8 percent coming from income and wealth taxes and 2.2 percent coming from indirect taxes. This compares with tax–GDP ratios of 15–25 percent in middle-income countries and 10–20 percent in low-income countries, making Iran one of the least-taxed economies in the world.[9] There is certainly considerable room for enhancing government revenues through efficiency improvements in the existing taxation system and the introduction of a value-added tax. This is essential not only to meet the extra spending requirements of the adjustment program, but also to sustain the core infrastructure investments needed for long-term economic growth.

Reform of charitable foundations

The commercial and charitable functions of the foundations that command considerable productive assets are incompatible. These functions must be separated. One approach would be to restructure the productive assets of the foundations into a number of independent companies whose shares are sold on the stock exchange. The funds raised could be reinvested in financial assets or held as shares of the newly created companies, with the revenues spent on public services and charitable activities. In this way the productive assets of the foundations would be managed according to commercial norms, and with the added efficiency and profitability more funds would be available to the foundations for charitable acts. There would also be the added advantage of transparency and accountability once the functions of the foundations are separated.

Industrial restructuring

The old public enterprises and semipublic charities are badly in need of restructuring. The continued existence of these industries in their present form is incompatible with the government's new export promotion strategy. It is imperative that an assessment of the commercial viability of these enterprises (with realistic shadow prices for their inputs and outputs) be undertaken. Under a new comprehensive industrial plan the government should help renovate key industries in which the country is likely to have static and dynamic comparative advantages. Of the remaining enterprises, those that are not a net foreign exchange drain should be maintained in the medium term, but attempts should be made to reduce overstaffing and improve efficiency through management and organizational reforms. Inefficient industries that are a net foreign exchange drain should be closed because they inhibit employment growth elsewhere in the economy. The privatization of public enterprises may proceed at the same time as or subsequently to such reforms.

Reform of labor institutions

Iranian labor relations and institutions are highly regimented and restrictive. The government imposes strict pay scales – indexed to the rate of inflation – on both public and private enterprises. This is particularly problematic during a period of rapid structural adjustment, when pay differentials need to be adjusted to the requirements of the market. Rather than being imposed by government decree, pay differentials and overall pay levels are best negotiated between employers and independent unions in a decentralized setting. Apart from ensuring better and more stable labor relations, this allows wage and employment outcomes to emerge in accordance with the realities of the marketplace, with efficient use of the information available to the workers and employers involved in collective bargaining. The workers councils in Iran are too centralized and politicized to be able to fulfill this function.

The labor law is also highly restrictive in terms of hiring and firing of labor. This is a major obstacle to the restructuring of old industries, and it inhibits rapid employment generation in the new, export-oriented industries. Given that the government has been unable to reform the labor law, a new, more flexible labor law should be introduced to cover (at least) enterprises that are established in the future. It should be recognized that the current labor law – contrary to what is often claimed – is not beneficial to the working class in general, and certainly not to the poor. The law only works to the advantage of certain interests that are linked to the organized labor institutions and, possibly, to the short-term interests of a small section of the working class in the organized sector.

Financial reform

As noted above, a major source of instability after the unification of the exchange rate was the overexpansion of bank credit to inefficient, loss-making enterprises. This outcome resulted from the problems facing the economic reform effort and the inability of the central bank to control credit expansion to different interest groups. To prevent this from recurring, the government should present a consolidated budget – including the accounts of public enterprises and semipublic foundations – to Parliament as a supplement to the government budget, with the credit position of the enterprises and foundations with the banking system separated from the accounts of the private sector. Full financial liberalization, particularly during a time of major reform and under current inflationary pressures, is not advisable. But negative interest rates should be avoided, and real interest rates in the banking sector should reflect the scarcity of capital in the economy. This is particularly important in Iran, where in the past the government and the central bank have been unable to control the rate of credit expansion in the face of political pressure from different interest groups.

Notes

1. Real wage increases are financed either by reducing the wages and consumption of other wage earners or by reducing the funds available for investment. When investment falls, other workers suffer as a result of reduced employment opportunities and slow productivity growth in the economy.
2. This measure of the real exchange rate is easier to calculate than the conventional measures for countries with multiple exchange rates and huge subsidies on input prices, and arguably a more meaningful one. For alternative measures of the real official exchange rate in Iran, see Pesaran, 1992.
3. Oil revenues increased from $9.7 billion in 1988 to $18.0 billion in 1990. This jump was partly due to price increases in the wake of Iraq's invasion of Kuwait and partly due to the expansion of output. Crude oil exports increased by 43 percent between 1988 and 1990, and by another 28 percent between 1990 and 1993, as production and export facilities damaged during the war were gradually restored.

4. Despite a more than 20 percent increase in crude petroleum export volumes between 1990 and 1993, oil export revenues fell from $18.0 billion to $14.3 billion during this time. Terms of trade deteriorated by about 20 percent between 1990 and 1993, implying an income loss of more than $3.7 billion.

5. The simplification involved a move from a seven-rate system to a three-rate system: the official exchange rate (70 rials to the U.S. dollar), the competitive rate (600 rials to the dollar), and the free market rate.

6. In fact, considering that the political situation in Iran dictates that the free market exchange rate is likely to have a premium over the equilibrium exchange rate, the unification of the exchange rate at the free market rate in 1993 could have amounted to an excessive depreciation of the exchange rate, rather than the opposite.

7. In this respect, the direct inflationary impact of the 1993 devaluation would have been relatively small, because the final consumer goods imports prior to the exchange rate unification were already traded at the free market rate, and subsidies for basic food items (bread, sugar, tea) were maintained after the unification.

8. As noted earlier, a distinction needs to be made between the impact of exchange rate devaluation prior to and after the exchange rate unification. During the earlier period, the main gainers from devaluation were the government, exporters, and the enterprises that benefited from a concessionary exchange rate on the input side but that sold their final product in the domestic market, where competing imports were converted at the free market rate. During the period of unified exchange rates these enterprises became the main losers, with the central government gaining the most.

9. In fact, disregarding the small oil-surplus economies (such as Kuwait, Saudi Arabia, and United Arab Emirates), Iran has the lowest tax–GDP ratio in the world. For example, in 1988 tax–GDP ratios in low-income countries such as India and Pakistan were 11.3 percent and 12.8 percent, respectively, and in other oil-exporting, middle-income countries such as Venezuela and Mexico they were 16.2 percent and 15.2 percent, respectively (World Bank, 1993).

References

Behdad, S., 1988. "Foreign Exchange Gap, Structural Constraints, and the Political Economy of Exchange Rate Determination in Iran," *International Journal of Middle East Studies* 20: 1–21.

Farzin, Y. H., 1995. "Foreign Exchange Reform in Iran: Badly Designed, Badly Managed," *World Development*, 23 (6): 987-1001.

IMF (International Monetary Fund), 1995. *International Financial Statistics*, Washington, D.C. : IMF.

Karshenas, M., 1990. *Oil, State, and Industrialization in Iran*, Cambridge: Cambridge University Press.

———— 1994. *Macroeconomic Policies, Structural Change, and Employment in the Middle East and North Africa*, Geneva: International Labour Office.

Karshenas, M., and M. H. Pesaran, 1995. "Economic Reform and Reconstruction of the Iranian Economy," *Middle East Journal*, 49 (Winter): 89–111.

Lautenschlager, W., 1986. "The Effects of an Over-Valued Exchange Rate on the Iranian Economy, 1979–1989." *International Journal of Middle East Studies*, 18: 31–52.

Mazarei, A., 1995. "The Parallel Market for Foreign Exchange in an Oil-Exporting Economy: The Case of Iran, 1978–90." *Working Paper*, 95/69, Washington, D.C.: International Monetary Fund.

Pesaran, M. H., 1992. "The Iranian Foreign Exchange Policy and the Black Market for Dollars," *International Journal of Middle East Studies*, 24: 101–25.

Riordan, E.M., U. Dadush, J. Jalali, S. Streifel, M. Brahmbhatt, and K. Takagaki, 1995. "The World Economy and Implications for the Middle East and North Africa Region, 1995–2010." paper presented at the World Bank workshop on strategic visions for the Middle East (June), Gammarth, Tunisia.

UNIDO (United Nations Industrial Development Office), 1994. *Industrial Statistics Database*, version 2.1. Geneva: UNIDO.

World Bank, 1993. *STARS*, version 3.0. Washington, D.C. : World Bank.

12 Policies and Economic Potential in the Countries of the Gulf Cooperation Council[1]

Hossein Askari, Maha Bazzari, and William Tyler

To ensure long-term economic security, countries whose economies are based on depletable resources must adopt policies that will enable them to maintain their standards of living after the resource is exhausted. For the countries of the Gulf Cooperation Council (GCC), development of a viable private sector to replace the public sector's large contribution to national output from oil is essential. Future prospects for these countries will be bleak unless appropriate policies are put in place before oil resources are exhausted.

Institutions and policies that enhance the business climate should be embraced and distorting economic policies should be eliminated. Government spending should be cut and indiscriminate subsidies should be reduced or abandoned. Other helpful policies include privatization of state enterprises, reduction of public sector employment, deregulation of markets (including the labor market), and establishment of a competitive real exchange rate.

During 1974–75 many observers predicted that the unprecedented transfer of wealth to oil-exporting countries would make many of these countries extraordinarily rich. Most of the optimistic predictions assumed that oil prices would not decline and that government policies would effectively transform this wealth into productive foreign or domestic assets. Nowhere was this oil more abundant, or growth more spectacular, than in the countries that make up the Gulf Cooperation Council (GCC) – Bahrain, Kuwait, Oman, Qatar, Saudi Arabia, and the United Arab Emirates.[2] Weighted average per capita incomes in the GCC countries rose from less than $1,000 in 1970 to $12,742 in 1976, dwarfing per capita incomes in the Republic of Korea

225

($740), Hong Kong ($2,730), and Singapore ($3,040) (World Bank, 1994b).

Table 12.1 Economic indicators, Gulf Cooperation Council, 1970–93

Indicator	Bahrain	Kuwait	Oman	Qatar	Saudi Arabia	United Arab Emirates	GCC total
Population, 1993 (millions)	0.5	1.4	1.7	0.5	16.4	1.7	22.3
Exports (billions of U.S. dollars)							
1970	0.2	1.7	0.2	0.2	2.4	0.2	5.0
1980	3.8	20.4	3.8	5.7	109.1	20.7	163.4
1993	3.7	10.5	5.4	3.4	39.4	23.3	85.7
Hydrocarbon exports (percentage of total exports)							
1970	78	94	100	96	100	96	94
1980	94	89	96	95	99	95	95
1993	70	95	87	77	96	70	83
Real GDP (constant 1985 billion U.S. dollars)							
1970	1.2	25.3	1.5	2.7	26.8	2.4	59.9
1980	3.8	30.7	5.0	5.9	111.0	28.6	185.0
1992	4.4	15.5	12.1	6.7	117.7	29.2	185.7
Real GDP per capita (constant 1985 U.S. dollars)							
1970	5,500	34,217	2,283	24,300	4,322	10,565	7,351
1980	11,290	22,409	5,081	25,691	11,843	28,365	13,931
1992	8,500	11,059	7,405	14,996	7,395	17,497	8,599
Average annual real GDP growth (percent)							
1970–80	13.7	2.5	13.4	9.1	15.7	31.0	12.2[a]
1980–92	1.3	−0.9	8.0	1.5	0.7	0.6	0.1[a]
1970–92	6.9	0.7	10.4	4.9	7.5	14.4	5.6[a]
Average annual real GDP growth per capita (percent)							
1970–80	8.9	−3.6	8.8	1.4	11.1	12.4	6.9[a]
1980–92	−2.2	3.6	3.4	−3.7	−3.6	−3.5	−3.4[a]
1970–92	2.9	0.3	5.9	−1.4	3.1	3.7	1.1[a]

a Weighted averages.
Sources: World Bank, 1994c; IMF and World Bank data.

Since 1976 income in the GCC countries has fallen, however, while income in other developing countries has increased. Average per capita income in 1993 stood at $12,012 in the GCC but had jumped to $7,526 in Korea, $12,971 in Hong Kong (1992 figure), and $19,286 in Singapore (World Bank, 1994c). This stagnation in per capita income can be partly explained by oil prices: in real terms petroleum prices were lower in 1993 than they were in 1975. Other factors have also been at work. None of the GCC countries has been able to diversify its economy away from an overwhelming dependence on oil, and none has developed sound economic policies.

Various economic indicators measuring the economic performance of the GCC countries since 1970 are shown in Table 12.1. By any measure change has been rapid; gross domestic product (GDP), GDP per capita, and export revenues have increased significantly, especially during the 1970s. Moreover, economic growth has been accompanied by a dramatic improvement in the welfare of the general population.

Under normal circumstances such rapid economic and social change would have to be accompanied by broadly based economic growth, a thriving private sector, and growing exports, most likely in high-income and price-elastic manufactured goods. In the GCC, however, GDP has at times declined at rates approaching those of a depression by OECD standards. For example, Saudi Arabia's real GDP fell from $111 billion in 1980 to $87 billion in 1985; real per capita income went from $11,843 to $7,001 over the same period. During 1980-92 average annual GDP per capita growth rates were negative in Bahrain (−2.2 percent), Qatar (−3.7 percent), Saudi Arabia (−3.6 percent), and the United Arab Emirates (−3.5 percent).

These developments can be attributed to several factors. The region's governments have pursued policies to rapidly benefit the average citizen – transforming an almost primitive infrastructure into that of a modern industrial state; enhancing basic social services such as health, education, and housing; developing a national defense; and financing sustained development. Although a great deal of success has been achieved in certain areas – especially in infrastructure development and in the delivery of social services – structural reforms and policies to promote sustainable development have not been put in place. The public sector is still dominant. The heavy dependence on oil continues. The participation of expatriate labor is high. Structural budget and current account deficits have emerged. These adverse developments have been exacerbated by declining real oil prices and revenues and high population growth rates.

The GCC governments have also paid insufficient attention to other necessary elements of a modern industrial state. Because institutions have not been adequately developed, transparency in decisionmaking is lacking. Efficiency considerations – in the education system, in health care delivery, in the functioning of labor markets – have been neglected. These issues were viewed as less critical when oil revenues were high, but have become increasingly urgent because oil prices have fallen over the past decade.

ECONOMIC POLICY IN DEPLETABLE RESOURCE-BASED ECONOMIES

The conceptual interpretation of net national product (NNP) in an economy is that it represents the highest level of sustainable consumption. In the development of the conceptual framework for national income accounting, extractive (depletable) industries are treated like any other source of national product, and the value of the extracted resource is thus added to national product at the point of extraction (that is, at the earliest point of production and sale).

This method of valuing the contribution of extractive industries in national income accounting, particularly in relation to maximum sustainable consumption, is ill conceived. To grasp why, imagine an economy that derives its total national output from depletable resources. If all the natural resources were depleted and consumed in the current year, conventional national income accounting would assign a high value to national product in the current year and a zero value in the subsequent year. This inconsistency was not important until the 1970s, when several oil-exporting countries began deriving a large part of their national product from oil.[3] This observation, in turn, has had profound implications for the interpretation of national output and for the nature and assessment of economic policies in natural resource-based economies.

An intertemporal model of a depletable resource-based economy

In order to derive the economic policy implications of this observation, we can assess how the conventional measure of NNP must be adjusted for a depletable resource-based economy or how much extra savings is required to compensate for resource depletion. These two assessments are theoretically identical in nature and rely on a simple notion. A large part of current NNP (derived from depletable resources) must be saved and invested in order to compensate for resource depletion, thus reducing conventionally measured NNP in order to derive maximum sustainable consumption (that is, theoretically correct NNP for a depletable resource-based economy).

For an economy that is 100 percent depletable resource-based, the ratio of conventional NNP to theoretically correct NNP is given by

$$Y/Y^* = 1/rT \qquad (12.1)$$

where Y is conventionally measured NNP, Y^* is theoretically correct NNP, r is real rate of return on investment, and T is life of oil reserves (in years).[4]

The result is intuitive. The higher the return that is earned on investments (that is, the greater the compensation for resource depletion) and the higher is T (that is, the longer the resource will last at the current rate of extraction), the closer are the conventionally measured and theoretically correct NNP. For an economy that is less than 100 percent depletable resource-based, this formula can be adjusted to

$$Y/Y^* = Y(\alpha) + (1 - \alpha)/rT \qquad (12.2)$$

where a is the proportion of NNP that is nondepletable resource-based.

An alternative way of looking at the problem is that depletable resource-based economies need a higher savings rate while the resource is contributing to national output in order to compensate for resource depletion.

For an economy as characterized above, the rate of required saving (to equate conventional and theoretically correct measures of NNP) is

$$S = 1 - rT(1 - \hat{S}) \qquad (12.3)$$

where S is the required savings rate and $\hat{S}$ is the desired post-resource savings rate. $\hat{S}$ establishes where the society wants to be when the resource is depleted (that is, the long-run savings rate). Similarly, for an economy that is not totally dependant on oil,

$$S = \alpha\hat{S} + (1 - \alpha)[1 - rT(1 - \hat{S})] \qquad (12.4)$$

This characterization of a depletable resource-based economy assumes that real oil prices increase exponentially at a rate equal to the real return on investment. (Although the equality is not a constraint and can be relaxed, the change in oil prices is an important unknown.) It also recognizes that uncertainty in oil prices, real rates of return, and the size of oil reserves are difficult to incorporate into the model. A simple approach to compensate for this deficiency is extensive sensitivity analysis. In general, however, uncertainty would call for higher rates of resource extraction and thus for even higher savings rates than those indicated (and an even lower theoretically correct NNP than without uncertainty).

Acknowledging these limitations does not affect the central message that, in order to maintain living standards, depletable resource-based economies must save and invest a significant portion of their current revenues from resource extraction to compensate for resource depletion over time.

Implications for savings and investment

The immediate policy implications of the analytical framework relate to savings and investment. The basic question is straightforward: Are the GCC countries attracting sufficient savings to compensate for the depletion of nonrenewable oil resources? Put another way, is the conversion of oil wealth resulting in the creation of sufficient productive assets to sustain future levels of consumption after the depletion of oil?

In terms of the model outlined above, the required savings rate, S, changes over time (as T changes with time); at the point at which the resource is depleted, $S = \hat{S}$. Thus it is possible that S may take on negative values in earlier years, when T is large, r is high, and $\hat{S}$ is moderate. But what should the savings rate be for GCC countries in order to achieve the necessary economic structural change today? Table 12.2 indicates the sensitivity of S to the contribution of oil to national output $(1 - \alpha)$, quality of investment (r), and life of oil reserves (T), which in turn depends on the size of oil reserves and on the rate of extraction (assuming $\hat{S} = 0.20$).

The actual and required savings rates for various values of r, using actual life of reserves and assuming $\hat{S} = 20$ percent, are shown in Table 12.3. Before examining GCC savings performance, some observations are worth noting. First, the dependence of individual GCC countries on oil $(1 - \alpha)$ and the expected life of oil reserves (T) vary greatly across countries. Second, the quality of investment (r) is critical for long-term economic performance in affecting the value of the required savings rate, yet it is difficult to assign a realistic value to r. To the extent that countries invest abroad, there are some useful indicators of historic returns for the United States (Ibbotson Associates, 1994).

Table 12.2 Required savings rates with different life of oil reserves, size of nonoil economy, and rates of real return

Share of nonoil economy in total economy and rate of real return	Life of oil reserves (years)				
	20	40	60	80	100
Nonoil economy = 40 percent					
$r = 0$ percent	68	68	68	68	68
$r = 0.5$ percent	63	58	54	49	44
$r = 0.75$ percent	61	54	46	39	32
Nonoil economy = 60 percent					
$r = 0$ percent	52	52	52	52	52
$r = 0.5$ percent	49	46	42	39	36
$r = 0.75$ percent	47	42	38	33	28

Source: Authors' calculations.

Table 12.3 Actual life of oil reserves, size of nonoil economy, and national and required savings rates, GCC (percent)

Country	Life of oil reserves (years)	Share of nonoil economy	National savings rate		Required savings rate			
			1980	1993	$r = 0$	$r = 0.005$	$r = 0.006$	$r = 0.01$
Bahrain	5	87	50	23	30	30	30	30
Kuwait	136	57	62	22	55	31	26	8
Oman	17	66	34	19[a]	47	45	45	43
Qatar	20	67	42	—	47	44	44	41
Saudi Arabia	82	63	51	27	50	37	35	25
United Arab Emirates	110	60	66	33[b]	53	35	31	17

— Not available.
a 1990 data.
b 1988 data.
Source: Authors' calculations based on World Bank, 1994c; British Petroleum, 1994; IMF data.

With the possible exception of Kuwait and the United Arab Emirates, most GCC countries have chosen to invest the bulk of their official foreign assets in the treasury bills of major industrial countries. Given the long-run (1926–93) average annual rate of return on U.S. Treasury bills of 3.7 percent and the long-run U.S. inflation rate of 3.1 percent, investment in Treasury bills would result in a long-term real return on foreign assets (r) of about 0.6 percent. To the extent that these assets are more diversified and better managed, r could be significantly higher. Although the return on domestic investments is impossible to estimate given the governments' distribution of sectoral investments and the small private sectors, it is unlikely that the aggregate domestic real rate of return has exceeded that of foreign investments.

Given these rough approximations for rates of return, several general conclusions can be made. First, the rate of required saving increases dramatically as life of oil reserves decreases, quality of investment declines, and dependence on oil increases. Second, an oil-rich country that makes unproductive investments ($r = 0$) needs a very high savings rate now to achieve a savings rate of even 20 percent when the oil runs out. Third, in comparing these results with actual figures, the assumed quality of the GCC countries' investment is critical. Depending on the value of this variable, they have saved more than enough or fallen far short of what is necessary.

Life of oil reserves has fluctuated as a result of changing extraction rates and new oil discoveries. At the low end is Bahrain, with five years of reserves remaining in 1993; at the high end is Kuwait, with 136 years of reserves remaining in 1993. Saudi Arabia and the United Arab Emirates each have about 100 years of remaining oil reserves, although extraction rates may rise faster than addition to reserves and oil substitutes could reduce the economic life of oil. The share of the nonoil sector in GDP varies among countries, although differences in these figures may stem partly from differences in the way these figures are defined. Finally, savings in all the GCC countries have declined since 1981, with national savings rates differing from country to country and fluctuating significantly from year to year.

Are savings rates adequate to compensate for oil depletion? Until 1981 savings rates appear to have been adequate. After 1981 the answer depends largely on what is assumed about the rate of return on investment. If real rates of return are assumed to have been 1 percent or more, then Bahrain and Oman are the only countries with inadequate savings. If real rates of return are assumed to have been 0.6 percent, Qatar and Saudi Arabia also have inadequate savings.

Implications for macroeconomic policy management

If the optimal or required level of savings is less than what is dictated by the need to compensate for oil depletion, the direction of policies should be changed. First, governments should cut spending and introduce a broadly based and progressive tax system to raise revenues and address current and intergenerational equity. Second, governments should pursue policies that stimulate private sector development, including deregulation of labor markets, privatization, and liberalization of financial markets. Third, governments should adopt exchange rate policies that increase the profitability of exports and thus encourage the development of export industries. These changes – which represent the minimum for beginning the move toward a modern industrial state – can be sustained only if the necessary institutions, with transparency of decisionmaking, are established.

Implications for the external sector

The external sector of an economy that depends on depletable resources differs from the external sector in other countries. The general presumption is that external accounts should be roughly in balance, and one would expect industrial countries to have a current account surplus and developing countries to have a current account deficit to finance economic development and growth.

For GCC countries the extraction and export of oil is tantamount to a the sale of an asset. The proceeds from oil exports are used, in part, to finance domestic development and export diversification. As a result the trade account is presumed to run a surplus while oil is being depleted, especially during the early extractive years. In fact, this is true for all the GCC countries except Bahrain (Table 12.4). Similarly, one would expect a persistent surplus on the balance of goods and services. Although service outflows (engineering, construction, consulting, and the like) can be expected to be large, oil export revenues and service inflows from foreign investment income should more than compensate. Furthermore, current account balances in the GCC countries should exhibit a persistent surplus during most of the extractive phase. (This may not be the case in the unlikely event that numerous and highly profitable domestic investments exist.)

However, several GCC countries – including Bahrain, Oman, and Saudi Arabia – have run current account deficits.[5] Bahrain's current account deficit can be explained by its lower reliance on oil and gas

Table 12.4 Trade and current account balances, GCC, 1980 and 1992

Country	1980		1992	
	Billions of U.S. dollars	*Share of GDP (percent)*	*Billions of U.S. dollars*	*Share of GDP (percent)*
Bahrain				
Trade balance	0.5	14.5	−0.3	−7.8
Current account balance	0.2	5.8	−1.0	−24.8
Kuwait				
Trade balance	13.9	48.7	0.1	0.4
Current account balance	15.3	53.7	−0.9	−4.0
Oman				
Trade balance	2.0	32.8	2.1	17.8
Current account balance	0.9	15.7	−0.4	−3.2
Qatar				
Trade balance	4.4	55.7	1.8	26.0
Current account balance	2.7	33.5	−0.2	−2.7
Saudi Arabia				
Trade balance	75.2	64.8	13.0	11.7
Current account balance	41.5	35.8	−19.4	−17.5
United Arab Emirates				
Trade balance	14.1	47.7	5.9	16.9
Current account balance	10.1	34.0	3.0	8.5
GCC total				
Trade balance	110.0	44.0	21.9	10.8
Current account balance	70.6	29.7	−18.2	−7.3

Note: GDP in current prices. Trade balance defined as trade in goods and nonfactor services.
Sources: World Bank, 1994c; IMF and World Bank data.

than other GCC countries, while Oman's is a reflection of the government's fiscal deficit. Also reflecting a serious fiscal imbalance is Saudi Arabia's current account deficit, which has persisted in every year since 1982. Although the rapid deterioration in 1990–91 was caused by the Gulf war, the persistence of the deficit is clearly structural and divergent from what could be expected given appropriate policies for a depletable resource-based economy. The policy change suggested by the current account deficit is clear – domestic spending and absorption should be reduced and nonoil exports encouraged.

Recommended policies for diversifying the export base

In addition to adopting appropriate policies for promoting private sector growth, governments must adopt a supportive real exchange rate policy if nonoil exports are to grow. A significantly overvalued exchange real rate will make exporting unprofitable, regardless of what other steps are taken. Real effective exchange rates in the GCC countries have depreciated since 1985, largely because of the depreciation of the dollar (coupled with fixed parities to the dollar). Still, exchange rates are not competitive enough to promote nonoil exports, which have shown little growth over the past twenty years.

GCC governments have historically argued that exchange rates are of little importance because oil is exported at an internationally set dollar price. While it is true that oil exports are largely unaffected by changes in the exchange rate, nonoil exports are unlikely to develop unless a competitive exchange rate policy or even more massive export subsidies are adopted. There is, however, a political dilemma. The private sector and the public have become accustomed to an overvalued exchange rate, which subsidizes domestic consumption. This method of subsidizing domestic consumption is inefficient, however, and hinders the development of nonoil exports. A more efficient way to maintain domestic consumption without affecting nonoil exports would be through direct fiscal transfers, as has been done in the U.S. state of Alaska.

Non oil exports have also been held back by overly generous government spending, which has increased inflation in nontradables (much of it not captured in official figures) and resulted in allocation of resources toward nontradables. This policy could be altered to support the growth of nonoil exports by providing production (output) subsidies to industries (for a limited duration) in which the countries enjoy a long-term comparative advantage.

THE ROLE OF THE STATE

The basic responsibilities and functions of the public sector are traditionally defined as providing public goods, promoting efficient resource allocation, maintaining macroeconomic growth and stability, and ensuring some norms of distributional equity (Musgrave, 1959). Although the extent of government contribution to domestic economic activity varies greatly across countries, in market-based economies the private sector is invariably the main contributor to national output. The underlying presumption is that the private sector provides goods and services more efficiently and that the public sector should provide goods and services or intervene in markets only when there is market failure.

The GCC governments, by contrast, have made income distribution a guiding tenet of their economic and political strategies. Oil revenues accrue to the state, and governments distribute these proceeds to citizens. The GCC governments have eschewed making direct payments to citizens, preferring to use the state apparatus to channel resources. This approach has created bloated public sectors, with extensive public employment and pervasive government involvement in the economy. Benefits are transferred to the population in several forms: public employment, limited taxation, a comprehensive welfare system, and generous direct and indirect consumer and producer subsidies.

These benefits, with their attendant distortionary effects, have had widespread and adverse economic and social effects. By introducing enormous distortions in product and factor markets, they have contributed to economic inefficiencies and resource misallocation. Questions of equity, compounded by the way producer subsidies are provided, have developed. Private sector development has been impeded. The work ethic has been eroded. A reliance on expatriate labor has subverted national initiatives. As a result the GCC economies can be classified as both market-based and command economies.

Public sector finances

In a depletable resource-based economy where resource revenues accrue to the government, it would be expected that the government would not run budget deficits during years of heavy resource extraction. This expectation is all the more important if there is no broadly based tax system in place.

An examination of revenues and expenditures for each of the GCC governments, however, reveals that this is often not the case (Table 12.5). All the countries have experienced budgetary deficits at some point since 1983. Oil provides the bulk of government revenues. Development expenditures account for a small share of government spending. Five of the six GCC countries are among the world's top military spenders (as a percentage of GDP). Thus spending patterns in the region do not conform to expectations for depletable resource-based economies, and these countries have achieved little diversification of their revenue base.

Table 12.5 Revenues, expenditures, and budget balances, GCC, 1970–92 (percentage of GDP)

Country	1970	1975	1980	1985	1992
Bahrain					
Revenues	30.3	30.3	33.6	36.2	28.5
Oil as a share of revenues (percent)	—	—	71.8	66.8	65.5
Expenditures:	26.4	26.4	27.4	36.5	37.2
Current	—	—	59.8	62.4	76.7
Investment	—	—	39.2	36.7	23.3
Budget balance	—	1.3	5.9	1.0	−7.2
Kuwait					
Revenues	36.5	71.6	89.3	59.0	47.3
Oil as a share of revenues (percent)	—	—	69.8	69.7	76.6
Expenditures:	—	23.5	27.7	47.7	71.3
Current	29.5	—	59.0	66.1	88.9
Investment	—	—	17.0	23.6	11.1
Budget balance	5.8	41.7	58.6	7.8	−35.8
Oman					
Revenues	40.1	53.3	38.8	38.7	39.1
Oil as a share of revenues (percent)	—	—	89.2	83.8	78.4
Expenditures:	36.8	57.9	38.8	50.1	40.3
Current	—	—	73.0	72.7	79.2
Investment	—	—	27.0	27.3	20.5
Budget balance	—	−9.9	0.4	−10.5	−13.2
Qatar					
Revenues	51.1	72.2	66.4	43.3	47.5
Oil as a share of revenues (percent)	—	—	87.8	84.5	70.4
Expenditures:	37.3	53.7	38.2	69.6	50.3
Current	—	—	71.8	75.6	89.2
Investment	—	—	28.2	24.3	10.8
Budget balance	5.7	18.5	28.1	−26.3	−3.4
Saudi Arabia					
Revenues	—	—	70.7	42.5	36.2
Oil as a share of revenues (percent)	85.3	—	75.5	66.2	76.8
Expenditures:	—	—	54.7	58.6	39.7
Current	—	—	48.8	40.5	69.2
Investment	—	—	51.2	48.8	17.4
Budget balance	—	—	21.5	−16.1	−8.9
United Arab Emirates					
Revenues	30.8	4.4	16.0	7.3	12.5
Oil as a share of revenues (percent)	—	85.3	95.5	83.3	88.4
Expenditures:	2.3	2.3	12.1	9.5	13.0
Current	—	40.6	49.8	63.9	78.1
Investment	—	—	50.1	36.1	21.8
Budget balance	1.5	1.5	2.1	−2.2	−3.4

— Not available.
Sources: IMF data; World Bank, 1994c.

Subsidies

Extensive subsidies – covering, among other areas, housing, health care, education, electricity, water, fuel, and capital costs – have also contributed to budget deficits in the GCC countries. Because these subsidies generate economic distortions and lead to reduced standards of living for future generations, they are inconsistent with long-term goals. Moreover, official subsidy figures grossly underestimate the true level of subsidies because they exclude many nonbudget items (such as fuel and capital subsidies and fiscal transfers for operating losses for electricity and water).

One way of classifying subsidies is by sector and type of subsidy (operating or capital). Operating subsidies require a cash outlay for current transactions and include subsidies for such items as wheat, essential commodities, electricity operations, desalination operations, and fuels (lost revenue). Capital subsidies are loans made at subsidized interest rates. The real amount spent on subsidies can be calculated by incorporating the multiplier effects of a dollar spent on domestic subsidies versus a dollar spent on foreign investment, the true value of the resulting output (at shadow prices), and so on. Because foreign exchange is not a binding constraint on GCC countires and there is thus no premium attached to foreign exchange earnings, foreign exchange effects are not applicable.

Data limitations make it difficult to estimate subsidies for each of the GCC countries. Moreover, estimation of the implicit subsidy embedded in water consumption – the largest single subsidy – depends on the opportunity cost used for nonrenewable sources of water, which account for about 70 percent of water consumption in the GCC countries. Still, rough calculations suggest their magnitude. Estimated subsidies in Saudi Arabia, for example, were $17.6 billion in 1994, compared with the official figure of $2.98 billion (Askari, 1990). The divergence between estimated and official figures can be explained largely by the exclusion of fuel ($6.64 billion) and capital ($6.56 billion) subsidies from official figures. In 1975 subsidies in Saudi Arabia accounted for 2.4 percent of GDP and 4.3 of oil revenues; by 1984 these figures were 36.1 percent of GDP and 68.4 of oil revenues. Fuel, electricity, and water subsidies account for the lion's share of subsidies in the GCC. The size of these subsidies varies dramatically from country to country, with Saudi Arabia providing the highest level of subsidies and Oman providing the lowest (Table 12.6). These subsidies have led to dramatic growth in the consumption of fuels, electricity, and water, with ominous implications. For water, rapid depletion of nonrenewable sources will increase the need for desalination plants. For electricity and fuels, given OPEC quotas on oil production, less oil is available for exports. The environment is also adversely affected and less oil will be available for future generations.

Table 12.6 Fuel, electricity, and water subsidies, GCC, 1980–92 (millions of U.S. dollars)

Country	1980	1985	1990	1991	1992
Bahrain	281	318	524	525	540
	(9.14)	(8.59)	(13.42)	(13.17)	(13.54)
Kuwait	1,035	1,100	1,571	1,716	1,729
	(3.63)	(5.13)	(8.77)	(15.33)	(7.95)
Oman	33	25	278	301	281
	(0.55)	(0.25)	(2.64)	(2.94)	(2.44)
Qatar	508	881	843	782	664
	(6.46)	(14.32)	(11.46)	(11.71)	(9.47)
Saudi Arabia	7,755	10,760	13,726	13,315	14,085
	(6.69)	(12.41)	(13.65)	(12.26)	(12.65)
United Arab Emirates	1,207	1,412	2,233	2,620	2,676
	(4.08)	(5.23)	(6.54)	(7.63)	(7.60)

Note: Numbers in parentheses are percentages of GDP.
Source: Authors' calculations.

Overall policy considerations

To achieve intergenerational equity, governments should pursue policies that ensure adequate savings, deliver high returns on an appropriate mix of foreign and domestic investments, develop social and physical infrastructure, promote competitive private and financial sectors, diversify the domestic economy and export base, and implement a broadly based tax system to diversify the government's revenue base.

Have GCC governments adopted these kinds of policies? In terms of savings, the experience has been mixed. The United Arab Emirates has consistently achieved levels of savings that are adequate to sustain consumption after oil wealth has been depleted (see Table 12.3). In most years Kuwait has had adequate savings; Oman and Saudi Arabia have had several years of adequate savings followed by years of inadequate savings. Only Kuwait has an explicit national savings policy to sustain economic activity after the depletion of oil, however – the government puts 10 percent of current oil revenues into a fund for future generations.[6] Given the expected duration of its oil reserves, Kuwait has the least obvious need for such a fund. These reserves proved invaluable during the Gulf war and its aftermath, however.

Regarding return on investments, it is difficult to judge the adequacy of returns on foreign investments without a breakdown of such investments. Domestic investments, often relating to large, energy-intensive industries (refineries, petrochemical plants, aluminum smelters), are often quite profitable, although their economic viability in the absence of substantial direct and indirect subsidies would be less certain. In addition, domestic investment has generally emphasized physical rather than human capital. Except for Kuwait, none of the GCC countries has a formal policy on the mix of domestic and foreign assets. Domestic expenditures (directly and indirectly through subsidies to the private sector) are generally pursued to the limit of absorptive capacity (and beyond), and foreign investments are made with the residual.

Social and physical infrastructure have been developed rapidly, with overcapacity in some areas and undercapacity in others. The social return on infrastructure is difficult to measure, however. GCC countries generally view physical infrastructure as a prerequisite to productive investment – with infrastructure in place and generous subsidies, it thought, a private sector will develop and provide needed employment for citizens. While it is true that infrastructure is important, private sector development requires complementary policies and programs, and public sector projects must be based on long-term comparative advantage.

As has been seen, the private sector in the GCC countries remains relatively small. Governments maintain a simplistic attitude toward private sector growth, relying on investment in infrastructure and indiscriminate subsidies. The results have fallen short of expectations. Moreover, regulations and conflicting government policies stifle the financial sector from participating in domestic growth and development.

Although public investments – and to a much lesser degree, private investments – have benefited nonoil exports, progress in developing nonoil exports has been slow, with petrochemicals the only significant area of success. Conflicting government policies have been the primary cause of slow progress. While subsidies have been generous, the form of subsidies has been inappropriate (input subsidies rather than output subsidies) and the GCC countries have adopted employment and exchange rate policies that do not support the growth of nonoil exports.

GCC governments have been reluctant to tax their citizens, but this luxury is no longer affordable. Moreover, a broadly-based, progressive tax system can be used to address both budgetary and equity issues. For instance, if a government favors rapid private sector development, it can address equity through taxes, by broadening and enhancing its revenue base. Tax systems would take about ten years to develop. If GCC governments delay the implementation of such systems, they risk financial conditions that could become much worse if policies are left unchecked. As it stands, no instruments are in place to promote intragenerational and intergenerational equity or broaden the government's domestic revenue base. Although there is no real poverty in GCC countries (at least among citizens), income distribution appears to be highly skewed.

PRIVATE SECTOR DEVELOPMENT

Infrastructure and subsidies have been the cornerstone of GCC governments' policies to foster private sector development and achieve social objectives. Government procurement practices and spending patterns also influence private sector growth. The coverage of these elements varies depending on a country's size, population, oil revenues, and policies.

Government subsidies to the private sector

Subsidies were introduced in the mid-1970s to distribute oil revenues and purchasing power to citizens. General government expenditures and later input subsidies were also targeted to help develop a viable nonoil sector. Over time the role of subsidies expanded to promote the private sector's role in economic diversification in all the GCC economies. Subsidies are targeted to enhance purchasing power, improve wealth distribution, achieve domestic stability, promote basic industries, and promote the private nonoil sector. GCC governments provide their private sectors with low interest loans, sell electricity and water below long-run average and marginal costs of production and fuels below opportunity cost, distribute subsidized land, and subsidize seeds and transportation for agriculture (Askari, 1990). Agriculture has also been subsidized through both input subsidies and price support for strategic commodities.

The main problem with input subsidies to industry and agriculture is that they misallocate economic resources and so distort production. A basic tenet of economic theory is that issues should be addressed at their source. Thus if subsidies are warranted, production subsidies – not input subsidies – are called for. Furthermore, only industries in which a country has a long-run comparative advantage should be supported, and even then only until they become globally competitive.

Effect of subsidies on the private sector

Subsidies have not achieved their desired goals. Instead, they have generated extreme economic distortions. Moreover, the wealthy have benefited the most (in absolute terms) from government generosity. Policies other than subsidies should have been used to attain the governments' goals. Direct transfers and progressive taxation could have enhanced purchasing power, improved wealth distribution, and achieved domestic stability. But governments did not have accurate censuses, most citizens did not know how to read or write and could not manage large fiscal transfers, and taxes were unpopular with the ruling elite and require a long time to be instituted. Overprovision of these subsidies resulted in product and factor market distortions that have added to economic inefficiencies, worsened resource allocation, increased income inequities, and lowered general welfare. Yet the private sector and the general public are accustomed to indiscriminate subsidies, and significantly reducing them and changing the direction of policies would be politically difficult.

Input subsidies have had other undesirable consequences. Consumption of electricity, water, and fuels has increased dramatically. In addition to the direct economic costs of these growing consumption rates, there have been attendant indirect costs, including air pollution and damage to underground aquifers from seepage of waste and rapid rates of withdrawal. Rapid increases in domestic consumption have also reduced oil exports and thus export revenues. More important, if the growth of subsidies goes unchecked, rapid population growth and subsidized prices will reduce export revenues even further by increasing domestic fuel consumption.

Subsidies must be cut. Long-run marginal cost pricing is the efficient way to price services (and net-bank price for fuels) for the private sector and households. Such pricing – possibly accompanied by output subsidies to the private sector and cash transfers to poor citizens – should be phased in over time to reduce undue hardships on the private sector and on the less advantaged members of society.

Creating a healthy private sector

The first prerequisite for the development of a healthy private sector is the establishment of the rule of law – that is, an environment in which no one is above the law and commercial laws are respected and enforced equitably by courts. Without this basic foundation business people will prefer to invest elsewhere. A second necessary element is the establishment of free and flexible goods and factor markets. A third prerequisite is a government that has a clearly defined economic program, promotes efficiency rather than political expediency, and is fiscally responsible. A fourth element is a business climate in which government economic policies are freely debated and discussed.

Much has been written about appropriate economic policies. Research into the miracle economies of East Asia has documented several broadly accepted lessons (World Bank, 1993b). These lessons include the importance of a market-oriented economy, fiscal responsibility, a tax structure that encourages investment, financial liberalization, export-oriented growth, appropriate credit expansion, flexible labor markets, relatively uniform and declining tariffs, provision of more opportunities for the private sector, and privatization.

Large quantities of depletable resource make the task facing the GCC governments both easier and more difficult. On the one hand, oil export revenues can finance investment and growth, thus reducing the need for external borrowing. On the other hand, maintenance of steadily growing net national product requires that the GCC governments transform their economic base into nonoil assets, through domestic or foreign investments.

Developing financial markets

To differing degrees the GCC governments have financed large projects and provided the private sector with low-cost and long-term financing. The governments' rationale for financing large projects has been twofold. First, the large capital requirements and potential risks were beyond the capabilities of a nascent private sector. Second, in certain areas pressing social needs required investments that small and developing private sectors were unwilling to finance. In addition, subsidies to the private sector were intended to stimulate rapid private sector development.

The provision of public sector financing for investment precluded the nascent financial sector from competing and operating in this arena. Banks eschewed medium- and long-term lending and concentrated on accumulating foreign assets and making short-term loans. The limited participation of commercial banks in domestic development has led many financial institutions in the GCC to place a significant portion of their assets in foreign financial markets. In addition, GCC stock markets have a short history, and market capitalization and depth are limited. Equity funding in the GCC is small because the private sector is small.

The private financial sector could play a critical role in promoting a healthy and vibrant private sector. For that to happen, however, governments would have to be committed to holding debtors accountable for interest and principal; financial deregulation would have to be introduced, including more freedom for commercial banks, abolition of interest rate ceilings, freedom of banks and nonbanks to issue instruments to meet investor needs, and freedom to establish private investment banks; and governments would have to withdraw from subsidized financing of the private sector.

Privatization

Privatization has contributed to private sector development and economic growth in many countries. While privatization is itself an important consideration for success, the economic context in which it occurs is also critical. Privatization is beneficial only if economic policies support private sector growth. Before introducing a broad program of privatization, the GCC countries should assess their overall economic policies and in particular their policies toward the private sector.

Saudi Arabia is the only GCC country that has privatized any public sector industries, first with the Saudi Arabian Basic Industries Corporation (SABIC) in 1984 and then with electric companies in 1985. Both entities continue to receive direct (the electric companies) and indirect (both SABIC and the electric companies) subsidies. Saudi Arabia is considering further privatization of public goods and service industries, including the telephone company and the national airline. The sequencing of overall policy reforms and privatization will be a critical factor in determining the success of these programs.

LABOR MARKETS

The rapid oil price increases of 1973–4 and the resulting rise in government expenditures caused severe labor shortages to develop in most GCC countries. These shortages were caused by two related factors. Increased government spending – especially for large public infrastructure projects – required an inflow of technical and professional personnel and blue-collar labor. Rapidly increasing government spending also led to substantial increases in personal incomes and private activities, requiring an immediate increase in professional, blue-collar, and menial labor. Shortages, concentrated at the lower and upper ends of the labor market, were ameliorated by an influx of foreign labor. The expectation was that the technical and professional labor shortage would continue for some time because of the long gestation period in developing indigenous substitutes. For blue-collar and menial labor the shortage was expected to stabilize and to decline as household employment stabilized and large projects were completed. However, the share of expatriate labor has increased, or at best stabilized, over time (Table 12.7).

Table 12.7 Expatriate labor as a share of total labor force, GCC, 1975–90
(percent)

Country	1975	1980	1985	1990
Bahrain	80.3	59.3	67.7	75.0
Kuwait	69.8	78.1	81.1	82.0
Oman	45.5	40.0	56.6	75.4
Qatar	85.5	81.6	75.5	81.0
Saudi Arabia	25.2	58.3	64.2	78.6
United Arab Emirates	81.4	89.7	87.6	83.5

Source: Gamelidin, 1994.

Blue-collar and menial workers come from India, Pakistan, the Philippines, Sri Lanka, Thailand, Malaysia, Yemen, and the Republic of Korea. Professional and technical workers come from Western countries and to a lesser extent from Japan and Arab countries outside the Persian Gulf. Other Arab countries provide teachers, professors, and managers of small enterprises.

Expatriate labor is concentrated in the private sector, for a number of reasons. The public sector mainly employs citizens, who prefer the public sector's bloated salaries. Other benefits of public sector employment – vacations, housing allowance, travel allowance, security – also have attracted citizens. Promotions and salary increases are less dependent on job performance in the public sector than in the private sector. Moreover, the private sector prefers to employ expatriates. Salaries can be lower, social security payments for expatriates are not strictly enforced in some countries, and employers can fire expatriates on the spot. As a result the public sector accounts for a significant share of nationals' employment, especially in Kuwait, Saudi Arabia, and the United Arab Emirates.

In the face of growing unemployment and underemployment of citizens, some GCC governments are pursuing two separate but related strategies: increased public sector employment and rules and regulations to induce the private sector to employ more nationals. These programs, carrying such monikers as Bahrainization, Saudization, and Omanization, have been popular with citizens but detrimental to private sector development and growth, since they are akin to a tax on the private sector. Given the region's declining oil revenues, budgetary deficits, and growing population pressures, government employment and current labor policies are unsustainable, and GCC governments should assess the long-run implications of their current policies.

Government labor policies

The GCC countries adopted different labor policies before and after 1984. Between 1974–75 and 1983–84, when oil revenues were high and the budget and current account enjoyed surpluses, governments allowed free inflow of expatriate labor from most countries; devoted resources to the education of citizens and provided scholarships for studies abroad; employed virtually any citizen seeking employment in the public sector; set salaries and benefits in the public sector significantly above those available in the private sector; and restricted participation of women in the labor force.

After 1984, when oil prices and growth rates fell, some GCC governments realized that constantly increasing public employment was neither sustainable nor desirable. Public sector employment benefits were reduced, most notably in Saudi Arabia, or increased less rapidly than in the past, and governments adopted policies to increase the employment of nationals in the private sector. Direct policies came in the form of pressures (not strict quotas) to employ nationals in government contracts; indirect policies imposed strict regulations requiring minimum local content on domestic contracts. At the same time, GCC governments reduced their financial support for nationals studying abroad and relaxed rules restricting female participation in the labor force.

GCC countries have also encouraged domestic population growth on the grounds that larger populations would provide a better national defense and limit the participation of expatriate labor. As a result the GCC's weighted average annual population growth rate was 5.1 percent during the 1970s. During the 1980s populations in the GCC countries grew by 4.8 percent, compared with 2.0 percent for all developing countries and 0.6 percent for industrial countries. Projections for the 1990s show a similar picture.

These policies have contributed to a number of distortions. GCC labor markets are highly segmented between the public and private sectors, between male and female workers, and between nationals and expatriates. Unemployment is emerging rapidly. Because nationals enjoy a competitive advantage in public sector employment, private employers that hope to attract nationals must offer employment packages that are significantly more generous than those required for expatriates. Conflicting and distortionary policies toward employment were not a problem during the boom years, but with declining per capita growth, rapidly deteriorating government finances, disappointing private sector growth, brisk population growth, and increased female participation in the labor force, employment of nationals will become a major social issue if it is not addressed. Moreover, rapid population growth will do little to displace expatriate labor, since nationals and expatriates cannot easily substitute for one another in the workplace.

Two emerging issues affecting the labor market should also be noted. First, the age structure of the GCC populations indicates that increasing numbers of nationals will be entering the labor force and seeking employment (Table 12.8). Especially in Saudi Arabia and Oman, a large proportion of the population is under the age of fifteen, resulting in a high dependency ratio. At the same time, rapid population growth and increased education mean that many more graduates joined the labor force during the 1980s than during the 1970s, and projections suggest that this trend will continue. The GCC countries will have to provide many more jobs for nationals; to be economically viable employment must be increasingly in the private sector. Second, the policy of providing free university education for nationals has

Table 12.8 Population structures, GCC, 1960–90
(percent)

Country	1960	1965	1970	1975	1980	1985	1990
Share of population less than 15 years old							
Bahrain	43.6	50.8	45.9	42.6	34.6	33.1	32.6
Kuwait	35.3	38.3	43.4	44.5	40.4	37.2	35.5
Oman	43.6	44.1	44.2	44.8	44.0	44.4	46.5
Qatar	35.6	30.0	28.8	28.1	27.9	29.1	31.0
Saudi Arabia	43.3	44.0	44.5	44.3	44.2	44.8	45.3
United Arab Emirates	41.8	38.2	35.0	28.3	28.7	30.7	30.7
Dependency ratio							
Bahrain	85.7	111	93.9	82.4	58.0	54.3	53.0
Kuwait	59.8	66.8	82.2	85.1	71.5	62.2	58.1
Oman	85.1	87.0	88.0	90.6	87.4	87.9	96.3
Qatar	69.6	70.0	65.3	65.4	50.0	55.2	58.3
Saudi Arabia	87.4	89.7	112	89.7	88.6	90.2	92.1
United Arab Emirates	85.1	67.8	59.6	44.0	42.6	47.4	48.0

Note: The dependency ratio is the sum of the population less than 15 years old and above 64 years old, divided by the population between 15 and 64 years old.
Source: World Bank data; Gamelidin, 1994.

produced a domestic labor force that is not equipped to work in the private sector. Government policies guaranteeing public employment have made many GCC nationals not consider future employment opportunities when choosing their studies. Instead nationals have concentrated on public administration, neglecting engineering, accounting, medicine, teaching, and other professions in demand in the labor market. According to a survey by the Saudi Chamber of Commerce, only 5,570 of the 16,259 Saudis that graduated from national universities in 1994 found jobs in the public sector. Increasing public sector employment and restrictive labor laws, although possibly ameliorating social problems in the short run, will prevent the transformation of these economies by reducing public savings and retarding private growth. A different approach is needed.

Recommended policy changes

Policymakers must implement a number of changes to increase the flexibility and efficiency of labor markets:

- The hiring and firing of nationals should be deregulated and the artificial gap between public and private sector remuneration should be abandoned.
- Subsidies that encourage rapid population growth should be eliminated. Such policies adversely affect future employment opportunities and place a heavy burden on natural resources. Moreover, given the fact that domestic labor and expatriate labor are not perfect substitutes, it is unlikely that rapid population growth will soon reduce the demand for expatriate labor.
- Public sector compensation should be cut and the size of the public sector workforce should be reduced through attrition.
- Pressures on the private sector to employ nationals should be eliminated and impediments to female labor force participation should be reduced. Female labor force participation is low in GCC countries (9 percent in Bahrain, 7 percent in Kuwait, 0.9 percent in Oman, 7.7 percent in Qatar, 3.2 percent in Saudi Arabia, and 1.6 percent in the United Arab Emirates). Easing the constraints on female participation will exacerbate unemployment problems. Still, such constraints should be systematically eliminated over the next few years because they will reduce the need for expatriate labor. In conjunction with these policies, stricter work permit requirements for expatriates should be adopted.
- Incentives should be established for nationals to pursue studies in fields in demand by the private sector. This should be a transition policy while labor markets are being liberalized and work permits for expatriates are being restricted. In the longer term free and flexible labor markets and the elimination of governments' distortionary salaries and benefits will encourage nationals to pursue studies that are in demand by the labor market.

POPULATION, RESOURCES, AND THE ENVIRONMENT

The projected rapid increase in GCC populations has significant economic and environmental implications. This growth will require well-formulated policies that generate higher savings and investment, increase private sector growth, and foster economic diversification. Unless productivity is enhanced, rapid population growth will limit the potential benefits of oil, gas, and other natural resources for nationals and exacerbate intergenerational equity. Population growth also has dramatic implications for the size of future subsidies and for pressure on other natural resources, especially water for domestic consumption and oil for exports.

Oil and gas resources

Kuwait, Saudi Arabia, and the United Arab Emirates are in a different league from the other GCC countries when it comes to oil reserves (see Table 12.3). In per capita terms, the United Arab Emirates and Kuwait are the best endowed, followed by Qatar. In Qatar gas reserves will likely turn out to be even more important than oil. As the international gas industry becomes increasingly important, Qatar's economic potential will improve. However, rapid population increases coupled with subsidized energy prices have resulted in explosive increases in domestic petroleum consumption, as noted earlier. If allowed to continue, such increases will reduce export availability and require costly production expansion programs, further straining national budgets.

Water resources

The availability of water in the GCC countries is limited by low and intermittent rainfall, limited sources of fossil groundwater, saltwater intrusion of aquifers, and the absence of permanently flowing rivers. Even without rapid population increases, water would become a critical resource need within the GCC. The natural scarcity of water in the region has been considerably aggravated by the implicit and explicit subsidization of water. With population pressures mounting, the depletion of water and its implications for the future are a source of great concern.

Agriculture accounts for about 85 percent of water consumption in the GCC (Table 12.9). During the 1980s water use in agriculture grew by an alarming 521 percent, an average annual rate of 18 percent. Water use is projected to grow 3.2 percent a year during the 1990s. This rapid growth in agricultural water consumption is a direct result of government policies to promote agriculture through direct and indirect subsidies.

Water consumption by domestic and industrial users has also grown rapidly. During the 1980s domestic and industrial consumption rose by 185 percent, an average annual rate of 11 percent, and is projected to grow 5.3 percent a year during the 1990s. Again, government subsidies and high incomes have encouraged rapid growth in water consumption.

Table 12.9 Actual and projected growth rates for water consumption, GCC, 1980–2000 (percent)

Country	Average annual growth rate, 1980–90			Projected annual growth rate, 1990–2000			Share consumed by agriculture		
	Agriculture	Domestic and industrial	Total	Agriculture	Domestic and industrial	Total	1980	1990	2000[a]
Bahrain	2.1	8.4	4.6	1.4	4.2	2.8	66.7	52.3	45.6
Kuwait	7.2	7.6	7.5	3.2	5.8	5.3	21.5	20.9	17.2
Oman	5.9	19.1	6.4	1.0	5.5	1.4	97.7	93.0	89.6
Qatar	6.2	5.4	5.8	5.4	5.1	5.3	54.5	56.2	56.9
Saudi Arabia	22.9	13.0	21.3	3.3	5.5	3.6	78.7	89.6	87.5
United Arab Emirates	5.4	9.0	6.6	4.0	4.4	4.1	71.0	63.8	62.7
GCC weighted average	18.0	11.0	16.6	3.2	5.3	3.5	76.8	85.8	83.2

a Projected.
Source: Authors' calculations based on Abdulrazzak, 1994.

Rapid growth in water demand has had two short-term effects. First, the rapid increase in wastewater has contaminated sources of groundwater. Even ignoring consumption, groundwater depletion is about three and a half times the rate of annual recharge of total fossil groundwater. Second, in order to supply household demand, there has been greater recourse to desalinated water, with its attendant costs.

Future water availability is questionable if the projected growth in water demand is not contained. As it stands it is difficult to estimate the life of groundwater in GCC countries. The quantity of reserves is questionable. The quality of water varies because of contamination. The long-term growth rate of water demand is unpredictable. In Saudi Arabia, assuming current practices and policies remain unchanged, proven reserves in renewable aquifers will be exhausted by 2005, probable groundwater will be depleted by 2015, and possible reserves will be gone by 2030.

Although circumstances in Saudi Arabia may be the most dire (because of the emphasis placed on agricultural uses of water and the ongoing depletion of groundwater reserves for this activity), conditions are not much better in other GCC countries. Based on simplistic – and optimistic – assumptions (5 percent annual growth rate in groundwater usage and no contamination), shallow groundwater resources will be rapidly depleted in all the GCC countries except Oman. Deep nonrenewable aquifers can provide an alternative, but at increasing cost and for a limited time.

Thus the implications for future water availability appear bleak. If policies toward water remain unchanged, water scarcity will become acute. Although the growing use of desalination will help meet some of the demand for water, the cost of desalinated water will demand a far-reaching adjustment. Some productive economic activities (most notably agriculture, but some industries as well) will be even less internationally competitive when groundwater is no longer available and water is priced at its opportunity cost. Since the subsidies required to keep these activities going may be enormous, the implication is that water-intensive activities will have to be shut down within about two decades.

The growing reliance on desalinated water implies a substantial financial burden in building new desalination plants. Because the potential burden of desalination plants may be excessive, it is useful to estimate future desalination requirements and their costs (Table 12.10). Table 12.10 is based on several simplifying assumptions. First, the average growth rates of water consumption for domestic and industrial uses are assumed to grow through 2015 at the rate projected for 1990–2000. Second, desalination is assumed to meet 70 percent of domestic and industrial water demand in 1995 (up from 55 percent in 1990) and to grow to 90 percent by 2015.

Table 12.10 Projected consumption of desalinated water, GCC, 1995–2015 (thousands of cubic meters)

	1995	2000	2005	2010	2015
Domestic and industrial demand	3,641	4,707	6,084	7,865	10,167
Desalinated water demand	2,549	3,509	4,829	6,647	9,150
Additional desalinated water demand over 1995		960	2,280	4,099	6,601
Cost of additional desalinated water[a] (millions of U.S. dollars)		3,617	8,595	15,447	24,879

a Capital and operating costs.
Source: Authors' calculations.

The rapid projected growth in demand for and costs of desalinated water are clearly ominous – and these figures do not even incorporate potential agricultural demand for desalinated water. Moreover, the figures in Table 12.10 grossly underestimate the likely cost of desalination. Desalination will probably have to provide more than 90 percent of domestic and industrial water usage by 2015. And, if nonrenewable resources are depleted by 2005 or 2015 (as predicted by some experts), desalination will have to satisfy some of the water demand in the agricultural sector.

The current water scarcity, rate of water usage, and overall outlook present several policy dilemmas. To address their growing water problems, GCC policymakers should reduce water subsidies now and bring rates in line with the full long-run marginal cost of production and distribution, reduce other agricultural subsidies for all forms of farming (except those that conserve water), reconsider policies toward rapid population growth and urbanization, introduce strict environmental measures to reduce contamination of groundwater reservoirs, and develop policies to use wastewater.

Notes

1. The authors gratefully acknowledge the support of the World Bank, the Petroleum Finance Company, *Petroleum Intelligence Weekly*, the Seattle Research and Training Center, the Gulf Organization for Industrial

Consulting, Dr. Martin Baughman, Dr. Philip Verleger, and an international engineering firm that has requested anonymity also provided invaluable assistance. Abdel-Aleem Sharshar and others at the World Bank provided useful suggestions but are in no way responsible for the views expressed here or for any shortcomings of this study.

2. Although rapid economic progress in the countries started in the early 1970s, the GCC was not formed until 1981.

3. See, for example, El-Serafy, 1989. This section relies heavily on Weitzman, 1990, and Askari, 1990. Similar treatments are presented in several recent World Bank reports, including World Bank, 1992a, 1993a, and 1994a.

4. This simplified relationship assumes that the expected growth in real oil prices is equal to the real rate of return on investment (real or monetary) and is based on an optimal rate of extraction where expected real price increases are equal to the social rate of discount (see Weitzman, 1990).

5. Kuwait also ran a deficit, although in this case it was clearly caused by events beyond its control (the Gulf war).

6. The Omani government established a similar fund, but it has repeatedly used it to finance current expenditures when faced with budgetary imbalances (World Bank, 1994a).

References

Abdulrazzak, Mohammed J., 1994. "Review and Assessment of Water Resources in Gulf Cooperation Council Countries," *Water Resources Development*, 10(1).

Askari, Hossein, 1990. *Saudi Arabia's Economy: Oil and the Search for Economic Development*, Cairo: JAI Press.

British Petroleum, 1994. *BP Statistical Review of World Energy*. London. BP.

El-Serafy, Salah, 1989. "The Proper Calculation of Income from Depletable Natural Resources," in Y. Ahmad, S. Serafy, and E. Lutz (eds.), *Environmental Accounting for Sustainable Development*, proceedings of a UNDP – World Bank Symposium, Washington D.C.: World Bank.

Gamelidin, Ahmed Ihab, 1994. "Labor Markets in the GCC Countries: A Survey," Washington, D.C.: World Bank.

Ibbotson Associates, 1994. *Stocks, Bonds, Bills and Inflation, 1994 Yearbook*, Chicago.

Kolars, John, 1993. "The Middle East's Growing Water Crisis," *Research and Exploration*, 9 (November): 44.

Musgrave, Richard A., 1959. *The Theory of Public Finance*, New York: McGraw-Hill.

Weitzman, Martin, 1990. "Net National Product for an Exhaustible Resource Economy," in Hossein Askari, (ed.), *Saudi Arabia's Economy: Oil and the Search for Economic Development*, Cairo: JAI Press.

World Bank, 1992a. "The United Arab Emirates: Policy Agenda for Economic Sustainability," Washington, D.C. : World Bank.

————— 1993a. "Bahrain: The Requirements for Economic Diversification and Sustainability," Washington, D.C. : World Bank.

————— 1993b. *The East Asian Miracle: Economic Growth and Public Policy*, A World Bank Policy Research Report, New York: Oxford University Press.

————— 1994a. "Sultanate of Oman: Sustainable Growth and Economic Diversification," Washington, D.C. : World Bank.

————— 1994b. *World Debt Tables*, Washington, D.C. : World Bank.

————— 1994c. *World Tables*, Washington, D.C. : World Bank.

Index

Abed, G.T.   3, 101–15
African, Caribbean and Pacific
    countries   173
Al-Ansari, M.J.   99
Al-Mahdi, S.   180–1
Algeria   8
Ali, A.   189
Anderson, R.E.   3
Aoun, General   118
Arab countries   245
Arab–Israeli conflict   140
Arabian peninsula   118
Arafat, Y.   106, 110
Armenia   171
Asia   7
    and Iran   203
    and Syria   148
    see also Central; South; Southeast
Askari, H.   6, 225–54
Association of Southeast Asian Nations
    (ASEAN)   19
Avins, J.   8
Azam, J.P.   187
Azerbaijan   171
Azhari, Minister   182

Bahrain   6
    see also Gulf Cooperation Council
Balkans   171
Baltic countries   173
Baroudi, E.   118, 122
Barro, R.J.   161
Bazzari, M.   6, 225–54
Behdad, S.   206
Berryman, S.E.   8
Beyhum, N.   121
Bruno, M.   189

Canada   143, 144
Celasun, M.   160, 162
Central Asia   171
Central and Eastern Europe   19, 173
Chabrier, P.   193
Charif, H.   119
Chehab, General F.   116, 117, 120
China   144
    see also Association of Southeast Asian
        Nations (ASEAN)

Chua, H.   195
Cleaver, K.   192
Collier, P.   186, 194, 195
Corm, G.   4, 116–33
Cuddington, J.   193
Cyprus   171

Daghestani, E.A.   145
De Santis, R.   160
Delgado, C.   192
Dervis, K.   162
Diwan, I.   2, 147, 150
Dornbusch, R.   189, 190
Dutz, M.   165

East Africa   203
East Asia   7, 8
    and Gulf Cooperation Council   243
    and Iran   203, 204
    and Jordan   84, 89
    and Lebanon   130–1
    and Morocco   21
    public financing   82
    and Sudan   189, 194, 195
Easterly, W.   185, 189
Eastern Europe
    communism   171
    and Egypt   53, 60
Economic Cooperation
    Organization   166
Economic Research Forum   1
Egypt   8, 53–77
    Central Bank   56
    and Eastern Europe   60
    employment   74–5
    environment   71–3; air pollution   73;
        land use   72–3; water pollution   72
    Environment Action Plan (1992)   71
    Environment Affairs Agency   72
    and European Union   59, 60
    external competitiveness, achievement
        of   59–62; domestic technology,
        augmentation of   62; trade alliances
        formation   59–61; trade network,
        reforming of   61–2
    Fifth Five-Year Plan   68
    Fourth Five-Year Plan   68

257

Egypt (*Cont'd*)
  gross domestic product (GDP) 55, 56, 57, 62, 63, 65
  gross national product (GNP) 62
  infrastructure 73–4
  and Jordan 79
  macroeconomy, adaptation of 56–9
  Mashreq–European Union agreements 59
  microeconomic measures 57
  Ministry of Education 67
  Ministry of Health 68
  nongovernmental organizations 71, 72
  and Palestine 109
  population growth 69–70
  poverty alleviation 70–1
  public financing 82
  real interest rates 58
  sectoral growth enhancement 62–9; agriculture 63–4; education 67–8; health 68–9; manufacturing 65–6
  Sixth Five-Year Plan 68
  socio-ethical measures 57
  and South Asia 60
  Specialized Agency 67
  strategy 55–6
  and Sudan 182, 183
  and Syria 144, 145
  taxation 58
  Third Five-Year Plan (1992–7) 55, 68
  Uruguay Round 59, 61
Eken, S. 122, 124
Elbadawi, I.A. 5, 178–99
El-Erian, M. 193
Euro-Mediterranean free trade area 19, 22
European Union 1, 2, 3, 8, 13
  Common External Tariff 173
  customs union 167, 172
  and Egypt 59, 60
  free trade agreement 25, 37, 173
  and Morocco 19, 21, 22, 23
  and Sudan 193, 195
  and Syria 143, 144, 148, 151, 152
  and Tunisia 48
  and Turkey 159, 165, 166, 169, 176

Farzin, Y.H. 217
Feyzioglu, T. 193
First, R. 182
Fischer, S. 185
Fontagné, L. 22

former Soviet Union 4
  Russian Federation 151, 153
  and Syria 136, 140, 144, 150, 151
  and Turkey 171
France 116

Gamelidin, A.I. 248
Gaza *see under* Palestine
General Agreement on Tariffs and Trade (GATT)
  and Morocco 14, 19
  and Tunisia 25, 27, 31, 33, 37
  and Turkey 159, 166, 169, 174
Generalized System of Trade Preferences 173
Georgia 171
Goel, R.K. 165
Golden, I. 144
Goldin, I. 19
Golladay, F.L. 8
Greece 161, 174
Griliches, Z. 160
gross domestic product (GDP) 7
  see also under individual countries
Grossman, G.M. 165
Gulf Cooperation Council (GCC) 6, 8, 225–54
  and Arab countries 245
  and East Asia 243
  economic policy in depletable resource-based economies 228–35; export base diversification, recommended policies for 235; external sector implications 233–4; intertemporal model 228–30; macroeconomic policy management implications 233; savings and investment implications 230–2; trade and current account balances 234
  export revenues 227
  gross domestic product (GDP) 227, 232, 236, 238
  Gulf War 234, 240
  and Hong Kong 226, 227
  and India 245
  and Japan 245
  and Korea 227
  labor markets 245–9; government policies 246–8; population structures 248; recommended policy changes 248–9
  and Malaysia 245
  net national product 228–30

and Organization for Economic
Cooperation and Development
(OECD) 227
and Organization of the Petroleum
Exporting Countries (OPEC) 239
and Pakistan 245
and Philippines 245
population, resources and
environment 249–52; oil and gas
resources 250; water
resources 250–3
private sector development 241–4;
financial markets, development of
243–4; government subsidies 241–2;
private sector, creation of 243–4;
subsidies, effect of 242–3
privatization 244
and Republic of Korea 226, 245
Saudi Arabia Chamber of
Commerce 248
Saudi Arabian Basic Industries
Corporation 244
and Singapore 226, 227
and Sri Lanka 245
state, role of 235–41; overall policy
considerations 239–41; public
sector finances 236–7; revenues,
expenditures and budget
balances 237; subsidies 238–9
and Thailand 245
and United States 231, 232, 235
and Yemen 245
Gulf countries 2, 4, 5–6, 136, 138, 140
Gulf War 171, 234, 240
Gunning, J. 195

Hag Elamin, H. 191
Hamdane, K. 131
Hamdouch, B. 2–3, 13–23
Hamilton, B.W. 161
Handoussa, H. 4, 77
Helpman, E. 165
Hoekman, B. 2
Hong Kong 226, 227

India 245
Indonesia 7
and Sudan 188
and Turkey 164
International Monetary Fund (IMF) 13
and Lebanon 122, 123, 127
and Morocco 14, 17
and Sudan 180
and Turkey 167, 174

Iran 1, 5–6, 202–23
and Asia 203
charities 218
conflicts 219
credits 218–19
and East Africa 203
and East Asia 203, 204
economic decline, causes and
consequences of 205–12;
postrevolutionary response 205–7;
productive efficiency and real
exchange rate 207–12
exchange rate reform and economic
restructuring 207, 212–19; booms
and busts 213–15; exchange rate
adjustments 215–19;
macroeconomic indicators 214
exchange rate unification (1993)
217–18
First Five-Year Plan (1989–93) 6, 202,
212, 213, 216, 217
foreign exchange 206–7
Foundation of the Oppressed and
Disabled 207
government controls 206
gross domestic product (GDP) 204,
205, 208, 213, 215, 217, 220
import boom (1991–2) 216
institutional reforms, suggested
219–22; charitable
foundations 220; financial 222;
fiscal reform 219–20; industrial
restructuring 220–1; labor
institutions 221–2
manufacturing 207–9, 210
and Organization for Economic
Cooperation and Development
(OECD) 203
per capita income 203, 204
public financing 82
raw materials 209–10
regional and international
perspectives 203–5
and Republic of Korea 204–5, 209,
210–11
Second Five-Year Plan 202
and Turkey 166, 171, 204–5, 209,
210–11
wages 209–10, 211
war with Iraq 202, 206, 212
Iraq 4
and Lebanon 118
and Syria 145, 148
see also Iran, war with

Iskandar, M. 118, 122
Israel 102, 104, 105, 106, 107, 108, 110
  Civil Administration 104, 109
  and Lebanon 123
  and Palestine 111, 112, 113
  public financing 82
  and Syria 140, 148
  and Turkey 173

Japan
  and Gulf Cooperation Council 245
  and Syria 143, 144, 152
  see also Association of Southeast Asian
    Nations
Jordan 8, 78–100, 101, 103, 106, 107
  Agricultural Credit Corporation 79,
    81
  Amman Financial Market 81, 95, 98
  Center for Vaccines in the Ministry of
    Health 87
  Council of Ministers 87
  Directorate of Petroleum in the
    Ministry of Energy's Natural
    Resources Authority 87
  and East Asia 84, 89
  Economic and Social Development
    Plan (1993–7) 85–6
  and Egypt 79
  Electric Power Company 81
  Electricity Authority 79, 87
  Encouragement of Industry Law 87
  future strategy 84–5
  government role, strategy for 85–8
  gross domestic product (GDP) 79,
    80
  Hotels and Tourism Company 88
  Housing Bank 81, 92
  Housing and Urban Development
    Corporation 79
  Industrial Development Bank 81, 87,
    92
  Industrial Estates Corporation 79
  Investment Corporation 81, 87, 99
  Irbid District Electricity Company 81
  Law 14 (1992) 95
  market-friendly strategy 85, 89
  Ministry of Industry and Trade
    regulations 87, 95–6
  Ministry of Post and
    Telecommunications 87
  neoclassical strategy 85
  new institutional economics 91
  newly industrialized countries 84
  and Oman 79

  Organization for Regulating the
    Telecommunications Sector 87
  and Palestine 106, 107, 109, 112
  Paper and Cardboard Company 87
  public entities suitable for
    commercialization 99–100
  public financing 82
  public governance, political economy
    of 88–91
  public sector reform 92–6; Amman
    Financial Market law 95; civil
    law 94; company law 94;
    import–export law 95–6; income
    tax law and administration 95;
    investment law 95;
    privatization 92–3; procurement
    laws 95; public universities 93–4
  public sector size and
    composition 79–82
  public shareholding companies 97–8;
    asset performance 97; growth in
    sales and fixed assets 98; rates of
    return 97–8
  Public Transport Corporation 79, 99
  Regulation 1 (1994) 95
  revisionist strategy 85
  Royal Jordanian 97
  social cohesion 89
  Social Security Corporation 81, 82
  and Southeast Asia 89
  state enterprises and corporate growth
    and performance 82–4
  Supplies Act 1993 95
  and Syria 144
  Telecommunications Corporation 79,
    87, 99
  Telecommunications Law 87
  value-added 81
  Water Authority 79, 99
  World Bank 85
Jorgenson, D.W. 160

Kabbani, O. 121
Kanaan, T.H. 3, 78–100
Karshenas, M. 5–6, 17, 202–23
Kasparian, R. 130
Khalaf, N. 124
Khalaf, S. 121
Kheir-El-Din, H. 4, 53–77
Kherallah, M. 144
Khoury, Ph. 121
Knight, M. 184, 185
Knudsen, O. 19
Kok, P. 183

Krueger, A. 194
Krugman, P. 194
Kuwait 6
see also Gulf Cooperation Council

Labaki, B. 130
Lahouel, M.H. 2, 25–49
Larsen, B. 7
Latin America 7, 8
and Lebanon 123
and Sudan 189, 190
Lautenschlager, W. 206
Layous, M. 147
Lebanon 7, 116–33
and Arabian peninsula 118
Bank of 124, 126, 127, 129
Bechtel 120, 121
Byblos Bank 129
Central Bank 116, 117, 123, 126, 129
Central Directorate of Statistics 116
Ciment Libanais 129
Council of Ministers 121, 122
Council for Reconstruction and
Development 118, 119–20, 121,
125, 126
Dar Al Handassah 120, 121
Directorate of Statistics 122
displaced persons 130
and East Asia 130–1
economic and social progress 117–19
and France 116
gross domestic product (GDP) 122,
123, 127, 132
Horizon 2000 Plan 121
income inequality 130
infrastructure 120
International Monetary Fund
(IMF) 122, 123, 127
and Iraq 118
and Israel 123
and Latin America 123
maimed persons 130
Maronite, Sunni, and Chia 118
Ministry of Planning 116, 118
National Unity 118–19
and Palestine resistance
movement 117
public health and education
systems 130
public transportation 130
reconstruction plan 119–31; budget
deficit and taxation policy 125–7;
dollarization of economy 123–5;
domestic financial market and status

of currency 128–30; economic
data, lack of 122–3; inflation
rate and exchange rates 124; real
estate boom and link to
savings 127–8; social
climate 130–1
Solidere 120, 121, 128–9
and Syria 130–1, 144, 147, 148
Taïeff agreement (1989) 118, 119
taxation 120, 131–2
unemployment 131
United Nations Development
Programme 122, 123
unskilled migrant workers 130–1
World Bank 118
Lebret, Abbé L. 117
Levine, R. 163
Libya 138
Loayza, N. 184, 185

Maddison, A. 163
Maghreb 2–3, 7, 21
see also Algeria; Morocco, Tunisia
Malaysia 7
and Gulf Cooperation Council 245
and Turkey 164
Maraslioglu, H. 160, 162
Martinez, A. 3
Marxism 91
Mashreq 2, 3–5
–European Union agreements 59
see also Egypt; Jordan; Lebanon;
Palestine; Syria
Mazarei, A. 216
Mediterranean 1, 2
Menassa, G. 117
Mexican peso crisis (1995) 19, 121
Moalla-Fetini, R. 193
Mohammed, N. 183, 185
Mohtadi, H. 7
Morocco 8, 13–23
adjustment policy 13–17;
achievements 14–16;
constraints 16–17
agriculture 18
Association of Southeast Asian
Nations 19
and Central and Eastern Europe 19
challenges 18–19
drought 18
and East Asia 21
economic liberalization 14
energy deficit 18
environmental deterioration 18

Moroccco (*Cont'd*)
  Euro-Mediterranean free trade
    area 19, 22
  and European Union 19, 21, 22, 23
  exchange control liberalization 14
  external options 21–2
  financial sector reform 16
  General Agreement on Tariffs and
    Trade 14, 19
  globalization 19
  gross domestic product (GDP) 14, 16,
    18, 20
  internal options 19–21
  International Monetary Fund
    (IMF) 14, 17
  London Club (1990) 17
  macroeconomic indicators 15
  monetary policy liberalization 16
  North American Free Trade
    Agreement 19
  Paris Club (1992) 17
  privatization 16
  public enterprise reforms 16
  public financing 82
  regionalization 19
  sector adjustment programs 17
  structural adjustment loan 17
  sustainable development
    achievement 20–1
  tax reform 16
  tripartite advisory committee 21
  Uruguay Round 19, 22
  World Bank 17, 19, 21
Mullin, J. 145
Multifiber Arrangement 175
Munla, N. 124
Musgrave, R.A. 235

Ndulu, B. 180, 188
newly industrialized countries 84
North America 144
  Free Trade Agreement 19
  see also Canada; United States
North, D.C. 90, 91
Numeiri regime 180, 181,
  182, 186

Oman 6
  and Jordan 79
  public financing 82
  see also Gulf Cooperation Council
Organization for Economic Cooperation
  and Development (OECD) 203,
  227

Organization of the Petroleum Exporting
  Countries (OPEC) 239
Özhan, H.G. 160

Page, J. 7
Pakistan 166, 245
Palestine 101–15
  Authority 101, 103, 104, 105, 107,
    109–14
  balance of payments 108, 113
  Council 109
  development strategy 111
  economic possibilities 106–14; full
    autonomy scenario 109–14;
    incremental scenario 107–9
  and Egypt 109
  external economic relations 112
  foreign direct investment 108
  governance and institutional
    reform 110–11
  gross domestic product (GDP) 108,
    113
  investment-friendly regulatory
    environment 113
  and Israel 111, 112, 113
  Jericho area 102, 103
  and Jordan 106, 107, 109, 112
  Liberation Organization 101, 102,
    104, 110
  Madrid Peace Conference 105, 106
  Oslo Declaration of Principles
    (1993) 101, 102–4, 105, 106,
    109; agreements, implementation
    of 103; stalemate
    development 103–4
  output growth 108, 113
  Paris Protocol (1994) 109
  public sector finances 113
  resistance movement 117
  stalemate, breaking of 104–6;
    fundamental approach 105–6;
    incremental approach 105
  unemployment and
    underemployment 108, 113
  West Bank and Gaza Strip 101–10,
    112, 114
Papandreou, N. 150
Peres, S. 148
Péridy, N. 22
Pesaran, M.H. 206
Philippines 245
Pio, A. 196
Portugal 174
Prebisch–Singer hypothesis 193

Qatar 6, 7
  see also Gulf Cooperation Council

Ram, R. 165
Ravallion, M. 189
Reinhart, C. 193
Renelt, D. 163
Republic of Korea
  and Gulf Cooperation Council 226,
    227, 245
  and Iran 204–5, 209, 210–11
  and Turkey 164
Riordan, E. 3, 6
Robinson, S. 162

Saudi Arabia 6
  Basic Industries Corporation 244
  Chamber of Commerce 248
  and Syria 144
  see also Gulf Cooperation Council
Sbaiti, A. 118
Schmidt-Hebbel, K. 189
Shafik, N. 1–8, 189
Singapore 226, 227
South Asia 53, 60
Southeast Asia
  and Egypt 53
  and Jordan 89
  public financing 82
  and Sudan 195
  see also Indonesia; Malaysia; Thailand
Spain 174
Squire, L. 147
Sri Lanka 245
structural adjustment 13
Sub-Saharan Africa 190, 192, 195
Sudan 2, 5–6, 178–99
  Addis Ababa peace agreement
    (1972) 180, 182, 186
  agriculture 181, 183
  Anglo-Egyptian Condominium 182
  Anya Nya movement 180
  civil war 178, 180, 197
  civil war, economic impacts of 182–6;
    costs 183–4, 185; potential peace
    dividends 184–6
  Closed Districts Area 182
  crisis management 178
  development, state's role in 195–7
  development strategy, complements
    to 189–95; agricultural
    development and environmental
    sustainability 191–3; debt
    relief 190–1; industrialization and

structural transformation 193–4;
    regional cooperation and
    integration 194–5
  and East Asia 189, 194, 195
  economic developments, recent
    179–81; economic indicators 179;
    macroeconomic indicators 181
  education 183
  and Egypt 182, 183
  and European Union 193, 195
  gross domestic product (GDP) 179,
    181, 184, 185, 188, 190, 191
  health 183
  and Indonesia 188
  International Monetary Fund
    (IMF) 180
  and Latin America 189, 190
  macroeconomic stabilization 187–8,
    190
  military spending 184
  Numeiri regime 180, 181
  oil boom 180
  oil production 183
  political and economic reforms 187–9;
    poverty alleviation 189; structural
    adjustment 188–9
  political instability 184
  Prebisch-Singer hypothesis 193
  and Southeast Asia 195
  and Sub-Saharan Africa 190, 192,
    195
  and Thailand 188
  Uruguay Round 193
  World Bank 180
Sukkar, N. 4, 136–54
Syria 8, 136–54
  agriculture 143
  and Arab–Israeli conflict 140
  and Asia 148
  Baath Party 153
  and Canada 143
  Casablanca conference (1994) 148
  defense spending 140
  economic growth 139, 147
  economic performance, recent 136–7
  economic pluralism 141
  and Egypt 145
  Elf Equitaine 137
  and European Union 143, 148, 151,
    152
  foreign exchange crisis 139
  and former Soviet Union 136, 140,
    150, 151
  gas reserves 137–8

Syria (*Cont'd*)
  gross domestic product (GDP) 137, 140, 142
  gross national product (GNP) 136, 145, 146, 151
  growth, challenges to 138–40
  growth, financing of 149–52; external debt 150–2; private capital inflows 149–50
  growth prospects 137–8
  and Gulf countries 136, 138, 140
  Investment Law 10 (1991) 139, 142, 150
  and Iraq 145, 148
  and Israel 140, 148
  and Japan 143, 152
  and Lebanon 130–1, 147, 148
  and Libya 138
  Ministry of Higher Education 145
  oil reserves 137
  Paris Club 152
  population growth 138–9
  public financing 82
  quantitative restrictions 142
  reform 139
  Shell 137
  stabilization and structural adjustment 141
  strategic economic issues 140–9; equity increase and poverty reduction 146–7; Euro-Mediterranean partnership scheme 148–9; health services, safe water and sanitation, access to 147; human resource development 146; international integration and export growth, promotion of 142–5; reform, acceleration of 140–2; regional integration participation 147–8; science and technology capability 145
  Supreme Council of Science 145
  tariffs 142
  textiles and clothing 143, 144–5
  and Turkey 171
  unemployment 146–7
  and United States 140, 143
  Uruguay Round 143
  World Bank 146, 150, 151
  World Trade Organization 143

Thailand 7
  and Gulf Cooperation Council 245
  and Sudan 188
  and Turkey 164

Tiktik, A. 160
Togan, S. 5, 159–76
trade-related aspects of intellectual property rights (TRIPS) 175
trade-related investment measures (TRIMS) 38, 174
Tunisia 8, 25–49
  Central Bank 45, 46–7, 48–9
  competition 26
  consumption duty 36
  Decree 89–442 (1989) 39
  deregulation of banking sector 45–7
  domestic production 29, 31, 32
  and European Union 25, 37, 48
  exporting firms 36–8
  fixed regime 42
  foreign trade law (Law 94–41) 26–7, 30
  General Agreement on Tariffs and Trade (GATT) 25, 27, 31, 33, 37
  gross domestic product (GDP) 35
  Higher Investment Commission 39
  horizontal objectives 26
  Housing Saving Fund 45
  imports 26, 27, 28
  income tax holiday 37, 38
  investment code (Law 93–120) 35, 36, 39
  investment regulation and incentives 26, 34–9; capacity licensing, removal of 38–9; new incentive system 35–8; old investment incentive system 34–5
  lending rates 46–7
  money market rate 47
  offshore firms 36–7
  per capita income 25
  price law (1970) 41
  price regulation 41–5; control at distribution stage 44–5; control at producer stage 43–4; control, extent of 42–3
  Price Regulatory Department 41–2, 43
  pricing system 26
  public financing 82
  public procurement policies 39–41; differentiated treatment of firms 40–1; transparency of rules 39–40
  restricted free regime 42
  self-certification regime 42
  structural adjustment 25, 27

trade liberalization 26–34;
  quantitative restrictions and
  licensing 26–30; tariff
  barriers 30–3; tariff binding
  33–4
trade-related investment measures 38
unrestricted regime 44
Uruguay Round 25, 27, 34
value-added tax 36
World Bank 28
World Trade Organization 37
Turkey 1, 2, 5–6, 8, 159–76
  and African, Caribbean and Pacific
    countries 173
  agriculture 161, 162–3
  and Armenia 171
  Association Council 172
  and Azerbaijan 171
  and Balkans 171
  and Baltic countries 173
  capacity expansion 163–5
  and Central Asia 171
  and Central and Eastern Europe 171,
    173
  Common Customs Tariff 172
  and Cyprus 171
  Economic Cooperation
    Organization 166
  education 161
  étatism 170
  and European Union 159, 165, 166,
    169, 176; Common External
    Tariff 173; customs union 167,
    172; trade agreements 173
  and former Soviet Union 171
  Framework Agreement 173
  General Agreement on Tariffs and
    Trade 159, 166, 169, 174
  Generalized System of Trade
    Preferences 173
  and Georgia 171
  and Greece 161, 174
  gross domestic product (GDP) 159,
    160, 161, 162, 165, 167, 170, 171
  gross national product (GNP) 159,
    163, 164, 166, 167, 176
  growth theories and growth
    analysis 160
  Gulf War 171
  income distribution 161
  and Indonesia 164
  international economic
    developments 166, 172–5;
    European Union, integration

with 172–4; multilateral
    agreements 174–5
  International Monetary Fund
    (IMF) 167, 174
  and Iran 166, 171, 204–5, 209, 210–11
  and Israel 173
  Kurdish nationalism 171
  labor force characteristics 161–3
  macroeconomic policies 166–71;
    foreign trade policies 169–70;
    investment incentives 168–9; public
    enterprise policies 170–1
  and Malaysia 164
  manufacturing 161
  mining 161
  Multifiber Arrangement 175
  and Pakistan 166
  payments crisis 1994 167
  and Portugal 174
  Prevention of Unfair Competition in
    Importation Law (1989) 169
  Protection of Competition 169
  protection rates 165
  public financing 82
  regional political developments 171–2
  and Republic of Korea 164
  restrictive wage policies 162
  savings 163–4
  Southern Anatolian Project 164–5
  and Spain 174
  State Institute of Statistics 163, 173
  State Planning Organization 160, 163,
    170
  and Syria 144, 171
  technical progress 165–6
  and Thailand 164
  total factor productivity 159, 161
  total value 160
  trade-related aspects of intellectual
    property rights (TRIPS) 175
  trade-related investment measures 174
  Treasury 170
  and United States 161, 176
  Uruguay Round 174–5, 176
Tyler, W. 6, 225–54

United Arab Emirates 6
  see also Gulf Cooperation Council
United Nations Development
    Programme 122, 123
United States
  and Gulf Cooperation Council 231,
    232, 235
  and Syria 140, 143, 144

United States (*Cont'd*)
  and Turkey 161, 176
Urata, S. 165
Uruguay Round
  and Egypt 59, 61
  and Morocco 19, 22
  and Sudan 193
  and Syria 143
  and Tunisia 25, 27, 34
  and Turkey 174–5, 176

van der Mensbrugghe, D. 19
van Eeghen, W. 2, 7
Villanueva, D. 184, 185

Wang, Z. 2
Waterbury, J. 8
West Bank *see under* Palestine

Wickham, P. 193
Wolff, L. 8
World Bank 1, 4, 13
  and Jordan 85
  and Lebanon 118
  and Morocco 17, 19, 21
  and Sudan 180
  and Syria 146, 150, 151
  and Tunisia 28
World Trade Organization
  37, 143

Yang, C.-P. 2
Yemen 245

Zahlan, A.B. 145
Ziesemer, T. 193